REAL ESTATE COUNSELING IN A PLAIN BROWN WRAPPER

- a practical guide to the profession

Jared Shlaes, CRE

Copyright © 1992 by the American Society of Real Estate Counselors of the National Association of REALTORS®. All rights reserved.

Opinions expressed in this publication are those of the author and are not necessarily endorsed by the American Society of Real Estate Counselors.

Printed in the United States of America

10 9 8 7 6 5 4 3 2 1

ISBN 0-939653-00-1

The illustrations in this book were created by John F. Hartray, Jr., FAIA

Members of the American Society of Real Estate Counselors are recognized as leaders in various aspects of real estate counseling. They are selected from the ranks of practicing counselors in business, the professions, government and academia. Membership is by invitation only, though applications may be self-initiated. The CRE designation (Counselor of Real Estate), a certification of the holder's good standing in the Society, attests to his or her expertise, reputation, and adherence to a stringent code of ethics. The Society offers quality publications, networking opportunities and educational programs.

American Society of Real Estate Counselors, 430 North Michigan Avenue, Chicago, Illinois 60611   312.329.8427

ABOUT THE AUTHOR

JARED SHLAES, CRE, a practicing second-generation counselor, brings to this book the wealth of real estate experience acquired in the course of a varied career that dates back to 1954, when he joined his father Harry Shlaes, CRE, in the Chicago office of the Lurie organization. Recently retired as Director of Special Real Estate Services for Arthur Andersen & Co., Shlaes previously headed Shlaes & Co., a real estate counseling and appraisal firm, after serving as Senior Vice President for counseling and appraisals of Arthur Rubloff & Co.

Shlaes has made significant contributions to real estate counseling and other related fields: computer software for property and portfolio analysis, appraisal theory, land use controls, historic preservation, downtown and neighborhood revitalization, development planning and urban design. He was a pioneer in the use of discounted cash flow analysis for investment real estate and sponsored the first lease-by-lease DCF program for portfolio management. A national authority on the economics of historic properties and the use of preservation easements, he was co-originator of the internationally admired Chicago Plan for landmarks preservation, a transferable development rights scheme which earned its authors the Louise L. and Y. T. Lum award of the Appraisal Institute. In his more ambitious years he developed a number of inner-city townhouse and apartment projects that brought him honors for their design excellence.

A widely published author, Shlaes was founding editor-in-chief of *Real Estate Issues*, the journal of the American Society of Real Estate Counselors, and received that organization's Louise L. and Y. T. Lum award for his advancement of knowledge. He has also served the Society as first vice president, editor of *The Counselor*, and chairman of the Education and Publications Committees. Most recently, he wrote Chapter 1, "Evolution of the Office Building," of the forthcoming book *The Office Building* published by the American Society of Real Estate Counselors, the Appraisal Institute and the Society of Industrial and Office Realtors Educational Fund.

CONTENTS

ACKNOWLEDGEMENTS

INTRODUCTION: WHY THIS BOOK?

PART I: THE BUSINESS OF REAL ESTATE COUNSELING

    2   Chapter 1 - WHAT COUNSELORS DO
    3   Counseling questions
    4   Typical counseling products
    7   What counseling costs
    7   Is counseling a profession?

    10   Chapter 2 - WHO COUNSELORS ARE
    11   Who can be a counselor?
    12   Skills the counselor needs
    13   Counseling careers
    14   Appraisers? Brokers? Counselors?

    16   Chapter 3 - THE COUNSELING INDUSTRY
    16   How it works
    17   Kinds of firms
    17   The sole practitioner
    18   The small firm
    19   In-between sizes
    20   Big firms
    21   The right size for you
    22   Professional societies
    22   The expanding market for real estate counseling

    25   Chapter 4 - COUNSELING ETHICS AND PRINCIPLES
    25   Why ethics matter
    26   Shlaes's rules
    27   Some counseling principles

PART II: SETTING UP FOR BUSINESS

    30   Chapter 5 - GETTING INTO THE GAME
    30   Beginners
    30   Getting an education
    32   Getting started
    33   Your first job
    33   Pay and working conditions
    34   Networks
    34   Getting ahead
    35   Established real estate professionals
    35   Making the switch
    35   Moving over, moving on

37	**Chapter 6 - STARTING THE BUSINESS**
37	Business or practice?
37	Rules for startups
38	Choosing a form of business organization
39	Sole proprietorship
39	Partnership
40	Corporation
41	Other possibilities
41	Choosing a business name
42	Twelve survival tips
44	**Chapter 7 - SPACE**
44	Where?
44	Which building?
46	How much?
46	Layout
47	Do you need a space planner?
48	An office in your home?
48	Office leases
50	**Chapter 8 - STAFFING THE OFFICE**
51	Traits to look for
51	Recruiting
52	Pay and other incidentals
53	Employees or subcontractors?
55	**Chapter 9 - COUNSELING TOOLS**
55	Equipment
56	Computers
57	Operating systems
57	Data sources
58	Computer software
59	Analytical tools
64	**Chapter 10 - YOUR PROFESSIONAL ADVISORS**
64	Lawyers and how to use them
64	Why do you need a lawyer?
65	How to be a good client and save money
66	Getting the most out of your accountant

PART III: RUNNING THE SHOP

70	**Chapter 11 - MINDING THE STORE**
71	Business pitfalls
72	Time management
74	Building team spirit
75	Keeping good people
75	Bad apples
76	Desk management
77	Files and work papers
79	Outside subcontractors
80	Suppliers

82	Chapter 12 - MINDING THE MONEY
82	Billing and collections
84	Danger signs
86	Cash flow problems?
86	Charitable contributions
88	Chapter 13 - INSURANCE AND WHAT IT'S FOR: RISK MANAGEMENT
88	Insurance
92	Other catastrophes

PART IV: MARKETING

96	Chapter 14 - WHERE WORK COMES FROM
98	How clients find counselors
98	The marketing plan
99	Finding your natural markets
100	How clients choose counselors
102	Creating the right image
103	Marketing alliances
103	Referral sources
104	Using the lemming effect
106	Chapter 15 - MARKETING TOOLS
106	The resume
107	Advertising
108	Publicity and public relations
109	PR goals and strategies
110	News releases
111	Surveys
111	Interviews
112	Additional words of caution
112	Public service
113	Professional and business groups
113	Meetings
117	Chapter 16 - MAKING THE PRESENTATION
117	Speeches
119	Hints for speakers
127	Chapter 17 - OTHER MARKETING IDEAS
127	Seminars
129	Articles and books
130	Structure and content
131	Style
131	Getting published
131	For love or money?
132	Brochures
133	Reminders
133	Getting on the lists

PART V: GETTING THE ORDER

136 Chapter 18 - SELLING THE JOB
- 136 Sales calls
- 137 Inquiries
- 138 Selling against competition
- 138 What makes prospects buy?
- 139 Questions prospects ask
- 140 Why they need you
- 141 Opportunities for counseling
- 142 Things prospective clients dislike

144 Chapter 19 THE INITIAL CONSULTATION
- 144 First blush
- 146 Freebies
- 146 The hidden agenda
- 147 Clients you don't need
- 148 Defining the problem and closing the sale
- 149 Types of problems
- 150 Steps in problem definition
- 150 Closing

152 Chapter 20 - FEES, BUDGETS, BIDS
- 152 Setting fees: How much?
- 153 Drafting the budget
- 155 Bidding
- 155 Competitive bidding
- 156 Regular clients
- 156 Negotiating the terms
- 158 Things to negotiate for
- 158 Payment arrangements
- 159 Time and expenses
- 159 Fixed fees
- 160 Staged and phased fees
- 160 Value billing
- 161 Retainers

162 Chapter 21 - THE PROPOSAL
- 162 Writing the proposal
- 166 Staged proposals
- 166 How long should the proposal stay open?
- 166 What the client will provide
- 167 Presenting the proposal

PART VI: THE ART OF COUNSELING

170 Chapter 22 - MANAGING YOUR CLIENTS
- 172 Things not to be with clients
- 172 Turning customers into clients
- 173 How to say things to clients
- 175 What clients don't like to pay for
- 175 Problems and complaints
- 176 Clients in a hurry?
- 176 Golf, booze, gifts and bribes

178	Chapter 23 - THE COUNSELING ASSIGNMENT	
178	The counseling process	
179	Planning the job	
180	Managing the job	
183	Chapter 24 - THE COUNSELING REPORT	
185	Some report-writing rules	
186	Use of confidential sources	
186	Quality control	
186	Presenting the report	
187	Oral reports	
189	Chapter 25 - CONFLICTS	
189	Conflicts of interest	
190	Testimony	
192	Depositions	
193	Other conflict situations	
193	Zoning and permit hearings	
194	Arbitration proceedings	
195	Negotiations	

PART VII: GETTING OUT

198	Chapter 26 - SALE, MERGER OR DISSOLUTION OF THE COUNSELING FIRM
198	Sale or merger
200	Liquidation
200	What's best?
201	Retirement

ACKNOWLEDGEMENTS

Nobody learns how to be a real estate counselor without obtaining help from many people. My father Harry Shlaes, an early CRE who died a quarter-century ago, was an important mentor. So in recent years has been my son Noah, also a practicing counselor. In their own way, so, too, were my long-deceased great-uncles George and Louis Lurie, self-made real estate men who never thought of themselves as professional counselors but found ways to let the thousands of people who benefitted from their advice provide suitable compensation.

John Robert White of New York City, a counselor of counselors and appraisers alike, taught me the importance of client management, proper fees and unbreakable ethics. James Gibbons of East Meadow, New York has been my valued advisor in these and a host of other matters. Abel Berland and the late Arthur Rubloff of Chicago, both prominent real estate men and counselors, taught me something about salesmanship and shared with me their remarkable ability to distinguish between the sheep and the goats. My eldest daughter Amity, a rising journalist and author, has improved my grasp of the written language; my younger daughter Jane, a human resources expert, keeps me in touch with the realities of individual feelings and organizational life. To all of them, my thanks.

Any book like this is to some extent a collective effort. I am grateful for the suggestions and enthusiasm provided by the American Society of Real Estate Counselors and the members of its Publications Committee. I also am deeply obliged to the Counselor's now-retired executive vice president Lois Hofstetter and especially to its staff vice president Linda Magad, who, through her editorial involvement, brought this book through to production.

I owe a huge debt to Chicago attorney-at-law Tobin M. Richter, who contributed to the text his time, ideas, legal knowledge and delightful humor. An equal debt is due John F. Hartray, Jr., FAIA, an eminent architect, skilled raconteur, deadly wit and boon companion, who created the lively illustrations. My thanks also go to Maureen Holtz and the word processing staff of Arthur Andersen & Co., who deciphered my often garbled manuscripts. Finally, I wish to express my appreciation to the Andersen partners, who graciously provided secretarial and administrative support for what turned out to be an unexpectedly time-consuming project.

Introduction

Why This Book?

Real estate counseling is such a new profession that few Americans have ever heard of it, even those who make a living in the land-and-buildings business. When they need help with real estate problems, most people look to friends and connections first, and then to any lawyers, architects, owners, builders, bankers, brokers, managers or appraisers they happen to know. What they expect to get, most of the time, is something for nothing. Sometimes they get it. More often, though, they actually get only what they pay for, if not less. "You don't pay for free advice," says the old saw, "until you take it."

Recognizing that there must be a better way, many individuals and companies are turning instead to professional counselors. These are experienced real estate experts who offer a special relationship to their clients: a relationship of trust that places a responsibility on the counselor similar to the one placed on doctors and lawyers. Like these other professionals, the counselor makes a business of looking after the client's interests, identifying his problems, outlining a corrective course of action and many times effecting a solution. The client gets the benefit of the counselor's knowledge, skills and attention without having to worry that a brokerage commission or a dealer profit will get in the way. In exchange the counselor, when everything goes right, obtains an agreed-upon fee plus the satisfaction of a job well done.

Readers can learn more about the basics of real estate counseling from the excellent publications listed in the References. Why, then, should they read this book? The answer is that there is almost nothing in print to tell the beginner how to enter and succeed in this fast-growing field. Between the plain brown covers in your hand are the practical things you need to know—most of them previously unmentioned in public—about real estate counseling as an art and a business. Here you will find laid bare the little secrets that aren't taught in any school, the how-tos and when-tos and what-fors that seasoned counselors have learned by trial and error, the bits of advice that can save you time, spare you mistakes and help you do a better job for your clients.

Like it or not, real estate counseling is a business as well as a profession. It must have money to pay the bills, feed the boss, support growth and sustain itself through lean times. Like other businesses, counseling lives on revenues that come only if it produces something people want and are willing to pay for. Counselors therefore have to offer a useful product, market it effectively and deliver the goods in order to get paid. This means, among other things, that they must hire and train employees, keep adequate records, control costs, send bills and collect payments, pay expenses and taxes, protect themselves against legal challenges and do whatever they can to keep the customers happy. In this book you will find enough about these and other everyday business concerns to save you time and money as you develop your real estate counseling practice.

Experienced counselors can expect to learn at least a few things that will improve their service to clients, raise their professional standing and sweeten their bottom lines. Others who are just starting out in counseling, or who are thinking about it as a full-time or part-time occupation, will learn enough about the field to decide whether or not it's right for them. Both kinds of readers, I hope, will arrive at a clearer understanding of counseling and what it can do for the public, which hasn't always been well treated by the real estate industry. Most Americans would agree that it's time somebody wised them up.

Part I

The Business Of Real Estate Counseling

Chapter 1

What Counselors Do

Even inside the real estate industry, few people have a clear idea of what real estate counselors do. This lack of awareness can be a real handicap when counselors talk with prospective clients. To make communication easier, let's briefly consider what counseling is all about.

The American Society of Real Estate Counselors, by far the leading organization in the field, offers the following definition of counseling:

> Providing competent, disinterested, and unbiased advice, professional guidance, and sound judgment on diversified problems in the broad field of real estate involving any or all segments of the business such as merchandising, leasing, management, planning, financing, appraising, court testimony, and other similar services. Counseling may involve the utilization of any or all of these services.

From this definition, you may gather that counselors do what brokers, salespeople, planners, managers, architects, builders, developers, appraisers and mortgage bankers do every day without thinking twice about it. There is a difference, though. When counselors offer their advice, or lend a hand to help a client, they do so on a strictly professional basis for an agreed fee, not for a commission or a profit.

Counselors spend much of their professional time playing doctor.

What kinds of things do counselors do? Too many to list without putting the reader to sleep. Here are a few of them:

- *Diagnosing the problem.* One of the most important tasks for the counselor is to find out what, if anything, is wrong or needs to be done. The counselor acts in the same way a doctor does when a patient comes in with a complaint or for a checkup. He identifies the nature and cause of any apparent problems so that treatment—or a health maintenance program—can start.

- *Getting the facts.* Doctors order and perform tests, talk to colleagues, look up unusual cases in the professional literature; so do counselors. Like doctors, counselors sometimes need to conduct a major study; at other times they may only need to make a few phone calls or visit with the client a few times.

- *Recommending solutions*. Once the problem and the facts have been disclosed, the doctor—and the real estate counselor—can recommend an appropriate course of action. The recommendation may be made in a formal report, a letter or a conversation. Often it consists of a strategy, a program, a set of standards or a bit of sage advice.
- *Helping the client*. Doctors and real estate counselors also are available along the way to help patients and clients solve their problems. For the counselor this help may involve searching out opportunities, negotiating deals, mediating disputes, testifying in court or selecting, recruiting, instructing and supervising the client's agents, contractors and employees.

COUNSELING QUESTIONS

Counselors are called upon to cope with a wide range of problems and opportunities. Here are just a few of the questions clients ask counselors to resolve:

- What is the best use of this property?
- Can I improve its performance?
- Should the property be left as is, rehabilitated or sold?
- Would it pay to subdivide the property before putting it up for sale?
- How should it be marketed?
- How should the marketing people be selected and instructed?
- Would a trade make better sense?
- Who are the likely buyers?
- What kinds of financing are available?
- How long should it take to sell?
- How should I deal with the toxic substance problems?
- What can I do to make the property more attractive?
- Should I rezone now or let the buyer do it?
- What are the chances of success for a development?
- How should I plan this development project?
- Is the project economically feasible?
- How will it affect the community?
- What are the risks?
- Where should I locate my new stores?
- Should I buy, build or lease?
- How much should I expect to pay?
- What should I try to accomplish in the negotiations?
- Can I improve the design of my real estate portfolio?
- What would be a fair way to divide it with my partners?
- How should we instruct the appraisers?

What clients hope to accomplish with the aid of counselors is to improve their positions as real estate owners, users, browsers, taxpayers or neighbors Achieving this goal may require counselors to make a choice, develop a plan, prove a point or cope with a challenge. It also requires counselors to identify their clients' opportunities as well as their problems and advise clients on how

to exploit them. Some clients have wealth they want to conserve and increase; others are still eager to make a pile of their own. Many just want to enjoy their lives more. Counselors try to help clients attain their objectives while earning an honest living—and, if they can, leaving the world better off.

Among the most valuable things counselors do for their clients, often without acknowledging them, are to:

- Prevent bad things from happening.
- Create heroes. Many a corporate ladder-climber or eager professional looks to the counselor for a way to look good.
- Rescue someone. When things are going badly, a client may need a life preserver or helping hand from the counselor.
- Remobilize the immobile. Clients who get stuck often need the counselor to redefine their problem or show them a way out.

Is this kind of work worthy of a responsible person's professional lifetime? You bet it is—not just because the counselor is helping other people but also because the counselor is dealing with an important subject matter: land and how it is used. What counselors do can have major consequences for their communities, affecting the way neighborhoods, towns, cities and regions grow and function. The real business of counseling isn't making money for the counselor or even the client. It's improving the well-being of other people and the areas in which they live and work.

TYPICAL COUNSELING PRODUCTS

What the counselor produces varies with the nature of the assignment. Sometimes it's a written report, but it also may take other forms. Among the possibilities: court testimony, comments made to the client while touring properties, help in preparing or implementing a land use plan, discussion of criteria to be used in selecting a store location, evaluation of an investment, advice about hiring an architect or appraiser. The counselor may be involved in almost any activity relating to real property—except the physical work associated with construction, maintenance and demolition—provided it is conducted on a professional basis for a fee, not for a commission or profit.

More often, though, the counselor's work product takes one or more of the following forms. The terminology used to describe these products is not hard-and-fast, and this list of counseling products is not exhaustive. The following discussion does, however, provide an overview of the most common types of counseling output:

> *Feasibility study*: A study intended to demonstrate to the client and any interested third parties whether or not a proposed development is feasible. It usually includes a description of the project, an analysis of its marketability, a set of financial projections, and a comparison of anticipated revenues against development costs to test whether the project is economically justified.
>
> *Market analysis*: An umbrella term for a variety of real estate studies; properly speaking, an analysis of a market, either in general or as it applies to a specific location or use. A counselor will prepare a market analysis when a client wants to know, for example, what retail sales volumes may be generated by a store in a designated area (without specifying the location and nature of the improvements to be constructed), or how well a particular fast-food outlet will perform. Elements of a market analysis for such a client may include a review of area demographics and retail sales statistics; an estimate of available purchasing power for individuals in relevant demographic categories; opinion research to determine customer characteristics and preferences; and, finally, a statement of anticipated sales volumes at the locations under consideration.
>
> *Highest and best use study*: An assessment of how land should be used for maximum profit or value, with due regard to public good. Through such a study, counselors explore land use possibilities and recommend the most promising.
>
> *Location analysis*: A study that explores the characteristics of a site or tests its appropriateness for a specific use, addressing such factors as zoning, utilities, foundation conditions, accessibility and prominence.
>
> *Site location study*: A search for and comparison of available locations for a proposed use: motel, bank branch, distribution center, chicken shack.
>
> *Development plan*: An outline of the activities needed to bring about a real estate development. Elements may include market research, design and development criteria, a zoning review, physical planning, cost studies, market and feasibility analysis, impact studies and the preparation of a formal plan setting forth the specific actions to be taken, the time line and the project management as the development goes forward.
>
> *Impact study*: A review of the effects of a proposed development or zoning change, usually prepared for planning and zoning boards and neighbors. Impact studies addressing these problems consider neighboring land uses and property values, seek out comparable situations in other areas and measure the likely effects of the project on traffic, school population, tax revenues, park utilization and other concerns.
>
> *Zoning analysis*: Ordinarily used in connection with proposals to change the zoning of a specific property or area, this kind of study may start with an evaluation of existing zoning patterns: Is there enough

Counselors produce a lot of written reports.

commercial land, for example, to meet the needs of the community? Is there too much industrial land? It also may consider the impact of the specific zoning ordinance or zoning change on neighboring properties, businesses and home owners. Sometimes the zoning analysis also involves a review of planning legislation, zoning administration and other matters.

Management review: An evaluation of the performance of the property management or asset management firm responsible for the real estate. This usually entails a physical inspection to check the condition and maintenance of the real estate followed by meetings with the manager and a review of administrative procedures, management records, tenant relations and operating information. The evaluation assesses management policies, personnel, administration, property maintenance, tenant selection, tenant performance and other relevant items.

Cost/benefit study: An assessment of the tradeoffs associated with a real estate decision. This type of study commonly assesses the tradeoff between the benefits and the costs that are expected to accrue from a decision. Counselors often study such relationships informally in connection with a broader problem, but they also may prepare formal cost/benefit reports with the help of consulting architects, engineers or cost estimators.

Portfolio analysis: Typically, the review of an existing or proposed real estate portfolio evaluates not merely the individual assets held, but also the asset mix, design and administration of the portfolio. The analysis also may furnish criteria to select properties and negotiate their purchase as well as to evaluate the performance of the portfolio manager. Sophisticated investment analysis techniques may be required, including sensitivity analysis to test the soundness of the property mix and to measure risks.

These and other kinds of studies can be combined in various ways to meet the needs of the client and the situation. Counselors frequently are called upon to be creative in finding new solutions that will serve the client's actual needs, not merely to prepare standard products that are somebody's idea of the way things are "supposed to" be done.

Any of these studies also may be involved in *litigation support*, a recognized service provided by many counselors. Litigation support helps the client and his attorneys sort out the facts of a case and prepare an effective presentation which may or may not involve the counselor's testimony. This type of work is sensitive and can have important consequences. Not every counselor is suited for it, as it requires, among other attributes, a retentive memory, the ability to organize masses of information, a thick skin, presence of mind and an agreeable, or at least convincing, courtroom demeanor. It also may require considerable research skills, unusual access to information and acknowledged expertise in the relevant areas of real estate.

WHAT COUNSELING COSTS

Fees for real estate counseling vary tremendously, depending on the scope and nature of the assignment, the availability of information and the reputation of the counselor. Sometimes fees may be keyed to results (see the discussion of "value billing" in Chapter 20). Assignments that call for an unusually high degree of responsibility or that can be done only by extremely capable people naturally command higher fees. So do urgent assignments that demand an unusual intensity of service or that tie up the counselor's office. Legal exposure—the extent to which the counselor must accept the risk of litigation associated with an assignment—is growing in importance as a factor that counselors must consider in deciding how much to charge.

Many counseling services can be folded into reasonably standard packages that carry established fee structures. Some services, though, cannot. Charges for these services are set by mutual agreement, often on the basis of the amount of time required to do the work. For more discussion on this sensitive topic, and on how to bid when bidding is called for, see Chapter 20.

IS COUNSELING A PROFESSION?

Yes and no. Real estate counseling is not yet well enough defined or recognized to be accepted as a profession on the same footing as law, medicine and accounting. There is no one standard advanced degree program or examination that qualifies an aspiring counselor for entry into the field, nor is there a universally accepted professional designation comparable to the MD, CPA or MAI. On the other hand, counselors do perform services in a professional manner and adhere to a code of ethics.

Part of the problem with real estate counseling at the present time is that any graduate program designed to train real estate counselors can equally well produce real estate developers, rehabbers, brokers, managers, appraisers, investors, syndicators and salespeople. What these occupations have in common is a body of knowledge and a set of skills that pertain to real estate in general. The counselor is presumed to have these skills, plus the ability to offer advice and support on a fee-for-service basis. As these latter abilities are best acquired by mentoring and experience, perhaps with the help of a few days' training, it's difficult to sustain the position that counseling expertise, rather than real estate expertise, is what counts. On the other hand, lawyers do many things besides practicing law, and many a doctor never sees a patient.

It's not unlikely that real estate counseling some day will be universally recognized as a true profession, but that recognition will come only after the industry establishes a reasonably credible set of professional standards and an entry examination comparable to the CPA and bar exams. Until then, the question will remain at least partly open.

References

ARTICLES

1. Bacow LS: Foreign investment, vertical integration and the structure of the US real estate industry. *Real Estate Issues* 15(2): Fall/Winter 1990, p 1.

2. Delaney CJ and Seldin M: Real estate in the 21st century. A Delphi perspective. *Real Estate Issues* 14(2):Fall/Winter 1989, p 1.

3. Pagliari JL: Real estate in 3-D: see it now! *Real Estate Issues* 15(2):Fall/Winter 1990, p 16.

4. Pittman RH and Seldin M: Real estate analyses using geographic data. *Real Estate Issues* 15(1):Spring/Summer 1990, p 32.

5. Rice, HH: The Legacy of the 1980s. *The Appraisal Journal*, LX(1): January 1992, p. 33.

6. Seldin M: Enhancing the quality of real estate decisions by use of the judgmental model. *Research on Real Estate*, monograph series, Kapplin, SD (ed) 1990.

7. Waller NG: Managing savings and loan portfolios. *Real Estate Issues* 11(1): Spring/Summer 1986, p 17.

8. Wunder GC: Restrictive clauses in shopping center leases: a review. *Real Estate Issues* 13(1):Spring/Summer 1988, p 29.

PERIODICALS

1. *The Appraisal Journal*, Appraisal Institute, 875 N. Michigan Ave., Chicago, IL 60611

2. *Business Facilities*, Group C Communications, 121 Monmouth St., Red Bank, NJ 07701

3. *Real Estate Issues*, American Society of Real Estate Counselors, 430 N. Michigan Avenue, Chicago, IL 60611

4. *Real Estate Review*, Warren, Gorham and Lamont, Inc., 1 Pennsylvania Plaza, New York, 10119

BOOKS

1. American Society of Real Estate Counselors: *Real Estate Counseling*. (Chicago, IL) 1988.

2. Selden M and Boykin JH (eds); *Real Estate Analyses*. (American Society of Real Estate Counselors and Dow Jones-Irwin) 1990.

3. Seldin M (ed): *The Real Estate Handbook*. (Homewood, IL: Dow Jones-Irwin) 1990.

4. The Appraisal Institute: *The Appraisal of Real Estate*, 10th edition. (Chicago, IL) 1992.

5. Blew JM: *Casebook in Real Estate Financing and Development*. (Glenview, IL: Scott Foresman and Co.) 1989.

6. Carn NG, Rabianski J, et al: *Real Estate Market Analysis: Techniques and Applications*. (Englewood Cliffs, NJ: Prentice-Hall) 1988.

7. Clapp JM: *Handbook for Real Estate Market Analysis*. (Englewood Cliffs, NJ: Prentice-Hall) 1987.

8. Halper S: *Shopping Center and Store Leases*. (New York: Law Journal Seminar Press) 1985.

9. McMahan J: *Real Estate Development*. (McGraw-Hill Publishing Co.) 1989.

10. Miles M, et al: *Real Estate Development Principles and Process.* (Washington, DC: The Urban Land Institute) 1991.

11. Saft SM: *Real Estate Development.* (New York: John Wiley and Sons) 1990.

12. Smith HC: *Real Estate Appraisal.* (Dayton, OH: Century VII Publishing Co.) 1987.

13. Welton K (ed): *Successful Leasing and Selling of Office Property.* (Lincoln Institute of Land Policy) 1985.

14. Welton K (ed): *Successful Leasing and Selling of Retail Property.* (Lincoln Institute of Land Policy) 1985.

15. Wills RK: *Case Studies in Real Estate.* (Englewood Cliffs, NJ: Prentice-Hall) 1990.

Chapter 2

Who Counselors Are

Practically anyone can profess to be a real estate counselor. Many people do who earn most of their living in other ways. The genuine article, however, is a qualified person who has adopted the counseling role and given up the chance to earn a commission or make a profit from a real estate venture in exchange for an agreed-upon professional fee.

Some counselors are executives from other fields.

These people often come from and remain in other areas of the real estate business. Lawyers, architects, developers, engineers, accountants, economists and others sometimes offer real estate counseling services. Probably the most common parallel career is that of the real estate appraiser, whose work overlaps the counselor's and whose professional formation is similar. The difference is that the appraiser's primary work is the estimation of value, while the counselor's is broader in scope and requires knowledge of other subjects.

Nothing (except possibly their employment contracts) prevents counselors from changing hats and acting as commission brokers, managers or dealers. When they do these things, though, they are not acting as counselors, and must make sure that their clients are aware of the change. Professionals who possess more than one hat owe to the world a clear statement that specifies which hat they are actually wearing so clients do not inadvertently hire a broker or a dealer when they really want a counselor.

Kinds of counselors. Counselors come in many forms. Some are part-time, some full-time; some are specialists, some generalists. Their skills vary greatly. Some are primarily researchers and problem-solvers; others are planners, diagnosticians, decision-makers, idea people, strategists, implementers, fighters or communicators.

Their backgrounds and experience are equally diverse. Counselors may come from almost any area of business, government, politics, social work, civic activity or academic life. Some will know most about shopping centers, others about various kinds of properties; some will be developers, others brokers, managers, appraisers, financial experts.

There is no single best background or kind of experience. The principal requirement is that the counselor be equipped to deal with the kinds of problems that most likely will be encountered and to perform the basic tasks of counseling. General intelligence, some degree of versatility, decent ethical standards and a genuine interest in the problems of other people will help to assure success.

WHO CAN BE A COUNSELOR?

Almost anybody. All it takes is a willingness to sell advice to someone who is willing to pay for it. So far, except where a real estate license is mandatory, no particular memberships, degrees or certificates are necessary, though that situation is changing. Until it does in your jurisdiction, the ticket to the real estate counseling profession is still free.

Many potential real estate counselors are merely interested in expanding their range of services; others want to make counseling a full-time occupation. Either choice is acceptable; after all, many of the best people in the field are sideline practitioners who spend most of their time in brokerage, development, management or appraising activities.

Part-time counselors may be executives in investment banking, management consulting or general real estate firms; others work for governmental bodies, insurance companies and large corporations. Still others practice in related fields such as law, accounting, architecture, engineering and financial planning. They enjoy sharing their expertise on a professional basis but don't want to make counseling their main occupation (although some may turn to full-time counseling after they retire).

While part-timers like these may be technically deficient in some aspects of counseling, they often offer more valuable services in the areas of their special expertise than better-trained but less-experienced full-time consultants. The standards to which they must adhere are mainly their own (and those of their clients!); so are their rules, prices and schedules. Their work may provide an additional source of income, but acts mainly as a diversion from their daily grind with opportunities for service and enjoyment.

Full-timers, on the other hand, must take counseling more seriously. Although individuals may enter the field directly from school, they are more likely to move into counseling from another area of real estate. Typically, full-time counselors are people who enjoy the professional orientation of the work, the opportunities to serve the community and the exposure to often complex and interesting real estate problems. Many appreciate the fact that counseling allows them to finish one assignment and move on to the next, rather than engage in a real estate management or development project that requires their attention over a period of years. Others—especially jaded brokers—enjoy the prospect that they will be paid a fee whether or not a deal is made.

Career counselors tend to be rather craftsmanlike in their approach to work. They like to think a problem through, dig out the data and present solutions to the problem in a convincing fashion. People who enjoy the hunt and the kill more than the selection of the bow and the placement of the arrow may be better off as developers, dealers or brokers.

SKILLS THE COUNSELOR NEEDS

The work of the counselor requires sharp skills and an appreciation of industry trends. Extensive reading is mandatory; so is attendance at educational programs and meetings of professional and business groups to assure constant access to current information.

Analytical and communication skills are essential.

Counselors need more than experience and technical proficiency in real estate and business matters; they also require specific counseling skills. Among these are the ability to:

- *Listen*. If you can't listen, you won't be worth much as a counselor. You must be able to pay close attention to what the client or the prospect is saying, to hear the music as well as the words and spot hidden agendas. Counselors must listen carefully in order to learn: What does the client really need—and why? How urgent is the problem? What possible solutions have already been explored? What connections does the client have that might be helpful—or troublesome? Who else is involved? Where is the client coming from emotionally? What personality traits is the client exhibiting? What does the client expect from this meeting—and from you? (For help with this aspect of counseling, see Chapter 19.)

- *Learn*. New information will mean little if you can't absorb it. You, as a real estate counselor, must be open to the facts and willing to apply new and different interpretations to them. You need to learn how to fit the facts into patterns you already know and combine well-known facts or concepts from different fields. For example, Newton recognized that falling apples had something to do with the movement of the planets.

- *Investigate*. Counselors must know where to look and how to dig for information: how to use a library card, hook into the computerized databases, tap a business connection. They also need to know how to ask questions in ways that encourage people to respond. This means framing the questions so they invite lengthy answers. The hard questions are saved for later in the conversation and posed in a nonthreatening way. Your tact and friendliness, as well as your persistence, will pay off when you are able to discover facts other people do not have, facts that may be essential to solving the real estate problem.

- *Analyze*. You can't make use of the information you collect unless you know how to identify significant facts and relate them to the problem. Computers will not give you all the answers, however indispensable they may be. You need to use all your mental faculties to think around and through a problem, expand a frame of reference or look at a problem from a completely new angle and test a variety of hypotheses before you move to a conclusion.

- *Synthesize.* Counselors need to pull the facts, analyses and interpretations together before they can take their answers to the client. You should be able to relate the use, value and potential of the property not only to the client's needs but also to such contingencies as the dangers of a falling stock market. If you can see the big picture, you will be especially valued as a counselor; if you can see only the small scenes, you probably should be doing something else for a living.
- *Communicate.* Real estate counseling services aren't worth much if the counselor can't make the client understand what he is saying. In some cases, you won't be effective unless you can reach the client emotionally as well as intellectually. Knowing how to present your ideas effectively is not a talent any of us is born with; it is a skill that must be developed through experience, education, training and reading. If you have trouble in this area, by all means work at it. Language, spoken and written, after all, is the best means we have to persuade and lead other people. (Chapter 15 contains useful tips on this topic.)
- *Maintain versatility.* Counselors must be flexible enough to confront many different kinds of problems from a variety of perspectives. There will be times when you'll need to call upon your skills in mathematics and logic, and other times when you'll need to rely more on your understanding of human nature. Having many strings to your bow lets you adapt to market opportunities and cope with a broad range of challenges. That's a formula for growth—and rising fees.

COUNSELING CAREERS

In large multi-office organizations such as national accounting and appraisal firms or the Federal government, the career path is obvious: hard work, adequate technical skills, professional integrity, team spirit and an ability to attract new business will lead to advancement. In smaller organizations the path may be less clear, but the counselor can generally enhance his reputation and improve his chances of promotion by working on larger and more sensitive assignments. Rising counselors may move sideways from time to time, joining a more hospitable firm or entering a related field such as asset management; many choose to launch their own firms. Meanwhile, as a counselor becomes more valuable professionally, he also will become better known and more important in the civic and business communities as a leader or a responsible participant.

Recognition may come more quickly to aspiring counselors who become members of established professional organizations (see Chapter 3). The CRE designation in particular carries special weight with people in the know; so does the MAI designation of the Appraisal Institute. But there is no magic, indispensable ticket in this field; the counselor's individual capabilities and personal reputation in the end will determine success or failure.

By far the most important single factor in counseling, as in other professions, is a rock-solid reputation for personal integrity. The dishonest counselor, or the one who fudges and cuts corners, will never build the kind of reputation that assures a successful career.

APPRAISERS? BROKERS? COUNSELORS?

As we have already seen, counselors provide other services besides advice. Many of these services are also provided by appraisers. Counselors conduct research, prepare marketing and development plans, testify in court and before zoning bodies, estimate values, and do other things appraisers often do in the course of their work. Appraisers, on the other hand, do many things that counselors claim as their specialties. In fact, the two fields overlap to such an extent that roughly half the members of the American Society of Real Estate Counselors hold the Appraisal Institute's MAI designation as well as the Counselor's CRE.

Counselors also act for their clients in many situations that impinge on the territory of other professionals. They frequently are retained to implement a client's programs, serving as the client's representative, agent or assistant in dealing with a wide range of problems. Counselors may even represent their clients in procuring or negotiating leases, easements and other property transfers.

Counseling, appraising and brokerage frequently overlap.

This particular form of counseling is rather uneasily accepted by the American Society of Real Estate Counselors because it so closely parallels the work of real estate brokers, who also research markets, view properties, identify likely prospects, draft and execute selling campaigns and negotiate deals on the clients' behalf. The difference is that the counselor in these cases works for an agreed-upon fee, not for a profit or on commission. The counseling contract provides that the counselor will be paid, usually at hourly rates or in a lump sum, for doing the work, whether or not a deal is made, though it often provides for additional payment if the campaign is successful.

"Transaction counseling" of this type can be desirable as well as legitimate. It assures clients that they will receive the counselor's full attention and allows clients to demand more in the way of research and planning than they can reasonably expect from a broker whose compensation is entirely contingent. Performance fees (see Chapter 20), which are payable only if and when a specified result is achieved, can make the counselor's total compensation equivalent to a brokerage commission. In the end, if everything goes right, the client is well served and the counselor well paid. If not, there will be at least a consolation prize, usually enough to cover project costs, for the counselor's efforts.

Does this leave everyone happy? Obviously not. The full-time commission broker sees this arrangement as a way to cut commissions and deprive him of his rightful compensation. Most career real estate counselors tend to agree with those who believe that this particular mix of advisory and operative services is acceptable; however, those who are active Realtors can understand and sympathize with the protests of their broker friends.

The fact that you may be engaged in transaction counseling, or any other kind of arrangement that provides for performance fees, does not excuse you from exercising the ethical behavior required of all counselors (see Chapter 4). The counselor, after all, is a trusted advisor to whom people turn for advice that is untainted by pecuniary and personal considerations. This role places a special burden upon the advisor, who must avoid not just the reality but also the appearance of bias.

Does a counseling career make sense? Not for everybody. There are other things you may do that offer bigger thrills, more power, even the chance to make more money when the times are right. The born salesman should sell; the born builder should build. Counseling is unlikely to make you king of the hill in a hurry. But for people who see themselves more as professionals than as entrepreneurs, who have a scholarly turn of mind and who enjoy facing a steady stream of new problems that invite creative solutions, counseling can offer a rewarding professional life.

Can you make it as a professional real estate counselor? Should you try? No one but you can answer these questions. Only you know whether you have the stuff and the desire to build a successful practice. Still, it never hurts to take counsel. Seek out people who are active in the field; find out what they think of your suitability as a counselor; get an idea of how they lead their business lives. Ask these individuals whether there is enough work in your specialty areas, and what your prospects are likely to be. After all, chances are the advice will be free!

References

ARTICLES

1. Langley SC: A CRE's viewpoint. *Real Estate Issues* 14(1):Spring/Summer 1989, p. 43.

2. Schwethelm AC: Counseling and eminent domain. *Real Estate Issues* 14(1): Spring/Summer 1989, p 25.

3. White JR: Counselors: professionally motivated business people. *Real Estate Issues* 14(2):Fall/Winter 1989, p 49.

BOOKS

1. American Society of Real Estate Counselors: *Real Estate Counseling.* 1984.

2. Seldin M, Boykin, J: *Real Estate Analyses.* (American Society of Real Estate Counselors and Dow Jones-Irwin) 1990.

3. Dilmore G: *Quantitative Techniques in Real Estate Counseling.* (Lexington, MA: Lexington Books) 1981.

Chapter 3

The Counseling Industry

The counseling field is expanding as fast as its markets.

HOW IT WORKS

Big changes are occurring in the business of real estate counseling, as they are in the overall real estate business. The restructuring and globalization of corporate America, the collapse of thrift institutions, the rise of pension funds and the opening of a worldwide market for financial products have dramatically affected property ownership and management. More and more, the real estate that was previously owned by local rich men who kept their finances to themselves has been disappearing into publicly owned investment pools administered by teams of financial professionals headquartered in distant cities.

This revolution has expanded the counseling industry, which for years was made up of prominent individuals who were occasionally called upon to address the problems of their most important customers and clients. Although many successful real estate practitioners still perform counseling on a part-time basis, more and more is being done by counseling groups large enough to serve the new institutional and corporate real estate marketplace. These groups can be found among major accounting firms, investment banking houses, financial institutions and appraisal organizations.

As buildings that used to be traded back and forth across a card table by local tycoons have become mere chips in the much bigger international game, the counselor has had to cover a larger area of the world. This has led to a wave of mergers and consolidations among counseling firms. The number of small- to medium-size firms has declined as large accounting and investment banking organizations have entered the business and established beachheads. With their tremendous resources and client networks, these large firms have been making rapid progress, despite conflict-of-interest problems and their often cumbersome administrative requirements.

The absorption of many well-known smaller counseling firms by larger ones is consistent with broad national and international economic trends. So is the assimilation of prominent individual counselors by accounting firms and financial conglomerates. Counseling firms and counselors are going where the action is. Large accounting firms, in particular, seem destined to attract more and more counseling work because they are accustomed to dealing with financial problems on behalf of clients, know how to administer professional people, have credibility as sources of financial information and understand the liability risks that are part of the business. Built into such firms are enormous client bases that can provide a virtually endless supply of new counseling assignments, subject to the conflict-of-interest issues that inevitably arise.

These changes can present a serious problem for counselors who must compete with growing giants in accounting and financial services to survive. For others, they represent opportunities to sell or merge their companies, and perhaps get a better job. As the big players jockey for position in this expanding field, they are aggressively seeking out leading real estate counselors as potential merger partners and employees.

In the end, of course, there always will be room for the individual counselor and the small firm. The flexibility, versatility and quickness of the small players ensure their survival even in a world dominated by giants. Those who have unique skills or expertise to offer will thrive in the new environment; they even may outlast some of their larger competitors.

KINDS OF FIRMS

Many different kinds of organizations provide counseling services, ranging from sole practitioners to large conglomerates.

The sole practitioner. Time was when the best real estate counselors operated entirely on their own, perhaps with a leg-person or two and a secretarial assistant. Some counselors still do. Often they are retired or semi-retired real estate practitioners: brokers, developers, mortgage bankers, financial executives or real estate officers with established networks that serve as sources of counseling business.

The lot of these sole practitioners can be difficult. While the administrative burdens they carry are light and the personal freedom they enjoy is considerable, such people generally are at the mercy of widely fluctuating work flows. They also are limited in the activities they can perform because they often cannot justify the expense of maintaining adequate support systems or providing a wide range of services. Problems involving large shopping centers, office buildings, industrial complexes, apartment projects and hotels may be too complex for them to tackle without help.

Sole practitioners pay a price for their freedom.

Some counselors have tried to solve this problem by working with subcontractors. However, subcontractors can be costly, they may not be available when you need them, and they don't always perform as expected. A counselor can, of course, pretend to have all the necessary knowledge and abilities; sooner or later, however, inadequacies tend to become apparent. If a counselor is good enough, he may be able to satisfy clients with problems that fall within his area of expertise. If he is cheap enough, the counselor may be able to attract clients willing to put up with second-class service. Either way, the sole practitioner often has a lonely professional life with many ups and downs.

The small firm. Small firms have been the rule in real estate counseling until fairly recently, for several good reasons. Counseling work is difficult to institutionalize; it requires a great deal of flexibility and often demands creative thinking. These characteristics give small organizations an inherent advantage over large firms which, by their very nature, are bureaucratic and rigid. Small firms also attract creative professionals, especially those who seek autonomy and professional satisfaction.

Working with a small firm can offer real pleasures to its clients and employees. Such firms can provide a broader range of expertise than the sole practitioner can, along with the camaraderie and mutual support that make the workday enjoyable. Unburdened by the large organization's administrative demands, small firms are relatively free to change location, and they are economical to operate. On the other hand, they lack the market reach, financial strength and the defensive capabilities of the big firm, and they seldom can afford to maintain the databases that increasingly are being required to perform counseling services responsibly.

Often small firms are organized as partnerships or Subchapter S corporations, although they may be sole proprietorships (see Chapter 6). If you are establishing or entering a partnership, be sure to pick your partners carefully. These are people with whom you will have to work day-to-day and on whose efforts and character your own fortunes will depend.

Ask yourself at least the following questions:

Choosing partners? Careful!

- Do I like these people?
- Can I depend on them?
- What qualities and clients will they bring to the venture?
- Are they financially responsible?
- Do they enjoy good reputations?
- Are they mature and stable?
- Can they stand up to a crisis?
- What will they add to the partnership?
- What will they add to my own capabilities?

If the answers to these questions don't give a reasonable promise of a successful, enjoyable and enduring relationship, take a pass. You have other options open.

In-between-sizes. The solo counselor and the very small counseling firm generally operate at a disadvantage. It takes a good-size team of counselors to provide the full range of services demanded by today's clients, who may have real estate interests involving many different kinds of property scattered across the country, if not the world. While every counselor is something of a generalist and some feel they can take on almost any problem that comes up, in reality it is only by marshalling the combined skills of a diversified counseling group or firm that a counselor can serve many clients adequately.

The required talents and experience can be organized in a number of ways. A common framework has one counselor and several staff people who collectively provide the necessary expertise. In this arrangement the lead counselor in effect conducts a professional practice with assistants, much like a lawyer in a solo practice who employs several trained clerks. This format allows the boss to enjoy a good deal of autonomy and enlarge the range of services he offers. It also can produce a better-looking bottom line than the counselor can generate alone.

Yet such a practice, however it may be expanded, lacks certain important attributes. Having only one principal, the practice cannot assure either clients or employees that it will continue to operate without him. These types of practices seldom name a successor who will head the firm after the principal retires, nor can they carry on effectively when the principal is sick, hurt or on vacation. Relying on only one counseling professional, they can stagnate from lack of new ideas and insights. Without the multiple networks that are available in larger organizations, the principal's knowledge of the marketplace and of industry trends can slip behind that of larger competitors. Perhaps worst of all, counselors in such practices seldom get the feedback and fresh inputs that are exchanged among professionals in larger firms. They may, as a result, fall victim to complacency based more on past glories than on present accomplishments.

Counselors who work on their own in large real estate firms, investment banking houses and other large organizational structures can overcome these drawbacks, at least to some extent. A better solution, though, is to work in a medium-size partnership or corporation that is set up to do counseling, perhaps along with appraising and consulting or some other related service. Such organizations have several principals who can swap stories and information, spur one another to greater achievement and step into the breach when the occasion demands. The group can be loose and flexible or highly structured, and can operate at many levels of professional sophistication.

However large, an organization remains essentially a personal practice until it is able to operate effectively in the absence of the principal. At that point—when other people are able to supervise the work, sign the reports, mind the store and attract new work—the group ceases to be a practice and becomes a business subject to the management principles that govern businesses everywhere.

Practice or business?

Such a company can survive the death of its founder or the disability of a key partner. Its business does not depend on a single person, nor does its overall administration. As a result, the company has stability, credibility and potential for growth. On the other hand, it may tend to lose flexibility, alertness and the ability to adapt quickly when circumstances change. Almost guaranteed is an increase in the amount of time that must be spent on internal communications and in the resolution of disagreements.

In terms of size, an individual practice—one lead counselor plus associates and staff—can seldom employ more than seven or eight people without encountering administrative and quality control problems. Practices with 12 to 15 employees need a strong second-in-command to serve as the principal's surrogate and potential successor. These practices also may find it worthwhile to install a good time-and-billing system, hire a database manager and begin to operate like a larger firm in other ways.

Big firms. The advantages—and disadvantages—of large organizations are considerable. Because the big guys are big, they can field enough troops for massive jobs that must be done quickly. They also have organizational depth, geographic reach and a variety of professional skills that few small organizations can hope to match. A large size usually means instant name recognition, a broad scope of services, formal training programs, good databases, sophisticated equipment and the likelihood that the organization will be around tomorrow to look after the client's needs. In the competition for corporate and institutional clients, the big guys usually win.

On the other hand, big firms and governmental agencies almost always lack the flexibility, the alertness and the enthusiasm of the small shop and its prompt decision-making; the boss of a large company, unlike the head of a small company, cannot make decisions on the spot without going through a lengthy chain of approvals. The big firms' deep pockets may make them especially susceptible to lawsuits. They also encounter conflict-of-interest problems more frequently than smaller firms and find it harder to maintain confidentiality in client matters. Some clients, in fact, do not believe a large firm can be trusted to keep their secrets or to put their interests first.

The economic performance of large counseling organizations also may be questionable. These firms can be difficult to manage profitably over the long term. Like small firms, they suffer because of the unpredictability of the work flow, which often varies with the business cycle and is subject to downturns in the firm's active markets and market areas. Another handicap is the large organization's vulnerability to price competition from leaner small firms and from sole practitioners who operate out of their kitchens.

The advantages of the large organizations nevertheless tend to prevail over the long run. Their succession problems can be easier to resolve than those of smaller firms; they are better able to serve big clients; they can promise growth which attracts ambitious staff people; and they can reduce costs and risks by diversifying functionally and geographically.

How large is large? In real estate counseling a small firm or work group may range in size from a minimum of two or three employees—one counselor, perhaps with a secretary and a leg person—to a maximum of eight or nine people. The medium-sized firm may have as few as eight or as many as 30 people; the large firm (in this small world) may include anywhere from 30 to about 300 people, 50% to 80% of whom are considered to be professionals. The possible combinations are numerous and can include professionals in planning, environmental concerns, law, financial management, accounting, marketing, architectural and general research services along with real estate counseling.

Your choice depends on you.

THE RIGHT SIZE FOR YOU

You need to choose a format for your counseling firm that fairly reflects your personality, your expertise, your clientele and your expected work load. Do jobs come in hard-to-predict batches, or do you have a solid group of retainer clients to assure a steady flow of revenue? Do you like to administer, or would you rather do the counseling work yourself? How easy is it for you to attract and hold good assistants and associates? Can your clients get by with occasional attention from you on matters about which only you are knowledgeable, or do they need a broader range of services than you can provide by yourself? Can you live with the fact that most practices in this field die with their founders, or do you want to leave something besides a memory for the next generation? How long do you want to work before you retire? How do you *really* want to spend the rest of your working life?

Not everybody wants or needs to expand his firm or services; those in their declining years often would just as soon leave things pretty much as they are. Most organizations, though, depend upon growth or the prospect of growth to attract, retain and develop good people. Young staffers, in particular, seek out growing organizations or those that show promise of expansion to give them better chances for rapid advancement.

Remember that not every organization has to be creative, efficient or enduring. Think realistically about your goals. It's hard for a large, tightly administered company to be creative, just as it can be hard for a creative organization to be efficient and well-administered. Your clients and friends can help you make good decisions about the kind of organization you should have. Once that decision is made, you can position yourself accordingly, hiring the people and seeking the clients who will move your firm in the desired direction.

Remember, too, that not everyone in your firm has to be the same. Even the most strait-laced firms can make room for an oddball or two, just as even the most free-swinging advertising and design firms need someone to keep the books. Mix and match as you think fit, but don't lose sight of your overriding goals or the fact that your public will tend to see your organization in simplified terms— as a reliable, efficient, creative, responsive, stiff, cheerful, brilliant or confused group of people—depending upon how you choose your people and present them to the world.

PROFESSIONAL SOCIETIES

The leading organization for real estate counselors, at least in terms of prestige, is the American Society of Real Estate Counselors (professional designation CRE), an affiliate of the National Association of Realtors. This group is open only to highly qualified individuals, and membership is by invitation only. The Counselors offer advanced educational programs, enforce a code of ethics and require members to maintain a high degree of general ability as well as excellent personal character. About half the members hold the MAI designation of the Appraisal Institute (see below); the rest come mainly from the ranks of developers, managers, brokers, investment bankers, insurance company executives, academics and full-time real estate counselors.

The Appraisal Institute is an organization of real estate appraisers that includes among its members many individuals who also do real estate counseling. Members of other appraisal groups, some of which are quite large, also include real estate counselors. There is still no well-recognized national association of real estate consultants or counselors that is comparable to the professional societies found in law, medicine, architecture and accounting. It obviously would be desirable to have such an association open to any reputable practitioner of good character regardless of Realtor status, but as yet no such organization has achieved wide recognition.

THE EXPANDING MARKET FOR REAL ESTATE COUNSELING

In today's global real estate environment, the future appears to lie with the large institutions and corporations that are taking over a growing share of the industry. These big players, with their sophisticated computer capabilities and trained staffs, have the data and the skills to track fast-breaking events around the world and reduce them to crunchable numbers.

What they often lack, though, creates opportunities for professional real estate counselors: detailed local knowledge, hands-on experience and seasoned practical judgment. These are precisely the qualities that qualified counselors can offer. Counselors can supplement the capabilities of a client's own staff in significant ways, bringing new ideas as well as new information to the table, verifying the staff's findings, substantiating or modifying its recommendations and adding a degree of professional objectivity that may not be available in-house.

Services of this type can be particularly valuable to institutions and corporations that are distant from the local marketplace and need thorough documentation. Fortunately for counselors, the institutional and corporate share of the total U.S. real estate inventory is large and will continue to expand, as indicated in a 1991 study for the Institute of Real Estate Management by Arthur Andersen & Co. Thanks to the deregulation of the financial community in the 1980s, the breakdown of the thrift organizations and the glut of commercial space that led to the financial collapse of the real estate industry in 1990-91, the big players—banks, insurance companies, pension funds and corporations—have greatly increased their direct equity ownership in real estate through purchase, foreclosure and mortgage loan workouts. These organizations consequently are natural candidates for counseling services.

There is no reason why this trend will reverse itself. The rapid accumulation of money in pension fund accounts, already totaling about $3 trillion, is still at least theoretically available for real estate investment. Real estate's mediocre experience has soured most funds on new real estate investment for now, but few expect to reduce their real estate commitments significantly, and many are looking ahead to further opportunities. Pension funds, like insurance companies and banks, are willing and able to pay for high-quality real estate services. They constitute an enormous and growing market for real estate counseling, one that appreciates expertise and accepts the fact that it costs money.

Other markets also are growing. Governmental agencies, as they struggle to deal with their own mushrooming space requirements (think of the possibilities in new jail construction alone, not to mention homes for the homeless and hospices for the AIDS patients), need help for themselves and for the constituencies they serve and monitor. These constituencies include banks, thrifts, local governments, small businesses, native Americans, women, and other minorities, criminals, the mentally ill, the poor, the sick, the old, the defense industry—the list goes on and on. Counselors have much to contribute in areas that concern government—including commerce, defense, parks, corrections, housing, economic development, urban renewal, planning, taxation and many others. The Resolution Trust Corporation, in particular, has become a veritable mother lode for auctioneers, asset managers, appraisers and real estate advisors of all sorts.

In the private sector, the increasing sophistication of property owners opens the door to further growth in counseling. Sellers, buyers, lessees, lenders, developers, operators and the officials who protect and police them are trying to make better decisions. So are brokers, managers, appraisers and other real estate professionals. The fiduciaries and custodians responsible for real estate held by syndicates, pension funds and insurance companies need backside protection as well as current information and, once in a while, meaningful outside guidance.

All signs indicate that the demand for real estate counseling services is on the rise and that it will continue to increase— through good times and bad—for the foreseeable future. Even during times of recession and in troubled markets, the need for real estate counseling is apparent. Like accountants, counselors are in a recession-resistant industry that can survive even a real estate debacle such as the 1984 oil patch collapse or the commercial property glut of 1989-90. Good times are ahead for good counselors.

References

ARTICLES

1. Blanchard K: Pondering a partnership. *Today's Office* 24 (1) Jun 1990, p 20.
2. Goddard RW: The rise of the new organization: doing business in the 1990s. *Management World* 19(1) Jan/Feb 1990, p 3.
3. Moss Kanter R: Partnerships and progress. *Modern Office Tech* 35(4) Apr 1990, p 14.

BOOKS

1. Arthur Andersen & Co: *Managing the Future*. (Chicago: Institute of Real Estate Management) 1991, pp 71-80.
2. Burstiner I: *The Small Business Handbook*. (New York: McGraw Hill) 1992.
3. Rosenthal L: *Partnering*. (Cincinnati, OH: Writers' Digest Books) 1983.

GOVERNMENT AGENCIES

Business and Pension Statistics, 1111 Constitution Ave, NW, Washington, DC 20224
Department of Commerce, 14th & E Streets, SW, Washington, DC 20230
Department of Housing and Urban Development, 451 7th St., SW, Washington, DC 20410

PROFESSIONAL SOCIETIES

American Association of Certified Appraisers, 7 Eswin St., Cincinnati, OH 45218
American Bankers Association, 1120 Connecticut Avenue, NW, Washington, DC 20036
American Federation of Small Business, 407 S. Dearborn St., Chicago, IL 60605
American Industrial Real Estate Association, 350 S. Figueroa, Los Angeles 90071
American Institute of Architects, 1735 New York Ave, NW, Washington, DC 20006
American Insurance Association, 85 John St, New York, NY 10038
American Society of Appraisers, 11800 Sunrise Valley Dr, Reston, VA 22091
American Society of Real Estate Counselors, 430 N. Michigan Avenue, Chicago, IL 60611
Appraisal Institute, 875 N. Michigan Avenue, Chicago, IL 60611
Building Owners and Managers Association International, 1201 New York Avenue, NW, Suite 200, Washington, DC 20005
Institute of Real Estate Management, 430 N. Michigan Avenue, Chicago, IL 60611
National Association of Corporate Real Estate Executives, 471 Spencer Dr S, West Palm Beach, FL 33409
National Association of Home Builders of the US, 15th and M Sts, NW, Washington, DC 20005
National Association of Housing Cooperatives, 1828 L St, NW, Washington, DC 20036
National Association of Industrial and Office Parks, 1700 N Moore St, Arlington, VA 22209
National Association of Real Estate Appraisers, 853 Broadway, New York, NY 10003
National Association of Real Estate Investment Trusts, 1101 17th St, NW, Washington, DC 20036
National Association of Realtors, 430 N. Michigan Ave., Chicago, IL 60611
National Society of Professional Engineers, 2029 K St, NW, Washington, DC 20006
Public Relations Society of America, 845 Third Avenue, New York, NY 10022
Realtors National Marketing Institute, 430 N. Michigan Avenue, Chicago, IL 60611
Relocation Assistance Association of America, 950 17th St., Denver, CO 80202
Society of Industrial and Office Realtors, 777 14th St., NW, Washington, DC 20005
Urban Land Institute, 625 Indiana Avenue, NW, Washington, DC 20004-2930

Chapter 4

Counseling Ethics and Principles

WHY ETHICS MATTER

Counselors are generally subject to standards of performance and ethics imposed by the Financial Institutions Reform, Recovery and Enforcement Act of 1989 (FIRREA), by state laws and by their own professional societies. They will need to look to their regulators for instruction about these standards, as the rules are too detailed and vary too much among jurisdictions to be discussed here. Apart from such formal constraints, counselors are subject only to general standards of good business and professional conduct.

There are two serious and legitimate purposes for standards of performance and ethics that have little or nothing to do with the regulators, politicians and jailers they support and the feelings of self-respect engendered by conformance with them. These purposes are: (1) the protection of the public, which is especially vulnerable to abuse by the professionals in whom it places trust; and (2) the maintenance of the profession, which depends for survival on the reasonable trust of its clients.

Without the safeguards provided by standards of performance and ethics, the standing of the profession would crumble, and the public would be at the mercy of the charlatans and cutpurses who wait in the wings. That is why we have a positive duty to respect these standards, whether or not they are enforced against us. Besides (though it probably should not be mentioned), a reputation for ethical behavior is attractive to prospective clients and helps present clients sleep easier.

Counselors who wear several hats (such as those of the broker, dealer, appraiser and mortgage banker) must be particularly careful that each client knows which hat is being worn at all times. It is considered unethical for a counselor to persuade a client to convert the counseling relationship to a brokerage or dealer relationship so that the counselor can collect a commission or turn a profit. That's because such a conversion may divide loyalties and eliminate objectivity. On the other hand, counselors usually have no reason to refuse a client who on his own initiative asks them to assume another role as long as the client understands the implications of the change.

Counselors who provide other services have to keep their hats straight.

The rules that follow, particularly as regards candor and discretion, may have to be tempered by common sense in conflict situations, especially litigation (see Chapter 25). A client's circumstances or a court order may force a counselor to disclose facts that should ordinarily be kept confidential. If so, the counselor probably can divulge the information without blame, but there are no guarantees.

SHLAES'S RULES

The following rules of real estate practice have been accumulated over many years of dealings with clients in many different situations.

- Don't lie. Don't exaggerate or over promise. Be straight with the client now and you will spare yourself grief later. You also will like yourself better, which tends to improve the quality and quantity of your sleep.
- Make full disclosure of any potential conflicts (see Chapter 25) and do so right away. Let prospective clients know about any involvements that may be related to the assignment. Such disclosure should include existing or previous connections to the people and companies involved with the problem, the likely solution to the problem, or nearby properties. Full disclosure not only is a key point of professional ethics, but also serves to impress clients with the breadth of your experience and business connections.
- Do the job quietly and faithfully. Clients expect and are entitled to discreet and loyal service. Keep their secrets and your promises. Try never to let the client down even when your attention must be focused elsewhere because of an emergency. Clients seldom forget a serious disappointment, and some view such disappointments as personal betrayals. In addition to keeping clients' professional secrets confidential, you have an obligation to be discreet about other things you may discuss, whether they are told to you in confidence or not. Don't be a blabbermouth.
- Honesty is essential. Candor can even be better, but it is rarer. Try to say what's on your mind, especially when it is important to the client's interests.
- Be diligent in performing the client's work; i.e., perform your counseling services thoroughly, honestly, carefully, promptly and at a fair price, which is a fee that is more or less commensurate with the work done, the responsibilities assumed, the urgency of the tasks performed, the knowledge and abilities required and the amount the market will bear.

It's important to remember that you have obligations to the public as well as to the client. If you are being asked to do something that, in your opinion, violates standards of civic responsibility, say so and, if necessary, resign from the assignment. The client should respect you all the more for doing so.

One further word: Be considerate toward your colleagues. This rule applies not only to people within your firm but also to other counselors in the outside world. Try to be helpful to them as a matter of professional courtesy and for the sake of their own potential value to you as friends and sources of information. Bread cast upon the waters in this context often comes back later with butter and jam added.

Here are four more good rules of ethics (The Four Big D's):
- *Define* the relationship. Make sure all parties to a counseling assignment understand who is the real estate professional and who is the client. Make sure, too, that the relationship is in fact professional and that the compensation arrangements are consistent with your responsibilities.
- *Disclose* any possible conflicts of interest.
- *Do* the work thoroughly so nobody can say that you cheated the client or that money was lost because of your carelessness.
- *Demand* no more than a fair fee for your work.

To these, some would add a Fifth D:
- *Don't* muddy the waters for your fellow counselors by calling into question the legitimacy of the counselor's role or the counseling profession.

SOME COUNSELING PRINCIPLES

The following characteristics of professionalism in real estate counseling also can help guide your work with clients.

> *Information.* Be sure you have enough. Don't depend entirely upon client-supplied information and secondary sources. Go into the field yourself or send responsible investigators to unearth the facts you need. Knowledge is power, true; in counseling, it is also safety. You will assure doing the best for your client if you do a thorough job of research *before* forming your opinions.
>
> *Logic.* Use it. A logical thought process, plainly described, will spare you many mistakes. Show the process to your clients, and chances are good you will be believed—and be *right*.
>
> *Economy.* Don't waste the client's time or money or your own. Write and speak cogently; don't take up time and space with unnecessary work or words. Use expensive, time-consuming illustrations and examples only when necessary.
>
> *Thoroughness.* Deal with all meaningful issues. Keep an eye out for smoke screens, tar babies and other hazards of the industry. Do your homework before you make your recommendations.

Organization. Plan your work and your presentation in an orderly manner. This prevents waste and improves credibility. It also makes you a better professional.

Responsibility. Remember for whom you are working and what you owe to that person, your profession and your own self-esteem. Take those responsibilities seriously. Other people will do the same for you.

Communication. Keep in touch with your clients, your staff, your colleagues and the world at large. Read, write, speak and listen. You must communicate effectively to do a good job as a counselor, and your clients will appreciate your willingness to keep them informed. Plan your communications with the listener or reader in mind so your message will have the best possible chance of getting through.

Timing. Time is a big factor in the real estate process. Keep control of it in your real estate counseling. Have things ready when they're needed, anticipate when other work may be needed and make sure your findings are delivered without delay.

Objectivity. Keep cool, stay straight. If you can't be objective, you aren't doing the job.

Skepticism. Appearances can be deceiving. So can information sources, including clients. Be on guard.

Sophistication. Keep current. Know what's going on in your own market, in the region and across the nation. Clients expect you to be up-to-date on the facts, personalities and technology associated with your industry.

Humility. There's no way you can know everything. If you acknowledge that fact occasionally, your clients will respect you all the more.

References

BOOKS

1. Beauchamp TL: *Ethical Theory and Business.* (Englewood Cliffs, NJ: Prentice-Hall) 1988.
2. DeGeorge RT: *Business Ethics.* (New York: Macmillan) 1986.
3. Gracian B: *The Art of Worldly Wisdom.* (New York: Currency) 1992.
4. Madsen P: *Essentials of Business Ethics.* (New York: Meridian Books) 1990.
5. Needleman J: *Money and the Meaning of Life.* (New York: Currency) 1992.

Part II

Setting Up For Business

Chapter 5

Getting Into the Game

How do you get started in counseling? Let's examine how the beginner in real estate or the established professional can get things going.

BEGINNERS

Starting from scratch in a career as a real estate counselor isn't easy, but it can be done, especially if you are able to locate in a major metropolitan center. Smaller cities seldom offer enough opportunities for counseling services to support a full-time professional, let alone a brand-new one. It's usually easier and more realistic for beginning counselors in small towns to enter some other area of the real estate business that allows them to develop knowledge of the trade as well as counseling capabilities.

Getting an education. It pays to have the right educational background. Until the death of Professor James Graaskamp, (CRE) who headed the Real Estate Center at the University of Wisconsin, there was no degree that gave quite as much credibility to novice counselors as that university's master's degree in real estate. Now other universities also offer degrees that are equally well regarded by real estate professionals. For a list of these universities and recommendations, consult the brightest young people you know in the counseling field or ask the American Society of Real Estate Counselors.

Some degrees are hotter.

A master's degree in real estate is by no means indispensable for success in counseling, and a doctorate even may be a drawback. Some of the best people in the counseling field lack a bachelor's degree, although that is becoming rare. The right job with the right company may offer such wide-ranging learning opportunities that you can progress more quickly as an employee than as a student. Young people with undergraduate degrees, strong natural abilities and some real estate background, or at least a deep interest in real estate, often do better than the holder of a graduate degree.

The degree doesn't have to be in real estate, though business training is helpful. Some of the best counselors grew up in other fields, taking degrees in history, philosophy, literature, music, engineering, mathematics, sociology, geography, urban studies and similar areas. These counselors bring to their professional activities a greater breadth of experience than can be gained in the typical real estate program. Education in real estate is fine to get you started in counseling, but it may not be the best kind of preparation for the long pull.

If you are planning to get an advanced real estate degree, choose a program that will give you a clear understanding of real estate mathematics, a working real estate vocabulary and a comprehensive knowledge of the legal, economic, social and physical aspects of the real estate field.

Before choosing a university, check it out. Who are the faculty? How large is the real estate school, and how does it fit into the academic structure of the university? Is the real estate school adequately funded? How are students selected, and where do they come from? What programs does the school offer? Does it emphasize academic research of a kind that is not likely to hold much practical appeal, or is it oriented toward real-life concerns? Do its courses seem likely to help move you quickly along your chosen career path? What do potential employers think of its graduates? Will the contacts you make be helpful later?

In addition to degree programs in real estate, you also will need to take advantage of other academic programs that will help you develop the ability to think clearly and express yourself well. Time spent developing financial and communication skills will be especially well rewarded; as a counselor with these skills, you will stand out in any crowd. Take your English and rhetoric courses seriously and seize every opportunity to polish your writing, speaking and debating talents.

Talk isn't always cheap.

Also try to come away from school with a good understanding of investment analysis concepts and tools as they apply to real estate. Familiarize yourself with discounted cash flow analysis, basic statistics and economics (see Chapter 9) and learn how to run the computer. A firm grasp of these fundamentals will help you to be professional on the job and provide a foundation for growth.

While still at school, you should be developing an acceptable business style (demeanor, manners, clothing, speech) and a sense of business ethics. You also should be improving your interpersonal skills and knowledge of practical psychology. At the same time you should be building your familiarity with real estate: What it is, how it operates, how it is owned and transferred, where value comes from and how it is created. These are the kinds of questions that will absorb the bulk of your learning time after you actually start working.

An important ability not often formally taught in schools is "groupmanship"—knowing how to get the maximum benefit out of a meeting, how to make your presence felt, when to speak out and when to remain silent, how to use formal and informal gatherings (see Chapter 16). These are skills that take practice. To begin acquiring them, join at least one campus organization (the debating society is a good choice) and visit off-campus meetings of political and civic organizations. Find out how these meetings are structured, how they are run and how they are used by individuals with their own public or private agendas. What you learn in such groups will carry over to the business world where corporate meetings, partnership meetings and gatherings of your fellow professionals are subject to similar rules. The abilities you develop and the friends you make also will be useful later on in your civic and marketing activities.

Find a good mentor if you can. It's traditional in the real estate business and in counseling as well. A senior who is worldly-wise, knowledgeable, thoughtful and interested in your professional growth can be of enormous value, accelerating your progress and helping you over the bumps.

Getting started. Like doctors and lawyers, some counselors simply hang up a shingle and declare themselves available. Most beginners, however, need the financial security, the support systems and the learning environment offered by a job in an existing organization (see Chapter 3).

You can try to start out directly in a real estate firm or counseling department that will help you acquire the basics before you move on, or you can take a job in some other area of real estate that will allow you to develop special expertise. Knowledge of shopping centers or hotels, for example, can be acquired by managing, selling, developing, appraising or financing those kinds of properties as well as by dealing with them as a consultant. Most of the best-known real estate counselors have extensive experience as practitioners, often in several different areas of real estate. Some of the most respected have done almost everything there is to do in real estate at one time or another. The knowledge gained through experience cannot be matched by a course of academic study.

It doesn't hurt to make a start in some related field. Economists, geographers, planners, investment analysts, architects, accountants, business consultants, lawyers, marketing experts, preservationists, engineers, builders, environmentalists and corporate managers often find that their training and experience can be brought to bear in real estate counseling. Some professionals from these fields move into counseling gradually, feeling their way along; others look for a job with an established company where they can build on their previous experience.

A classic avenue to real estate counseling is by way of real estate appraising. (The CRE designation of the American Society of Real Estate Counselors is not for beginners.) Working appraisers often can broaden their efforts to include at least part-time real estate counseling, while senior appraisers often do a good deal of it. The CPA and CPM designations can be helpful, as can degrees in law, business and engineering.

Your first job. In choosing a first job beginners should look for a firm or company that offers opportunities for rapid learning, personal growth and client contact. Don't get stuck in an organization that won't let you grow or that doesn't use the full range of your abilities. While a certain amount of nose-to-the-grindstone scutwork will not hurt, too much time spent on run-of-the-mill tasks will stunt your ability to respond to fresh situations. Set realistic goals for yourself. If they cannot be met in your present circumstances, move on. (For more on where and how to start, see Chapter 6.)

Work for growth as well as money.

Where to go. Your first job can be sought in the usual ways: through family connections, friends made at school, formal interviews with campus recruiters, help-wanted ads, the grapevine. A better way, however, is to learn enough about the industry to identify a few companies that are attractive because of the work they do, the reputation they enjoy or the opportunities they offer to beginners. Seek out these companies; make your interest known by presenting a carefully thought-out description of your qualifications and how you can be useful to the company. You may be surprised at the welcome you receive.

Should you look for a small company, a large one, a pure counseling firm or some sort of mixed organization? The answer depends on you and your ambitions. A small firm will give you a quicker start and put you in direct contact with a variety of work situations and clients; a large one may offer better training programs, bigger clients and more important assignments (see Chapter 3).

Major insurance companies have acted as launching pads for many top counselors. So have family real estate firms, investment banking houses and national brokerage concerns. There probably is no bad way to start—provided your employer has a good reputation and will allow you to grow.

The job interview. The employment interview is not just an opportunity for displaying your wares; it's also a way of learning more about the company so you can form a sound judgment about the wisdom of accepting employment there. Have a list of questions in mind about the company and its work and make sure you are satisfied with the answers. Asking these questions not only will give you what you need to know about the company but also will demonstrate to the interviewer that your interest is serious.

Pay and working conditions. Salary shouldn't be the only consideration when choosing a job. When you're starting out, look for opportunities to learn, grow and advance. Consider the reputation of the company: How will it look on your resume when the time comes to move on? Pay attention to the working environment: Are people happy, spreading their wings, working hard? Consider who your bosses will be and your chances of finding good mentors and opportunities to develop your skills. The right working environment is far more important than take-home pay at this early stage in your business career, except when family obligations force you to go after the top dollar. Generous vacations and fringe benefits also are nice, but remember they are only temporary perks and that you are in this business for the long haul.

Networks. No matter where you begin working, be sure to set about building the networks you will need for friends, contacts, information, business and future jobs. One place to start building these networks is through your professional society. Another good place is through the local chamber of commerce, where you'll meet fellow professionals as well as business prospects. Realtor boards, churches and synagogues, clubs and civic organizations are all worth exploring. Follow your own judgment—and your own interests—in deciding which organizations will be important for you.

Take an active part in the organizations you join. Bread cast on the waters now, in the form of committee work and the attention you pay to the members and activities of the group, may take a while to return, but eventually it will come back with interest. You'll also welcome the support you get from your networks and the friendships you build.

Getting ahead. In any organization certain things will be important to your advancement. This book doesn't pretend to be a comprehensive get-ahead manual, but it can offer at least a few suggestions:

- *Develop a recognizable expertise.* Pick some aspect of the field that really interests you and work at it until you know more than anyone else. You'll be noticed both for what you know and for your diligence.
- *Be visible.* Clients and bosses have no way of recognizing who you are unless they can see your work and you, at least occasionally. Make sure that when you accomplish something, others know what was done and who did it.
- *Be straight.* People who are devious and excessively calculating seldom are appreciated.
- *Pick your projects.* Choose projects where you can learn something, meet new people and, if possible, make a favorable impression.
- *Don't be a slacker.* Everyone appreciates hard work and persistence.
- *Don't be afraid to blow your own horn* once in a while. Many a light goes out for lack of air and spectators.
- *Stand up when the situation calls for it.* Nobody likes a wimp; everybody admires a person of character and principle.

As you go along, take care to build a good resume. Seek out assignments that will add to your credibility as well as to your skills and knowledge. Write for trade and professional journals when you have something to say; give speeches when you get the chance. Ask yourself what a prospective counseling client would like to see on your biographical statement and work to put it there.

ESTABLISHED REAL ESTATE PROFESSIONALS

Making the switch. Brokers, developers, managers, lawyers, appraisers and others with a good grounding in some aspect of real estate may find it harder to enter into full-time real estate counseling than fresh university graduates with advanced degrees. Often it's easier for real estate professionals to enter the counseling field as part-timers and treat counseling as a sideline, one that may or may not become a full-time occupation but will add a dimension to their business lives and provide an enjoyable way of earning extra income.

Most people actively engaged in real estate find that they are called upon from time to time for advice. Often they give it for nothing, as "part of the service." This practice is bad for two reasons: first, because it tends to be underappreciated; second, because it seldom produces revenue for the advisor. The cure for this, and an excellent way to break into real estate counseling, is to let the would-be freeloader know that you'll be pleased to assemble the necessary facts, think through the problem and provide a responsible answer to the question, in exchange for a sensible fee.

Some people object to such fees; others respond positively to the suggestion. Corporate executives and businesspeople are accustomed to paying for advice; they use lawyers, accountants and other business professionals all the time and understand that good advisors are worthy of their hire. Even those who don't usually pay for advice can be shown that an unpaid advisor may be less trustworthy than one who takes the responsibility seriously and expects to be paid for it.

Letting your clients and business contacts know that you are available for professional real estate advice and support services is the first step in the process (see Part IV: Marketing). This can be done in conversation, by letter, through the media and in other ways (see Chapter 15). It may take a while, but if you are able to deliver services that clients value, your reputation and your business will grow.

A more forceful entry into the counseling field may be advisable. Get your credentials together, develop a marketing plan and launch a campaign to let the world know about your special qualifications. Who knows? The world may be waiting for your services.

Moving over, moving on. As your practice develops, you may find that your business framework is inadequate—too small, too confined in its operations, underequipped or insufficiently staffed to provide a full range of counseling services. In such cases, unless you can persuade the company for which you work to build the capabilities you need, it may be advisable to make a switch.

If you aren't ready to start up your own practice, you may find it practical to join an existing organization, possibly as a partner or a part-time consultant. Small,

More than one way to get in.

medium and large firms in a number of metropolitan centers attract a wide variety of work and may welcome your overtures, particularly if you can bring them new knowledge about a particular aspect of the industry. Another option may be to create your own organization, perhaps by opening up a sole practice with a secretary and one or two part-time or full-time associates. It's a good way to test the waters and can lead to great things.

References

ARTICLES

1. Clodfelter R: Preparing potential entrepreneurs for tomorrow's world. *Business Education Forum* 44(7): Apr 1990, p 30.

2. Mackay H: A career road map: running the show. *Modern Office Tech* 35(7): Jul 1990, p 12.

EDUCATIONAL SOURCE

Directory of Educational Institutions, Accreditation Commission, Association of Independent Colleges and Schools, Suite 600, 1730 M St., NW, Washington, DC 20036

BOOKS

1. Boe A: *Is Your "Net" Working?* (New York: John Wiley and Sons) 1989.

2. Costanzo WK: *Getting Hired. How to Sell Yourself.* (Portland: Carolina Pacific Publishing) 1987.

3. Krannich RL: *Network Your Way to Job and Career Success.* (Manassas, VA: Impact Publications) 1989.

4. Steingold F.: *The Legal Guide for Starting and Running a Small Business.* (Nolo Press) 1992.

5. Weiss A: *Million Dollar Consulting.* (McGraw Hill Publishing Co.) 1992.

Chapter 6

Starting the Business

BUSINESS OR PRACTICE?

Before you begin planning the details of your new counseling business, give a little thought to your goals, situation and resources. What, in fact, do you hope to accomplish with this undertaking? Where do you stand in terms of experience, connections, reputation and financial condition? Do you have the friends, the skills and the knowledge to make a fast start? Do you have the cash and credit to tide you over until the business gets up to speed?

Even if the answers to all these questions are positive, you still need to do a little soul searching to make sure you're making the right career decision and to help determine your capital requirements, office location, company structure, equipment and staffing needs and marketing strategies. How much does money matter to you? What about professional recognition? Personal growth? Enjoyment? Leisure time? How competitive are you? How hard do you want to work? Will this be a professional practice based on your own skills, a partnership or a full-blown counseling organization?

The choices you make will be influenced by your personality and by the available markets. What kind of person are you? Will your ego and financial needs (or those of your associates) force you to grow? If so, how much growth can your community support? Are you the kind of person who does well running a large organization? Do you really want to have more than a local or regional practice? (See the discussion of company size in Chapter 3.)

Large or small, your startup business will be subject to certain unofficial rules.

RULES FOR STARTUPS
- *Keep the nut low.* There's no need to open your counseling business in a suite of fancy offices with every accessory in place and a horde of underoccupied people. Rent what you need, grow when you must, conserve your cash for rainy days. These rules apply to professional staff just as much as they do to furniture and equipment. Don't take on permanent employees who won't be slightly overworked; hire independent contractors until you know you want full-time people for the long pull.

- *Stay loose.* Who knows how things will develop? In six months you may find yourself out of business—or operating at twice the volume you predicted. You may even find yourself in a different business entirely. Avoid committing yourself prematurely to a path that may turn out to be the wrong one.
- *Hire wisely.* The people who join you now will be important to your early success and will probably become key people in your growing organization. Choose them for their adaptability, eagerness, intelligence and professional skills. After all, work of entirely new kinds may come from unexpected quarters, and your employees will have to cope just as you will.
- *Have enough cash on hand* and line up more in case you need it to cover slow periods and unforeseen problems. Try by all means to have funds on hand to tide you over for at least three months of operation; you'll appreciate the cushion.
- *Build your credibility quickly.* Line up an important client or job, take on a civic responsibility, score a success or two as promptly as you can. Show the world that you are to be taken seriously.
- *Have a marketing plan.* Follow it diligently, even at times when you think you're too busy. Remember that the lag between the marketing effort and its payoff can be several months—or years.
- *Develop key referral sources.* Call on them, write them, take them to lunch. Don't let them languish because of neglect. These individuals can help you make a fast start and grow. The list of key referral sources probably should include your law firm, your bank, your accountants, your trade association and your business friends.
- *Work hard* and demand hard work from your people. Long hours, as well as tight budgets, are typical of successful startups in every field, even though you may think they won't be necessary in your case.
- *Be alert to your competition.* Know who they are, what they are doing, how much they charge. You'll be bidding against these people, so you'll need all the information you can get about them.
- *Become a real expert*, if you aren't one already. Read the trade journals, follow the economic news, take courses to strengthen your weak spots. Clients will quickly recognize your expertise—or lack of it.
- *Focus on the big things*, even while looking after the little ones. Go after the big account, the big job, the big connection that will get you started in a big way. Too many businesses stay small and marginal because their owners aren't willing to aim high enough for success.

CHOOSING A FORM OF BUSINESS ORGANIZATION

The general rule for startup businesses is to keep them as simple as possible.

When deciding how to organize your startup business, the rule is: "Don't do more than you have to." Why spend money and time unnecessarily on lawyers, franchise taxes, separate bank accounts and corporate filings? Keep your life as simple as you can, though no simpler. If the nature of your business requires that you set up a partnership or incorporate, by all means do so. Just remember that it will cost you.

There are three basic business options: (1) sole proprietorship, (2) partnership, and (3) corporation. Each has its advantages and drawbacks.

Sole proprietorship. With a sole proprietorship, you own the entire business. This lets you call the shots as you think fit and make only a few administrative demands on yourself. You can't have partners or stockholders, but nothing prevents you from hiring all the employees you can afford. All the board meetings can be held in your office, home or car. You get 100% of the deductions and pay 100% of the taxes. You don't have to make filings (other than your own personal tax forms), unless you go under a different name and have to complete assumed name certificates, because the proprietorship has no legal existence apart from you. Upon your death, it may be harder for your estate to transfer ownership, but if what you are selling is mainly your own personal talents, you'll take those with you anyway.

Your liability protection comes primarily from insurance (see Chapter 13). While insurance won't guard your assets against the just demands of ordinary creditors, it should provide reasonable protection against claims arising out of your negligence and incompetence or the ingenuity of someone else's lawyer.

As the business grows and you get older, you absolutely must obtain the assistance and advice of an accountant and a lawyer with demonstrated skills in small business organization and estate planning (see Chapter 10 on the value of lawyers).

Partnership. The main difference between the partnership and a sole proprietorship is the involvement of two or more owners. How the proportions of ownership are distributed (50/50, 90/10, 40/30/30, etc.) is up to the partners, but if nothing is specified in the partnership agreement, the distribution is assumed to be equal among all partners.

A partnership does not pay federal taxes (the partners pay taxes as individuals), but it must file an information return. Its defenses against liability are the same as those of the sole proprietorship, but these defenses are complicated by the fact that each of the partners is fully liable for all the debts of the partnership, jointly and severally, to the full extent of his assets. This is troublesome as a business matter because any of the partners presumably can bind the partnership, even to a major obligation, without the consent of the others. Each partner owes the others a fiduciary duty to refrain from engaging in a competitive business without obtaining the consent of all partners.

While a partnership can be created merely by going into business with another person and sharing profits, it makes no sense to do so without a well-thought-out partnership agreement drafted by a competent attorney. Such an agreement offers at least some protection in case one or more of the partners dies, gets sick, retires or just gets tired of the business. The sad fact is that, even with a good agreement, you are not likely to withdraw from a partnership without incurring scars. Because the buyout and termination provisions are especially critical, they should be carefully examined by the partners as well as the attorneys who will draft the partnership agreement. These provisions also must be properly funded to avoid major problems.

On the question of attorneys: It can be dangerous to have just one lawyer represent all the parties to the partnership agreement. Unless all partners contribute the same in terms of time and money and consent to the use of the lawyer and the basic terms of the partnership, conflicts of interest will arise. In such cases it's better for each partner to have his own attorney, even if all the attorneys for the partners work for the same law firm.

Taxes can make the difference.

Corporation. A corporation is treated in law as a legal person with an identity separate from its owners. It may have one or many shareholders, each of whom has a specified claim on corporate earnings but ordinarily has no personal liability for corporate debts. Because it is a taxpaying entity, with an income tax rate that may well exceed the personal rate, the corporation can cost its stockholders tax money they otherwise would not have to pay. A compensating advantage is that, within certain limits, money kept in the corporation for corporate purposes, such as investment in machinery and equipment, is not taxable to the shareholders until it is paid out as salaries or dividends. With good tax planning, the corporate form sometimes can work to the owners' advantage.

Small corporations usually qualify for "Subchapter S" status, which means that their income is not taxed to the corporation itself but only to the shareholders, though a corporate return must be filed. Subchapter S requirements are very strict, and the rules that govern these corporations are full of pitfalls for the unwary. Be sure to get expert advice before filing for Subchapter S status.

Corporations offer other kinds of benefits. For one thing, they confer a degree of protection against personal liability, as the stockholders are not individually liable for the corporation's debts. The value of this shield may be slight, as a small professional corporation soon finds that any kind of long-term commitment or any activity requiring significant credit cannot be accomplished without the backup of personal guarantees. The best protection against personal as well as corporate liability for tort and negligence claims is insurance. If a risk cannot be insured against, the hard fact is you probably will have to bear it.

Corporations do, however, require some diligence. They must, for example, maintain up-to-date records. The privilege of incorporating a business is granted by the state, which wants to be able to find out what a corporation is up to. If the pages of the minute book are blank, you have corporate amnesia, which can cost you dearly. If you decide to incorporate, do it in your own state, where your lawyer knows the rules and maybe the judges, unless someone points out a very compelling reason to incorporate in another.

Other possibilities. There aren't really any to speak of. A limited partnership is an investment vehicle, not usually a practical form of business organization. If you have a "silent" partner who is contributing funding but is not participating in the operation, you may consider this vehicle, but not otherwise. Trusts have their uses, but they don't generally include the operation of an active counseling business.

You must be sure to talk to your lawyer about all of these issues (see Chapter 10 on how to choose and work with legal counsel). The discussion here is far from complete, and it makes no attempt to deal with all legal and tax ramifications.

NOTE: The foregoing is based on materials provided by Tobin M. Richter, Esq., who assumes no responsibility for the author's editing or comments.

CHOOSING A BUSINESS NAME

This is a tricky matter because the name you choose has legal, marketing and prestige implications. Pick with care, and check the soundness of your choice before you adopt it.

Legal concerns. Your business name must be sufficiently different from the names of other businesses already in operation to be safe from challenge by existing companies. "Real Estate Counseling, Inc." may or may not be used by an existing company, but chances are high that another firm bears a name resembling it. Better to call your organization "John Q. Smart and Friends," especially if that correctly describes the firm. Safest of all are new combinations of sounds and letters. "RECoServ, Inc.," "RECoCorp" or "RecSI" may do if they haven't already been adopted by some counseling, record distributing or wrecking company.

Sole proprietors can use their own names without much risk, unless the names are well known (even a hamburger maker whose last name is McDonald will hear from another company of similar name if he puts it on his restaurant). Impersonal names ("Blanktown Realty Counselors," "General Advice Partnership") must be formally registered with the state, county or city where you do business, depending upon local laws. This procedure is not necessarily difficult or one that requires the services of a lawyer. Corporate names take on legal standing when the documents of incorporation are filed, something you can do yourself. Most people, though, wisely leave this task to the attorneys who assist them in forming the corporation (see Chapter 10).

Corporations can give protection but require attention.

It pays to be different.

Marketing advantages. Will the name appeal to clients and prospects? Does it accurately describe the ownership of the company or the services it offers? "Blanktown Real Estate Counselors" will do a fair marketing job in Blanktown, but it may not mean much to potential clients who think of Blanktown as a jerkwater community. "John Q. Dunderhead & Co." works best if John Q. has an established reputation or if his name has an honorable ring to it. Least appealing to most prospects are overambitious or pretentious names: "Universal Counseling" may be right for an international firm, but it is not suitable for a one-person office in a small town. Dual names—"Dunderhead and McDonald"—follow a discernible trend among law firms, creating the risk that people will think you and your partner are lawyers.

A matter of prestige. Common sense helps here. You want to sound solid, respectable and intelligent, but you don't want to appear to be bigger or smarter than you are. "Space Age Counselors, Inc." or "Very Best Advice Company" will convince few prospects of your importance. On the other hand if you are strong enough to carry the weight, a name like "Real Estate Research Corporation" or "Economic Research Associates" (both exist) will do you no harm.

TWELVE SURVIVAL TIPS FOR STARTUP COUNSELING BUSINESSES

1. *Keep your eyes peeled.* Something good—or bad—may be coming.
2. *Look for opportunities,* especially the kind that offer immediate profits or good upside potential: important jobs, active clients, promising new specialties.
3. *Take no major risks.* You're not General Motors; you're a small business, even if you are in a big company, and can't afford big losses.
4. *Work hard.* Others are doing it, too.
5. *Stay lean.* You never know when you'll need money for something quite unexpected.
6. *Keep your promises.* Be on time with reports, at meetings, when repaying debt. Meet your payrolls.
7. *Watch your cash.* It isn't the accrual earnings that count in bad times; it's what you have left to live on. Plan for your needs.
8. *Take all profitable jobs*—but go after retainer business hardest. It'll help stabilize your cash flow.
9. *Get cash in front.* Especially when a client is from another state.
10. *Market constantly.* People not only need to know what you do, they also need to be reminded that you exist.
11. *Have fallback positions ready.* If you lose a battle, you still may be able to win the war.
12. *Respect yourself.* You'll charge more, do better work and build a better reputation than you will if you act like a wimp.

References

ARTICLES

1. Blanchard K: Pondering a partnership. *Today's Office* 24(1) Jun 1990, p 20.

2. Goddard RW: The rise of the new organization: doing business in the 1990s. *Management World* 19(1): Jan/Feb 1990, p 3.

3. Moss Kanter R: Partnerships and progress. *Modern Office Tech* 35(4)Apr 1990, p 14.

BOOKS

1. Gumpert DE: *How to Really Start Your Own Business.* (New York: Inc. Publishing) 1992.

2. Rosenthal L: *Partnering.* (Cincinnati, OH: Writers' Digest Books) 1983.

3. Silvester JL: *How to Start, Finance, and Operate Your Own Business.* (Homewood, IL: Dow Jones-Irwin) 1992.

Chapter 7

Space

WHERE?

The location of your counseling business doesn't matter much except in terms of convenience for you, your staff and—if they drop in often—your clients. A prestigious address is nice and may help with recruiting other professionals, but adds little, if anything, to the credibility of your business. It also may be costly not only to you but to clients who may not want to pay extra to support an expensive office locale. Some of the best firms in the country occupy secondary locations.

You do have your own comfort to consider and that of your hardworking colleagues. Pick a spot that is close to the places they visit often: title records, libraries, key clients. Don't choose a location that is physically dangerous or will raise too many eyebrows. If at all possible, pick an address that's handy to a variety of facilities: restaurants, health clubs, shopping, museums. Such a location will help make your employees' breaks more enjoyable, and may encourage them to get to the office earlier in the morning.

Where's lunch?

Getting in and out of your office building at the beginning and end of the day and at lunch time is an important consideration. So is accessibility to visitors and employees; if it's too hard to get to your office, people may avoid coming in. Access to public transportation and to a ready supply of parking spaces and taxis will make everybody's day more agreeable.

WHICH BUILDING?

If you are design-conscious, or want to seem so, you may choose to locate your business in a well-designed building. Office rent in these buildings is often no higher than the rent elsewhere, and an office in one of them may be good for your firm's image (see Chapter 14). New or old, well-designed or not, the building you select should reflect the fact that you are a real estate counselor who knows the difference between quality and junk. A building that is handsome, solidly constructed and properly maintained will do you credit (but see Chapter 14 for some additional thoughts about image).

Buildings, of course, are sold from time to time, so there are no guarantees about the performance of your future landlord. It nevertheless pays to select a building that has a competent and deep-pocketed owner who will be inclined and able to keep it in good shape. It helps if the landlord has offices in the building, so when things go wrong they are likely to be corrected quickly. If the owner (or a major tenant) is also a client or may become one, so much the better.

A good office selection checklist will reduce your chances of making a serious mistake. If you don't have one at hand, here's a beginning:

- Column spacing: Is it large enough?
- Modularity: 5' x 5' is best for most tenants.
- Ceiling height: 8 feet? 8 1/2 feet? 9 feet? Higher ceilings create a better impression, especially for large offices.
- Elevator service: Is it frequent? Fast? Reliable? Available after hours?
- HVAC: Is it of high quality? Quiet? What is the availability and cost of after hours service? Are there individual controls?
- Floors: Are they level? Large enough to allow for expansion? Solid?
- Floor load capacity: Is it high enough?
- Partitions: Are they reasonably soundproof? Designed for low-cost floor-plan changes?
- Lighting: Is there enough? Is it the right kind? How flexible is it? How wasteful?
- Building storage: Where? How much? At what cost? Subject to flood?
- Security: Are there guards? Electronic systems? Is there proper administration and training of security teams?
- Service: How good? What kinds?
- Mail and dispatch facilities: Are there regular messenger service pickups? Where is the nearest post office? Federal Express pickup?
- Tenants: Are they compatible with your firm? Established clients? Possible sources of new business? Providers of things you regularly buy?
- Maintenance and housekeeping: How frequent? How thorough? How prompt in response to complaints?
- Washrooms: Are there enough? Are they properly maintained? In the right places? Attractive? Secure? Clean?
- Eating and recreational facilities: How good? How costly? How available?
- Facilities for the disabled: Does the building conform to the applicable laws?

A word on mechanical systems: Make sure your space is well provided with equipment that works, is reliable and doesn't make too much noise. A breakdown of the heating system on a cold day (or the cooling system on a hot one) can put you out of business. Why take the chance?

HOW MUCH?

While space needs vary, one principle is worth noting: Have plenty. Your business probably will grow, and even if it doesn't, consultants need more room than you think. Besides, spacious areas are good for morale and productivity.

Staff-level consultants don't need much individual space. A small office or even a cubicle will do, provided reasonable steps have been taken to minimize extraneous noise. Each consultant should have enough room to accommodate a couple of good file cabinets, a computer station, a telephone, in- and out-boxes, some books and a place to spread out papers concerning the job in progress.

More is better.

This setup assumes there is enough conference and work space elsewhere in the office to hold meetings and tackle big projects. It also assumes there is a central library, or at least a place where books and information files are maintained. Individual consultants who hold frequent small meetings will need more space than lone wolves and others whose work is done mainly outside the office or requires little interface with the rest of the staff.

The smaller the firm, the larger the area that should be allowed per person, as small firms seldom are able to afford adequate conference and work rooms and must often use the boss's office or some makeshift area for these functions. Large firms are able to fine-tune their space planning and reduce the allowance per person to something under 200 square feet; small ones often can allow 300 square feet or more per person.

LAYOUT

Efficiency is important, but so is flexibility. However carefully you plan, there's no way to predict exactly how you will use office space, so be sure to allow for change. Think in terms of movable partitions and uniform finishes, including floor coverings, that will let you juggle functions and spaces without incurring major costs. And plan for expansion, just in case it happens.

Your reception area does not need to be large, but it should be comfortable, well lighted, properly ventilated and tastefully appointed. Lavish furnishings are not indicated unless the overall design of your office demands them.

It's convenient for most firms to have a conference room off the reception area so meetings can be held without disrupting the activities of the office and so the receptionist can double as host. If at all possible the conference room should accommodate 12 to 15 people, the largest group that will permit a good general conversation. The room can be used for luncheons and seminars as well as business meetings and special projects. Additional conference and workrooms also may be distributed around the office as convenience dictates.

A small kitchen adequate for heating soup and making coffee will allow you to serve sandwiches or cold cuts at lunch and provide better caffeine infusions than can be had in the offices of many competitors. It also will encourage your employees to bring their lunch and provide a place to keep the pop cold.

Open, flexible and suitable.

The general rule is to lay out the office so people who work together have work spaces that are as close as possible. Don't make your employees spend a lot of time and energy scurrying around the office in search of one another. A relatively open plan allows people to see who is in and what they are doing. This kind of layout can be accomplished without loss of acoustical privacy by using plenty of glass, which gives workers who occupy interior cubicles some feeling of connection with the outside world and perhaps a view of the outdoors through the window in the boss's office.

Completely open office layout plans don't work very well for counseling firms. Clients need the real and psychological privacy offered by enclosed work areas. So do most staff people, particularly those who are located next to frequent telephone users or to individuals who must deal with noisy complainers.

Sound is a factor in productivity and morale. There naturally will be a certain degree of noise when the office is busy, but there shouldn't be so much that thinkers and production workers become distracted. Carpeting and acoustical ceilings go a long way toward solving noise problems. Additional acoustical panels, wall hangings and window draperies also may be necessary, but should not be overused. Don't try to create a place that is quiet as a tomb; you don't want to be thought of as dead.

The office layout should consider how employees will circulate. People will be moving around quite a bit in your offices and should find it easy to do. Make the connections between important functions clear and convenient. Word processing, for example, should not be stuck somewhere in the back of the office but brought close to the consultants who will be working with it. The boss, too, should be centrally located if possible, partly for better control but mainly so others can see that the boss is working and available.

As to light: Natural light too frequently is ignored. Use it where you have it. High-level general lighting is seldom necessary; most people like to work with localized lighting they can turn on and off. A relatively low level of general lighting can be supplemented by work-directed spotlights and lamps. Fluorescent lighting costs less than incandescent, but if you use it, be sure to select tubes that project a warm or neutral color, not the old-fashioned fluorescent fixtures that produce icy blue light.

DO YOU NEED A SPACE PLANNER?

Many offices are laid out by professional space planning firms which offer architectural and interior design skills and may even extend their services into areas normally belonging to personnel and business consultants. These space planners can help formulate your design criteria, estimate present and likely future space needs, analyze your operation in search of greater efficiency and plan your communications facilities. Given the chance, they also will cut your hair, select your clothes and take you to lunch.

The good space planners do an excellent job and charge generally reasonable fees, often based on the number of square feet to be planned. To find them, check with major leasing brokers, building managers and multioffice space users who have extensive experience in this field. Before hiring a space planner, get a list of the planner's clients, visit their premises and talk with them. How satisfied are they? How well organized is the space planning firm, and how responsible was it about keeping its promises? Was the space ready on time? How does it look and work?

AN OFFICE IN YOUR HOME?

It's probably not a good idea to have your principal office at home unless you already have an established clientele and would rather save money than position yourself for growth. Clients don't particularly mind meeting consultants in their dens, but generally would rather entrust their jobs to a counselor with a staff and professional offices near important sources of business and information. Usually this means a centrally located office in a conventional office building or at least in an attractively converted loft, residence, store, school, church, bathhouse or YWCA.

A home office does have certain advantages that cannot be matched in the downtown setting. The cost is low, the refrigerator is close at hand and the commute is short, and maybe your spouse will answer the phone for you. On the other hand, it is said that distance lends enchantment. Think about it and take your pick.

OFFICE LEASES

You may already own a building or want to buy one for your counseling business. If so, fine; you know what to do. If not, chances are you will have to rent space in somebody else's building. As a professional real estate counselor, you shouldn't need a lot of help on leasing, but here are a few pointers anyway:

- *Get all the free rent and other concessions you are entitled to.* The landlord may be annoyed but will think more of you as a professional.
- *Get the space built exactly to your needs.* Office landlords often will handle rebuilding for small tenants, especially those who have space to sublet or those whose buildings are in the rent-up stage. While starting up your business, try to let the landlord pick up the tab.
- *Get as many options as you can*—for renewals, for expansions, for early cancellation. Landlords want to keep their own options open, so they will discourage the use of renewals, expansions, cancellations, etc., especially with small tenants. It's nonetheless worth it to try getting some. The right renewal options will allow you to take the space for a short initial term, which reduces

your problems if you must discontinue or relocate the business. Cancellation clauses give you a way out in case things go sour. If you think you may die in the near future and don't want to encumber your estate, ask for a death clause.

- *Look after the fine print.* You don't want to discover at an inconvenient moment that the landlord has rights to your space, your assets and your body parts that you didn't know about. What an embarrassment for a self-declared expert!
- *Don't neglect sublease opportunities.* Tenants who want to get out of their leases make soft negotiators. As a startup or small business, you often can make do with a relatively short-term lease arrangement. Consider profiting from these circumstances to negotiate for cheap rent plus free remodeling and other goodies. There's a good chance the original tenant—and the landlord—will be delighted to accommodate you.
- *Remember that you may have prestige value.* Some landlords, especially those with buildings that need the boost, may want to brag about being good enough to attract a savvy space expert like you. You can take advantage of their eagerness.
- *Have a lease,* even if the landlord is an old friend. Friends sometimes forget important details of their agreements, especially when it's convenient. Besides, leases of more than a year usually aren't enforceable unless reduced to writing.

References

BOOKS

1. Crane R, Dixon M: *The Shape of Space: Office Spaces.* (New York: Van Nostrand Reinhold) 1991.

2. Scott R: *How To Set Up and Operate Your Office at Home.* (New York: Charles Scribner's Sons) 1985.

3. Tweedy DB: *Office Space Planning and Management. A Manager's Guide to Techniques and Standards.* (New York: Quorum Books) 1986.

PERIODICALS

Modern Interior International, Grosvenor Press International, London

Modern Office Technology, Penton Publishing, 1100 Superior Avenue, Cleveland, OH 44114-2543

Chapter 8

Staffing the Office

You can't do everything yourself. Even if you could, it wouldn't be good business. Law and accounting firms grow and thrive by supplementing the skills of their partners with the hard work of salaried associates and staff who actually may know more about the subject matter than the partners themselves. This know-how can increase the chances of the job being done right. Proper use of associates and staff can also improve the incomes of the company's partners while giving the young a chance to prove themselves.

Choose aces, kings and queens.

Many counselors prefer to work alone, but most have learned to delegate at least some of the tasks they undertake. An important aspect of business policy is the selection and development of good employees. The right choices can help the business grow, improve its financial performance and assure its future after the counselor retires to greener pastures.

Insecure individuals or professionals often choose inferior associates in the hope that the boss will look better by comparison. In reality this practice makes the employer appear to be a poor judge of character and talent. Clients easily recognize the talents of associates and appreciate the counselor's ability to identify and retain good people.

Clients also appreciate the broadened range of services counselors can offer by employing a well-diversified high-quality staff. If your own primary expertise is in real estate investing, for example, you may want to seek out assistants who are expert in taxation, management, development or planning to supplement your own skills.

Try to see to it that every new person knows something you don't and can do something you can't. Why hire someone who adds nothing to your organizational strengths except a body on the chart?

TRAITS TO LOOK FOR

You don't want people who are unwilling to work. You also don't want people who will cause too much friction or be a drag on your firm. Will the new person mesh well with your team? Does he have the curiosity, the drive, the brainpower and the emotional soundness to grow within your organization and pull his own weight while learning?

Don't disregard your intuitive reactions to prospective hires. If you don't like a person, your clients probably won't either. Is he alert and interested? Adaptable? Efficient? Responsible? Curious about the things that need to be learned? Does he have a sense of humor? The ability to hold up under pressure? Initiative? Interesting things to say? Does he know enough about the field to get a good start in your shop or to fill a gap in your organizational structure?

At least in the beginning, try to hire individuals who are intelligent, articulate and naturally curious. Don't insist on real estate experience if the person brings something relevant to the group. A person with a background in law, construction, geography, history, architecture, mathematics, planning or historic preservation can be useful if he can write well and meet your other criteria. People with undergraduate degrees in real estate, while they may be fast starters, sometimes are too narrowly trained to make good counselors. An undergraduate degree in some other field, followed by a graduate degree in business, law, planning, economics or real estate, is probably the best preparation.

Secretarial, word processing, research and administrative personnel should be chosen with just as much care and respect as professionals. They are every bit as essential to the success of your business. Look for lively, flexible individuals with well-balanced personalities, sharp minds and a willingness to pitch in. Such people may be expensive, but they are worth the extra money because they come through when the chips are down (as the chips often are in counseling). If you can find someone who is interested in the business and hopes to become a professional one day, so much the better. He will learn faster.

RECRUITING

Where can you find people? Just about anywhere. Counselors in small counseling shops usually don't have the time to engage in formal recruiting efforts at local universities, but large counseling organizations often find the effort to be worthwhile. Want ads work sometimes; you may even find a good employee by checking the "situations wanted" column. The best recruits, though, usually come through referrals generated by your own people because they are interested in bringing in colleagues with skill and work habits compatible with their own. Particularly if you're getting along in years, younger staff will be better acquainted with the current talent pool than you will. Ask them to help. They will be valuable in recruiting and judging new hires and you will be strengthening their self-confidence and the cohesiveness of your firm.

In talking with prospective employees, don't be shy about asking appropriate questions and offering relevant information. You want the prospects to know as much as possible about your style of work for the same reasons you want to know as much as possible about theirs. Don't hire someone who isn't going to like the way you work or whose work habits will upset the office. Give the prospects all the interviews they or you need to assure a good fit.

Don't neglect to check references, either. Ask previous employers about personality traits as well as performance records. How well did the candidate stand up under pressure? How much initiative did he show in new situations? How reliably did he meet deadlines and honor promises? How did clients feel about the candidate? What did co-workers say? How often did he get sick, and when? How did the candidate feel about travel and getting his shoes dirty?

Be careful in your hiring (and firing!) not to fall afoul of the increasingly complex requirements of the law. Talk to your attorney about the risks. The Small Business Administration, the American Management Association and the U.S. Chamber of Commerce may also be helpful.

PAY AND OTHER INCIDENTALS

Be generous. It will come back to you in better work, longer hours and greater loyalty. Find out what the competition pays and offer at least a little more. When hiring new people, try to make sure they will be better off with you than they were with their previous employer. A less-than-adequate salary almost surely will turn out to be false economy.

Pay enough, give enough.

Providing health insurance and other routine fringe benefits is good for the organization as well as the employee because they help make employees feel secure and fairly treated. Find out what other firms are doing and don't hesitate to seek professional advice. You may have legal obligations you don't know about.

Review the staff's compensation at frequent intervals, offering raises whenever you can to show that you notice their progress. Most of us tend to lag behind the job pay market, particularly during inflationary times, and to underappreciate how fast employees are growing as professionals.

Bonuses are an excellent way of rewarding hard work and unusual achievement. Unexpected ones are best; routine annual bonuses too often are considered to be part of the ordinary compensation package, while on-the-spot rewards can be linked directly with superior performance. A small counseling shop can issue a bonus when the money is there and the opportunity arises; a large organization may have to be more systematic.

Real estate counseling can be demanding work, so a certain leniency in vacation and travel policies is appropriate. Encourage your good people to attend meetings of their professional societies, and allow them to tack on a vacation day or two if the meeting is in a pleasant place or near one. A working trip to Paris or Honolulu can be almost as good as a vacation and will be appreciated as such. That doesn't mean, of course, that the customary three or four weeks off with pay, depending upon length of service and other factors, won't be required.

Employees should be encouraged to pick up the tab for their own professional society functions unless you require them to attend or feel the employee is entitled to a freebie by virtue of outstanding service or longevity. You may agree, of course, to reimburse employees for specific professional memberships and educational programs or for attendance at functions that will be useful to your organization and clients.

EMPLOYEES OR SUBCONTRACTORS?

Small counseling offices often use part-time and occasional help who may be added to the payroll as employees, paid by the job or hired as contractors for major tasks. Clients may or may not care whether your people are full-time employees. Business prudence generally dictates that you keep your permanent staff at a size that can be supported by your usual flow of work and that you supplement with freelancers and independent subcontractors when necessary. This arrangement provides a degree of flexibility and reduces the risk of a business collapse during slack periods.

It also can reduce bookkeeping tasks (you must withhold federal and state taxes for employees but not for independent contractors) and out-of-pocket cash, as independent contractors may not be covered by your state's workmen's compensation law and are supposed to provide for their own social security.

The Internal Revenue Service, which likes to use employers as collection agents, understandably wants to know about any independent contractors you hire for more than a few days a year. If you pay more than a certain amount to any individual, whether you consider that person to be an employee or an independent contractor, the IRS will require you to complete Form 1099. Objective criteria distinguish between employees and independent contractors, so you cannot escape responsibility for workmen's compensation insurance and withholding taxes just by announcing that you consider your staff to be independent contractors.

Watch the rules.

The IRS is especially leery of long-term arrangements with independent contractors, because they may be used by employers to escape payroll and withholding taxes. Such arrangements sometimes persist long after they have served their original purpose, and the IRS will seek payment of all taxes that should have been paid during the years the arrangement was in force. The axe, when it falls, can be painful.

Your choice of independent contractor or employee status for counseling personnel also should be affected by insurance considerations. Make it a point to discuss in detail with your insurance agent the work your people will be doing and the terms of their contractual arrangements. If you can, include both contractors and employees under your errors-and-omissions coverage, as the mistakes of an independent contractor easily may result in a lawsuit against you. You also may want protection against automobile accidents and other third-party risks as well as against any mishandling of client funds—or your own.

If you are going to use independent contractors, be sure to have each contractor sign a written agreement that specifies the duties to be performed and the compensation to be paid and that emphasizes the agreement is for specific services, not employment. Pay independent contractors lump sums for identifiable tasks rather than by the hour or day; treat them as you would outside contractors, even if they occupy desks in your office; make them provide their own tools and equipment as outside contractors would; and let them manage their own work and time. The more your relationship with independent contractors resembles a contract for outside services rather than an employment agreement, the less the IRS is likely to intervene.

Be particularly cautious about trying to convert an employee into an independent contractor; this step should not be taken without first obtaining expert advice. Remember that state governments and the IRS have reasons to disapprove of questionable independent contractor arrangements and that the rules and definitions of independent contractor status can vary greatly. If in doubt about these matters or what you should do when trouble arises, by all means discuss the matter with your attorney and with the National Association of Realtors, which makes information on the topic available to its members.

References

BOOKS

1. Barrons: *Conducting Better Job Interviews*. (New York: Barron's Business Success Series) 1992.

2. Bell AH: *The Complete Manager's Guide to Interviewing: How To Hire the Best*. (Homewood, IL: Dow Jones-Irwin) 1989.

3. Byham WC and Cox J: *The Lightning Power of Empowerment*. (New York: Fawcett) 1992.

4. Garfield C: *Second to None: How Our Smartest Companies Put People First*. (Homewood, IL: Business One Irwin) 1992.

5. Wendover RW: *Smart Hiring*. (Englewood Cliffs, NJ: Prentice-Hall) 1989.

6. Worthington ER: *Staffing a Small Business. Hiring, Compensating, and Evaluating*. (Milpitas, CA: The Oasis Press) 1987.

7. US Department of the Treasury. Internal Revenue Service: *Tax Guide for Small Business*. Publication 334. (Washington, DC: IRS).

Chapter 9

Counseling Tools

Every counselor needs a tool kit that includes adequate equipment, good software, up-to-date data sources and a number of useful analytical techniques.

EQUIPMENT

Every counselor who can use one should have a lightweight laptop or notebook computer with a hard disk and modem, plus a reasonable array of software including spreadsheet, database management, desk management, word processing, communications, statistics and investment analysis. If your staff counselors have other hardware or software preferences, hear them out before insisting on what you are using now, but remember that incompatibility among computer systems can be a serious handicap in an office.

Most firms today have telefax equipment, which has become essential in modern business communications. Many have electronic voice communications and electronic mail, both of which are real conveniences and timesavers. Cellular phones, pagers and similar gadgets will help track your clients and your employees, if you can tolerate the interruptions. You also should investigate the new portable units that combine these and other functions.

It's wise to insist that staff counselors provide their own hand calculators, cameras and other incidental equipment such as flashlights, measuring tools and pocket dictating equipment. This policy minimizes arguments about lost or damaged items and gives each staff counselor the sense that he is investing in the work and the firm. Larger items should be purchased by the firm, except, perhaps, for a counselor's briefcase computer.

Cheaper can be better.

Computers. The new notebook and laptop models are excellent; some actually come with enough incidentals and essentials to serve as the counselor's only computer, especially when they can be plugged into larger keyboards and monitors in the office. You don't have to buy the most expensive, though; most current units will be obsolete soon, anyway. Choose one that has readily available service, a fast main processor, an easy-to-use keyboard, a good hard disk drive, a sufficient amount of disk space and random access memory and a built-in modem with telefax capability. Color is a big plus, but it adds cost and may not be necessary. If you plan to use Windows or OS/2 as your working environment, be sure to insist on a fast enough microchip, a big hard disk and plenty of memory.

The 3 1/2" diskette is excellent and durable. Don't be deterred from using a laptop that requires small diskettes because you've been using only 5 1/4" floppy diskettes in the office. You can buy a unit that will transfer information from the larger to the smaller disk easily and quickly.

Local area networks (LAN), while helpful, are not indispensable in small offices. Diskettes can be hand-carried or sent back and forth. Exciting new packages are appearing that connect several people by modem or LAN so they can work on the same reports from a distance, a real time-saver. Modems are useful for all sorts of other activities, including connecting with electronic mail systems and commercial databases.

If you plan to do desktop publishing, make sure that someone in the office is interested in it and willing to do it; then choose your equipment accordingly, selecting, at a minimum, a good laser printer, a high-resolution monitor, extra RAM and disk space and a mouse. Remember that service, compatibility and ease of use are at least as important as a system's technical features and the manufacturer's reputation. Don't let yourself be seduced into buying something that won't work in an emergency.

Some large offices prefer a mainframe or minicomputer with workstations and terminals for individual consultants. Most can do better with personal computers that can be upgraded, replaced and perhaps linked by a LAN, without making a major investment in hardware. Central computer systems have real advantages, but they do break down occasionally, and when that happens, nobody can use them. Besides, the basic requirements for computerizing real estate counseling—spreadsheets, word processing, database management and the like—are all cheaper and easier to do on personal computers. Data sharing, central storage and distributed printing, which are the reasons most businesses invest in mainframes and minis, can be done on networks, without getting any new software.

Why a computer on every desk? Partly for ease of use, partly for encouraging staff counselors to learn the ins and outs of the computer and to find new applications for it. These days a staff counselor who can't do discounted cash flow analysis, who doesn't understand basic statistical concepts and who writes with a pencil rather than a word processor is considered professionally handicapped.

Bear in mind that undergraduates in most universities have used personal computers since the early 1980s; some colleges require students to buy them. You therefore are entitled to demand that young hires possess basic word processing and spreadsheeting skills. Existing staffers should also be urged to become technically proficient.

Operating systems. For real estate counseling MS-DOS-based systems are still the best choice. Spreadsheets, word processing and database management can be run on Macintosh, Windows, OS/2, and UNIX operating systems, all of which have important advantages; however, most specialized real estate programs run best on MS-DOS.

DATA SOURCES, COMPUTER SOFTWARE AND ANALYTICAL TOOLS

Real estate counselors make use of a great many data sources and tools, too many to be discussed here or even listed. This book is not a text on real estate investment analysis but on the art and business of counseling. For more information on analytical methods and techniques, see the excellent *Real Estate Counseling, Market Analyses, The Appraisal of Real Estate*, and Gene Dilmore's wonderful cookbook for counselors (all cited in the References).

Data sources. Your office library, job files and personal contacts are only the beginning of a comprehensive collection of data sources. The U.S. government and its agencies, especially the Department of Commerce, also are excellent sources of information, as are many state and local agencies. Public libraries, trade association libraries, including the National Association of Realtors library in Chicago, university libraries and the files of your professional colleagues are valuable. So are the many computerized databases accessible by modem. Among them are the following:

> *Lexis-Nexis.* These parallel database services, the first aimed primarily at the legal profession and the second at the general user, are both offered by Mead Data Central, 9443 Springboro Pike, P.O. Box 933, Dayton, OH 45401, (513) 865-6800. Lexis incorporates, among many other databases, a property records file (ASSETS) for six California counties, three Chicagoland counties and a number of collar counties around New York City. Doubtless other such files will follow. Nexis, more useful to many counselors, includes several years of back files of such publications as *Business Week, Business Month, Newsweek, U.S. News and World Report*, the *Chicago Tribune, Investor's Daily, Financial World* and (one example from a large collection), *Dayton-Springfield Business Life*.
>
> *Dialog.* This general database service is offered by Dialog Information Services, Inc., 3460 Hillview Avenue, Palo Alto, CA 94304, (800) 334-2564 or (415) 858-3785. Dialog includes many files of interest to counselors, including libraries on architecture, associations, business economics, business news, U. S. companies, energy, geology, public affairs, tax and accounting and the full text of 18 newspapers. Among its numerous databases are Arthur D. Little Online, *Books in Print*, the

Federal Register, PTS U.S. Time Series, Econbase time series and forecasts, and newswires including AP, UPI and Reuters.

CompuServe. An on-line bulletin board by subscription only is offered by CompuServe, Inc., 5000 Arlington Centre Blvd., Columbus, OH 43220, (1-800-848-8199). Information is provided on almost any subject area.

Other important databases, not all of them available on computer, include those maintained by Dow-Jones (publishers of *The Wall Street Journal* and other business publications), Standard & Poor's, *The New York Times*, Real Estate Data Incorporated (REDI), and a variety of research bureaus, private firms, business organizations, governments and governmental agencies. Of great and growing importance are geographical information systems (GIS) based on the U. S. Census. These data systems are available through a number of service companies and allow users to map census data for all parts of the country in considerable—and often valuable—detail.

COMPUTER SOFTWARE

Lotus 1-2-3. This software is still the most popular general purpose spreadsheet and analytical system among real estate professionals. Other similar systems are available and some, notably Borland's Quattro Pro and Microsoft's Excel, may be better. Lotus, however, is well established, has reasonable graphic capabilities and interfaces readily with a wide range of other software packages. It also is relatively easy to learn, doesn't cost much and is well supported by the manufacturer.

WordPerfect and *Microsoft Word*. These powerful word processing tools are well adapted to real estate counseling report production. The later versions of these software packages handle book-length reports easily and have graphics capabilities, though Word still has some disturbing bugs. Wang systems, aging fast, are used in many offices. Other packages may work equally well, but for one reason or another have not found favor in the market. As a result, few word processing people know how to use them. Once you decide on the word processing software for you, use it in all your personal computers and make sure everyone in the office is attuned to it. Your word processing people can help you make a good choice.

Harvard Project Management. Still very popular, this package is always on the verge of being overtaken by others. Read the literature and check with other users before you make a choice.

Paradox. This database manager is gaining in popularity. Other capable and well liked DBMs include Dbase, RBase V and DataEase. Many more specialized packages are available. For use in keeping track of your schedule, contacts and work lists, try MemoryMate, a bruit-force program that is easy to learn and use, does the job and doesn't cost much. Other more sophisticated desk managers can do far more, but take some getting used to.

ProJect and *Office 2*. These programs allow lease-by-lease discounted cash flow analysis of properties. ProJect is harder to learn and more expensive, but has greater power and flexibility. Office 2 may be preferable, although it is aging fast, for occasional use or use by people who don't have the time to learn ProJect. Spreadsheet templates exist in profusion and can be useful if you don't have the time or the inclination to develop your own, but the templates lack the power of the commercial packages.

Desktop publishing. With a little practice, a reasonably capable personal computer and a laser printer, anyone can produce professional-looking graphics, reports, slides and exhibits. The technology costs little and is not hard to learn. It greatly improves the appearance of your written work and is fast becoming standard in the industry. Because desktop publishing hardware and software are evolving so rapidly, no programs are listed here; refer to your neighborhood desktop publishing hobbyist or consult the magazines read by computer buffs for specifications, prices and critical opinions.

Negotiator Pro. A new entry available from Beacon Expert Systems Inc., Brookline, MA, this program conducts you or your client through any standard type of negotiation. It can take into account not only the specifics of a situation but also the personalities of the negotiators, including you. Like other expert systems, Negotiator Pro attempts to do things as a genuine expert would do them, given enough time and the right facts. It'll never replace a skilled negotiator, but it can help anyone plan and execute a good strategy.

Paper Works. This new program from Xerox links your computer to any fax machine. With it, you can fax a document from the field to your office computer for storage or for distribution to any number of locations. You can also call up any document from your home-office hard disk and fax it to yourself, wherever you may be. For traveling counselors, this can be a real godsend.

Many other software packages are available to meet your specific needs: project managers, graphics programs, analytical programs, communications software, GIS front ends and expert systems, to name just a few categories. Because new products are appearing at a rapid rate, don't be satisfied with the suggestions that appear here; ask around, read the magazines, try out what's available. You may find something cheaper as well as better. But remember: Untried new software may have bugs that make it worse than worthless in a pinch. It therefore usually makes sense to go with the established workhorses.

ANALYTICAL TOOLS

Following are a few of the tools commonly used in counseling assignments.

Discounted cash flow analysis: The basic tool of the investment analyst, DCF reduces the anticipated stream of income and expenses associated with a property or portfolio, or the cash flows associated with the ownership position being evaluated, to their net present value, using standard compound interest algorithms. The method is described in many publications (for example, *Real Estate Counseling*, cited in the References). It is based on the formula:

$$PV = CF_1/(1 + Y) + CF_2/(1 + Y)^2 + ... + CF_n/(1 + Y)^n$$

where:

PV = present value;

CF = the cash flow for the period in question;

Y = the periodic yield or discount rate used; and

n = the number of periods in the income or cash flow projection.

DCF estimates property value, loan value, equity value, leased fee and leasehold values and the values of other interests in real property. Because it is widely applied to stocks, bonds and other investments, it is familiar to investment analysts and financial institutions and used by corporate financial officers to make capital allocations as well as to value corporate assets. DCF can be done with software packages such as ProJect, Office 2 and Lotus 1-2-3, but in many cases it can be performed on a financial hand calculator such as the Hewlett Packard HP12C, available in most cities for less than $100.

Statistics and probability. The data analysis and projections associated with many counseling assignments require some understanding of statistical methods and the laws of probability. Retail sales volume and rental income forecasts, for example, may require the analysis of historical patterns using statistical inference. Regression analysis can be used as an aid in estimating property values and as a means of relating pairs of variables or even multiple variables (with the help of multiple regression). Multiple regression, which usually requires computer help, is a powerful tool for sorting out the factors that create value in different parcels of real estate, a great help in analyzing "comparable" transactions. Probability analysis allows counselors to study populations and predict events.

Sensitivity analysis and optimization. The significance of any particular variable in a projection—property taxes in discounted cash flow analysis, for example—can be tested by changing the variable and measuring the impact of the change on the conclusion. In the case of DCF the result is usually an estimate of current property value. Sensitivity analysis and optimization allow the analyst to test the effect of a property tax increase, for example, on the value of property today; it can be used equally well to test the wisdom of a specific rehabilitation or development project.

As any DCF analyst knows, the impact of the assumptions made about the ultimate selling price of a property may have a greater or lesser effect on property value depending upon a number of factors that can be sorted out in this way. Similarly, the best size of a projected office building, the best mix of uses in a mixed use project or the most profitable scheduled room rates for a hotel can be established by testing the possibilities, either in gross common-sense terms or with a computer.

Risk analysis. Several techniques are used to analyze and assess risk and weigh the risks associated with an investment against the likely rewards. For a brief discussion of this and the other tools mentioned here, see *The Appraisal of Real Estate* (cited in the References).

Rating grids. These grids are used to reach many different kinds of decisions by numerically rating individual factors associated with a decision and totaling the results, as in the following example:

Factor	Option One		Option Two		Option Three	
	Prop A	Prop B	Prop A	Prop B	Prop A	Prop B
Location	7	8	9	9	8	9
Land size	6	7	4	5	4	6
Visibility	4	2	9	7	6	5
Neighborhood rating	7	6	6	8	6	4
Accessibility	3	8	7	6	4	3
Utilities	9	4	6	7	9	8
Price	4	4	7	6	9	8
Distance from downtown	5	5	9	9	4	6
Total	45	44	57	57	50	43

An analysis of the totals produced by rating grids suggests which option and property should be chosen; in this case it's Option Two. Critical to the process, of course, are the identification of the relevant factors and the assignment of correct ratings.

Network analysis. Methods such as the Project Evaluation and Review Technique (PERT) and Gantt charts are used in network analysis, which is well suited to planning and managing real estate projects and conducting extended real estate counseling assignments. They help the analyst identify the critical path and plan for uncertainties associated with the assignment. While large-scale analyses require computer support, smaller ones can be performed with ordinary flow charts.

Measures of investment performance. Real estate investment is judged in terms of a number of criteria: cash return on the initial investment (a.k.a. the current yield; in appraisal parlance, the overall rate of return, going-in return or equity return); internal rate of return (IRR) or yield rate; payback period. For a more complete discussion, see *Real Estate*

Counseling, Gene Dilmore's *Quantitative Techniques in Real Estate Counseling* or *The Appraisal of Real Estate* (cited in the References).

Investor criteria. In addition to the measures listed above, investors consider factors such as risk, upside and downside potential, size, internal and portfolio diversification, tax factors, leverage, timing and appropriateness to specific situations in terms of resources, preferences, abilities and constraints. Investors also may wonder whether the opportunity is fairly priced in market terms or how the price relates to replacement cost.

Development planning. Developers and their backers think and act something like investors, but they have additional concerns, such as the qualifications and track record of the developer, the availability of suitable personnel, the quality of the site and the project, the suitability of project planning, the appropriateness of market timing and strength, the adequacy of cash planning and contingency reserve requirements, the nature of political and community relations problems and the need for (or fear of) the public relations consequences of their involvement.

These and other developer concerns can be systematized on computer; some developers actually have brought their software to a high state of sophistication. Programs of this type, which are essentially expert systems, can function as project monitors as well as planning tools. Commercial software packages can handle parts of the job, but none does it all. If you are serious about having a comprehensive version of this tool in your kit, you probably will have to build it yourself.

References

BOOKS

1. Bender H: *PC Tools: The Complete Reference*. (New York: Brady) 1992.
2. Daniel W: *Business Statistics. Basic Concepts and Methodology*. (Boston, MA: Houghton Mifflin) 1986.
3. Goldman N: *Online Information Hunting*. (New York: McGraw Hill) 1992.
4. Dayton D: *Computer Solutions for Business*. (New York: Harper and Row) 1987.
5. McWilliams P: *The Personal Computer in Business Book*. (New York: Quantum Press) 1984.
6. *MS DOS Portable Library*. (Orem, UT: Microsoft Press) 1992.
7. Niedermiler-Chaffins: *Inside Novell Netware*. (New York: New Riders Publishing) 1992.
8. Norton P and Jourdain R: *PC Problem Solver*. (New York: Brady) 1992.
9. Sochats K and Williams J: *The Networking and Communications Desk Reference*. (New York: SAMS) 1992.
10. Spurr WA: *Statistical Analysis for Business Decisions*. (Homewood, IL: Dow Jones-Irwin) 1967.
11. *US Census Population and Housing Characteristics*.(San Diego, CA: National Decision Systems) 1990.

12. US Department of Commerce, Bureau of Economic Analysis: *Survey of Current Business*.11. *The Winn L. Rosch Upgrade Bible*. (New York: Brady) 1992.

13 *The Winn L. Rosch Upgrade Bible*. (New York:Brady) 1992.

14. Wood L and Blankenhorn D: *Bulletin Board Systems for Business* (New York: John Wiley and Sons) 1992.

PERIODICALS

1. *Compuserve Information Service*, Compuserve, Inc., 5000 Arlington Centre Boulevard, Columbus, OH 43220

2. *Home Office Computing*, Scholastic, Inc., 730 Broadway, New York 10003

3. *PC World*, PC World Communications, Inc., 501 Second St., 501 Second Street, San Francisco, CA 94107

4. *Portable Office*, IDG Communications/Peterborough, 80 Elm St., Peterborough, NH 03458

CHAPTER 10

Your Professional Advisors

LAWYERS AND HOW TO USE THEM

Anybody can find a lawyer; the trick is to find the one who can help you the most. This means you will want more than professional competence; you may also want a lawyer who can act as a friend, general advisor, sounding-board and possibly even as a source of business and referrals. (Not all lawyers will be willing to send you their clients, who may, after all, blame *them* if your work turns out badly or who may accuse them of a conflict of interest. This would be an embarrassment in the best of circumstances. In the worst it can result in litigation and force both the client and you to look for other lawyers. Still, it won't hurt to choose an attorney who is affiliated with a firm that serves the kinds of clients you hope to attract.)

Don't be shy about asking questions when considering a lawyer or a law firm.

Ask questions not only of the lawyer, but also of his clients. How well qualified is the firm in the kinds of work you want them to do? Do they have the right experience? Are their charges affordable and fair? If at all possible, pick a lawyer who has been down your kinds of roads before. The fees will amount to a lot less.

WHY DO YOU NEED A LAWYER?

Here are just of few of the many things a competent lawyer can do for you:

- Help you choose and form an appropriate business structure
- Check possible company names for conflicts
- Draft contract forms and contracts
- Keep corporate records
- Advise you about insurance and taxes
- Help arrange financing and negotiate workouts

- Coach you for expert testimony
- Plan with you for your succession
- Assist you through merger and acquisition discussions
- Look after your estate

You, of course, can take care of some of these activities yourself or get advice on them from your accountant and other advisors. On the other hand, it doesn't hurt to keep a smart, legally trained person informed about your affairs and get him to take a personal interest in them. One day you may find that the expense is more than worth it.

You also can take many steps to reduce your legal costs.

HOW TO BE A GOOD CLIENT AND SAVE MONEY
by Tobin M. Richter

While it may seem hard to believe, how you behave as a client can make a material difference in your legal fees. One way or another, all lawyers charge for their time, even time spent in telephone conversations with you, including those calls that catch them at home. They also want to collect for their out-of-pocket disbursements. Talk to them in detail about how they charge, and while you're at it, find out what it costs for them to make a photocopy or reproduce a picture. If you're a heavy user of such things and can get the work done more cheaply on your own, you'll save money.

It may not be possible to budget for your needs in advance, but you should discuss with your lawyers precisely what your objectives are and how you want them approached. Lawyers waste a lot of time with clients who aren't sure what they want, muddling along and running up bills until the client's objectives finally become clear. Don't just call your lawyer because you have a car phone and things are dull on the expressway. Have a plan before you turn on the meter. When the time comes for a meeting, make sure that you or your lawyer knows what the agenda will be.

Take the time to discuss with your lawyer what things you can do for yourself, perhaps with a little guidance. Sit down with him or her to review typical contract forms, purchase orders, dunning letters and similar items. The lawyer will let you know when to call for help and when you can safely proceed on your own.

Finally, don't be afraid to spend money where it will produce efficiency and savings in the long run. Many clients don't like to pay lawyers for the initial research needed to prevent costs and trouble later on. Unfortunately, there is no surer way of creating inefficiency, waste, high legal fees and bad results than to embark on a project without it.

Once you have established a relationship with a lawyer, start thinking about his law firm as an opportunity store waiting for you to browse. Make friends in the firm; spend time with those friends, learning what they do and how you may be able to work with them. If nothing else, they can help you learn more about their field and your own.

The same comments apply to your banker and accountant. Both have much to say in directing the service needs of their customers and clients. When those clients need real estate counseling services, your name should be among the first they provide, unless they have a policy against referring clients to one another. You can find out such things before you sign on, so don't forget to inquire and state your preference.

Use your professionals.

GETTING THE MOST OUT OF YOUR ACCOUNTANT

If you are already in business, you may know all you need to know about this topic. If not, a few words of advice may be useful.

Accountants are: (1) valuable professionals who can keep you out of trouble; (2) potentially useful business consultants; and (3) expensive. You can save money, and still get full value, by keeping your own books with the help of a standard software package designed for small-business personal computer users. If you are computer phobic, you can do the same job manually with the help of readily available handbooks. Only if you and your employees lack the skills—or consider your time too valuable for this sort of thing—should you use an accountant for bookkeeping tasks that can be done more economically by clerical staff.

Make sure, though, that the person to whom you turn over your routine bookkeeping chores is competent and trustworthy. Much as you may trust your secretaries and administrative assistants, you seldom will find them to be reliable bookkeepers. If you plan to use a bookkeeping service, be sure to check its references beforehand. Watch what your bookkeepers are doing, make sure they are properly instructed and, unless you have the time to do it yourself, have an accountant oversee the work.

Whether you do your own bookkeeping or farm it out, you may need the help of a trained tax advisor unless you are qualified to prepare your own tax returns. Tax laws are changing so quickly that you may find the advice of a knowledgeable accountant will more than justify the cost, especially since that chore is now entirely computerized in most accounting firms. You can, of course, prepare the returns on your own computer, but there is wisdom in having them at least reviewed by a tax expert.

You also may want an accountant's assistance to prepare your balance sheets, minimize your taxes and help you analyze your costs and improve your financial picture. Bear in mind that most accountants don't know your business as well as you do, and some have kept nose to grindstone for so long that they can't see very far ahead. On the important issues, you'll have to think for yourself.

Accountants, like lawyers, usually charge on the basis of the time they devote to your affairs. As their hourly rates can be high, it pays to set budgets and limit the amount of time they can spend on your affairs without consulting you. The structure of many accounting and law firms encourages their employees to put in as much billable time as they can, so be forewarned.

Accounting tasks that must be done, whether by you, your bookkeeper or an accountant, include:

Journal entries. These record the daily events in your money system: bills sent, bills received, money flows. One journal may be sufficient, but several may be needed to cover different kinds of activities.

Posting to ledgers. Journal entries must be entered in ledgers, i.e., books that keep track of individual departments and accounts.

Balancing and verification. Totals must be checked, and ledgers and journals must confirm one another.

Cost calculations. You need to know what it costs to do business: per day, per hour, per job.

Scheduling accounts payable. It also pays to know how much cash you'll need for suppliers and when it'll be needed.

Sending invoices and statements. A good billing system brings in money quickly, which helps to improve profits and assure solvency.

Preparing tax returns and supporting documents. Uncle Sam can be nasty if you don't do a good job in this department.

Generating reports. Balance sheets, profit and loss statements and interim reports help to increase profitability and reduce risk.

Software selection. See Chapter 9 if your accountant doesn't have the right answers.

Do it yourself where you can.

On the subject of computer software: many good bookkeeping and accounting packages are available and well supported. Features vary, so be sure to discuss your choice with other users and your accountant before you commit yourself. Remember that it's the cost of learning, running, and maintaining the system that matters, not the cost of the software, so don't buy on the basis of price alone.

You may want to inquire about a recently issued small business package from Intuit, Inc., the company that sells the popular checkbook program Quicken. Its Quickbooks sounds ideal for the small practice: easy to learn, understand and use. A related program, Quickpay, looks after the payroll if there is one. Unfortunately, Quickbooks can be scary to accountants, as it allows the user to go back and change entries after the month has been closed out on the books. They may insist on a more accounting-oriented package like Businessworks or Peachtree. If Quickbooks catches on as expected, though, the accounting professional will have little choice but to catch on — quickly.

Remember that accountants are valuable not only to make sure you pay your taxes but also to help you determine financial facts that may be vitally important to your business. Among them:

Sales volume. These figures can tell you how much you are selling, how often your sales occur, where they come from, how large your sales run and if sales are getting better or worse.

Cost of sales. This is the amount it takes to get and to perform each assignment. Analysis of these figures will help you decide what kinds of business to pursue and what kinds to drop.

Overhead costs. This is the cost of being in business: rent, utilities, telephone, postage, secretarial services and the like. The information can be used to price your services and determine how much business you need to attract just to cover expenses.

Markup and profit calculations. If you know what your costs are, you will be able to figure how much business you need to generate before you start making money and how much you need to reach your profit goals.

Good figures can help enormously in planning your business activities and evaluating potential new business, and they can provide early warnings of trouble. Even an accounting firm that fails to keep close track of its figures can find itself in deep water, wondering how it ever got there. Don't get caught in that position.

References

BOOKS

1. Finkler SA: *Finance and Accounting.* (Englewood Cliffs, NJ: Prentice-Hall) 1992.

2. Goozner C: *Business Mathematics. The Easy Way.* (New York: Barrons Educational Series) 1991.

3. Kravitz WW: *Bookkeeping The Easy Way.* (New York: Barrons Educational Series) 1990.

4. Livingstone JL: *The Portable MBA in Finance and Accounting.* (New York: John Wiley and Sons) 1992.

5. Scioletti DL: *Legal Decisions for CPAs and Business People.* (Dubuque, IA: Kendall/Hunt) 1979.

6. Siegel JG, et al: *The McGraw Hill Pocket Guide to Business Finance.* (New York: McGraw Hill) 1992.

7. Sitarz D: *The Complete Book of Small Business Legal Forms.* (New York: National Home Business) 1992.

Part III

Running The Shop

Chapter 11

Minding the Store

Every business needs somebody to make sure things go as they should. In a small business that somebody is usually the proprietor. As your business grows, you'll assign at least some of these burdens to other people, but no matter how large you get, you'll never be able to rid yourself of these duties completely. Chief executives who forget to check the store now and then eventually find themselves with nothing left to sell.

Among the things the storekeeper of a professional firm must do are manage his own time and that of his people, keep records, maintain databases, deal with subcontractors and suppliers, send invoices and see that bills are paid, watch the cash, pay the bills, see that the place is properly insured and protected and keep the customers happy. Some of these tasks have been touched on in earlier chapters; most are discussed in the following chapters under a variety of labels. The subject of marketing (buying the ads and putting out the signs) and other essentials take up most of Parts IV, V and VI of this book. For even more information on these topics, you can consult the excellent books about time and business management by Peter Drucker and Tom Peters (see References).

Here are a few pointers for use in minding your counseling store:
- Keep a close eye on the cash. It tends to dribble away otherwise.
- Get the money now, or at least as soon as possible.
- Prepare for tomorrow, which usually comes.
- Ask the right questions if you want the right answers.
- Check clients, employees and sources before you accept them, not when it's too late.
- Never assume. You and another party may have entirely different things in mind.
- Touch the bases. Who else ought to know about what you're doing? Who else can throw light on the subject?
- Try something different occasionally. It might work.
- Have enough clients. With too few, you'll find yourself high and dry when they desert you or retire.
- When a lemon presents itself, look for the opportunity to make lemonade. It's often there.
- Remember your friends. If you don't, sooner or later they will become your enemies.

- Keep track of the competition. How much are they charging? Have they found a way to do things better? Are they after your clients?
- Build your successors. Nobody else will, except your executor or a creditors' committee.

BUSINESS PITFALLS

You'll also need to watch out for pitfalls. Here are 18 to guard against:

1. *Handshake agreements.* These are dangerous unless you know the client well and have at least some degree of mutual trust. Get the particulars in writing and spell out the details, or you may find that the client's recollection differs from yours.
2. *Underbidding.* Prepare a job budget before you issue a quote and check to see what the market thinks the job is worth. A bid that is too low can cost your reputation as well as money.
3. *Underbilling.* If the job takes longer than you expected because of something the client does or fails to do or because you encountered unexpected circumstances, don't hesitate to let the client know what happened and revise your bill. When the client alters course while the job is underway, get a change order and charge for it.
4. *Overpromising.* Don't make commitments you can't meet, and don't promise more than you can deliver. You may make a sale by overheating your sales pitch, but you probably won't like what follows.
5. *Relying too much on others.* Clients can't always be counted upon to keep their promises; neither can employees or subcontractors. Probe, check, verify before you make a commitment that depends upon other people. You may need to pin down clients, in particular, before you start, to make sure that you get the information and materials you need to perform on schedule.
6. *Chasing too many birds in the bush.* The bird in the hand is usually more nourishing. Don't pass up a good small job while waiting for a big one to materialize.
7. *Lawsuits.* These eat up more than the fees consumed by lawyers; they also can absorb your time and energies, prevent you from undertaking profitable assignments, demoralize your shop and depress your family. Take every precaution to minimize the likelihood of becoming entangled in anybody's litigation, except for money.
8. *Overdependency.* A business with one or two clients is a business in trouble, even when it is profitable. The clients may prove to be loyal, but your overdependence on them will lead you to make compromises and concessions that, in the end, will impair your ability to perform.
9. *Overspecialization.* You can't afford to overspecialize. In the first place, clients can have so many needs that you'll need to be versatile to address their problems. In the second place, you'll risk a business breakdown if your usual sources of work dry up. You may be able to

regroup after such a loss, but sometimes there's no choice but to retire to another climate.

10. *Procrastination.* Learn not to put off what needs doing now and to put off the rest only when absolutely necessary.
11. *Laziness.* You can't make it without hard work—your own and that of the people around you.
12. *Carelessness.* Everybody makes mistakes now and then—a person who isn't making mistakes isn't working—but that doesn't excuse you from being careful. Pay attention. It'll save you grief.
13. *Weakness.* You have principles; stick to them. When they are challenged, let the world know you take them seriously. Nobody respects a pushover.
14. *Hiring the wrong people.* Get the best you can find. It'll pay in the long run. Turnover and training cost time as well as money.
15. *Quitting too soon.* Everybody suffers occasional setbacks. Winners look past them, fix what they can and persist.
16. *Undercapitalization.* Have enough initial capital not just to cover your immediate needs but to provide a decent reserve for rainy days—and slow months.
17. *Failure to anticipate.* Plan ahead for cash needs, space needs, client demands and legal challenges.
18. *Neglecting your reputation.* Because bad news occasionally pops up in the wrong places, it pays to check your own reputation from time to time. Draw a credit report on yourself and your company; have a third party check your references; see what the local banks and chamber of commerce have to say about you. Don't make the common mistake of using a reference who will have unkind words to offer when someone calls to inquire about you.

TIME MANAGEMENT

Professional firms have little to sell except time and results. Think for a moment about your doctor, your lawyer, your accountant. Essentially what they do is spend time on your problems, sometimes solving them. You pay them for their time at rates that reflect your confidence in their ability to succeed.

Sometimes an accountant, more often a lawyer, will base his fee partly or wholly on results. Counselors can do this, too, under certain conditions (see the discussion of value billing and performance fees in Chapter 20). Usually, though, counselors charge only for their time.

For that reason you have little choice but to keep track of your business day in quarter-hour segments and require that any professionals who work for you do the same. Time tracking arrangements don't need to be elaborate; simple logs will do. However, if you do a lot of time-based billing, you can find better ways to keep track of your hours. What you must remember, and get your people to understand, is that time—always and inescapably—is money. If you can't charge for a service, and charge enough, your business will fail.

Your firm may have a good computerized time-and-billing system in place. If you don't, you can buy or create a system of your own or do without the computer and manually keep your own time records. Your accountant can set you up, if need be.

Time = Money

A detailed log is advisable for four principal reasons:
1. It will provide a record to back up your time-based invoices and tax returns.
2. It will give you the information you need to prepare good job budgets and bids (see Chapter 20).
3. It will allow your staff to get the information they need for putting together time-based invoices and keeping track of the time spent on fixed-fee jobs.
4. It will remind you that your time is valuable and that you should bill as much of it as possible to clients.

Once you know how you are spending your time, you can seek out ways of managing it more productively. Here are a few suggestions:
- Before you start each day, make a list of your priorities in descending order of importance. Interruptions and new items of business are inevitable, but you can at least try to start at the top of the list and work your way down. You may find that the things at the bottom of the list don't need to be done at all.
- Find ways to group tasks that belong together (same time, location, subject matter, equipment, data sources, people). That way you won't have to do things twice or begin too many things at the beginning.
- Finish the tasks you start. If you have too many projects on the table at once, you may give each only a lick and a promise every now and then. You'll lose time with multiple starts while the projects drag on.
- Establish routines for your assistant and yourself that minimize unnecessary interruptions, which cost you not only the time it takes to deal with them but the time it takes to get back in the swing of what you were doing.
- Dodge people you know will waste your time, especially unexpected callers who are just looking for a little company or a free bit of advice. Even worse are "friends" (read "exploiters") who always have a non-paying project they want you to undertake.
- If you find yourself hung up on a decision, don't spend too much time mulling it over. Get help or reduce the problem to its simplest form and list the pluses and minuses in writing. You'll soon see your way clear.
- Learn to say "no" to things you don't really have time to do. It's your own time priorities that count, not usually those of other people—at least not those of the people you see at work. And remember: Someone else's failure to plan does not constitute *your* emergency.

- Make written plans for your big projects, attach tickler dates and enter them in your personal schedule. Also ask your assistant to nag you about important project dates as they come up.

BUILDING TEAM SPIRIT

Your people want to enjoy their work, just as you do. Help them by creating a collegial environment where they can feel good about each other and themselves. Every counseling group is a team; team players need to help one another and save their competitive instincts for use against other firms.

Administration ≠ Management

You can encourage team sentiments by treating your associates and employees as you would family members: with respect, support and fairness. Ask for their advice, applaud their successes and show them how to turn their failures into learning experiences. Reward stand-out performances, but not to such an extent that you create jealousies and upset others.

Be careful not to *over*administer and *under*manage your people, as many large firms tend to do. These practices cut into morale by making employees feel regimented, meaningless and insecure. A good organization, at least in the counseling field, develops the team by recognizing and developing its employees. The organization should allow each person to feel important, useful and special; it should give each person a clear sense of what he is expected to contribute and a reasonable belief that his accomplishments will be properly noticed.

Among other things, this responsibility requires you to tell them how your organization works and what it is about. Make sure your people understand and share your goals. Let them know how the group is structured and how they fit into it; spell out the rules so everyone can respect and remember them. By the time you finish with such an orientation, each team member should have a good idea of his responsibilities and of how performance is measured in your shop.

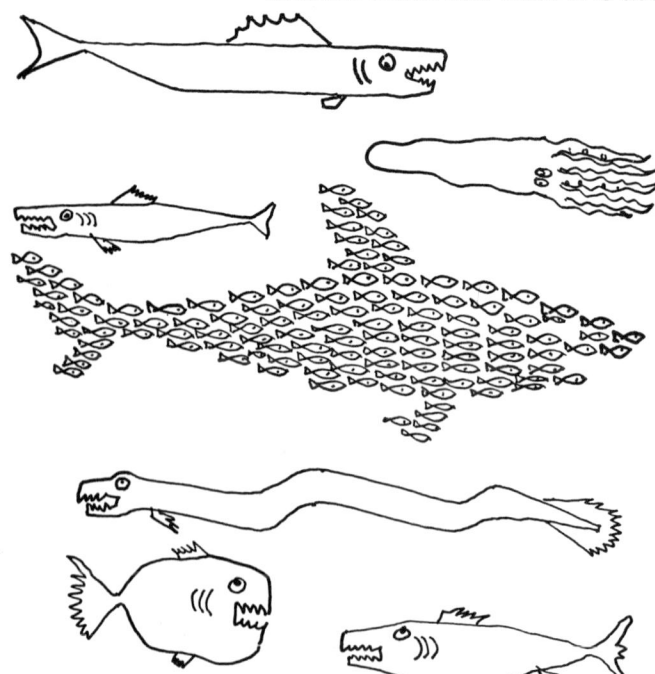

Good office groups socialize away from the workplace. Encourage this tendency with scheduled and spontaneous outings, office parties, special T-shirts and sports costumes. Such outside activities and uniforms build feelings of loyalty and pride that strengthen the organization.

A team approach to client assignments helps to assure good performance and, at the same time, builds the collaborative spirit. The client knows that if one team member is unavailable, another who is acquainted with the job can follow up if need be. Meanwhile, the junior member of the team receives mentoring and moral support from the senior member; the senior member, in turn, receives professional backup.

The best long-run morale builder is a consistently high level of quality and performance. Excellence should be your aim. There's nothing that builds confidence and pride in employees like belonging to a first-class team, whether it is large or small. Your people know that such teams are likely to grow and prosper. They will take satisfaction in their team membership even in the early, slow days of development, and they will be willing to wait for better days—and perhaps a better deal—in the knowledge that good things are bound to come soon.

Confucius pointed out long ago that a well-run country will have difficulty preventing foreigners from entering. In company terms a well-run organization will be attractive to good people, making recruiting efforts easier. There is no magnet for a talented person as powerful as a professional group of high quality, especially if it provides a warm, friendly, challenging and creative working environment—and gives promise of rapid growth.

Keeping good people. If the pay is generous and the working conditions right, people generally will stay with you at least for a few years. To cement their loyalties, you may want to offer profit sharing and a percentage of ownership in the company after a period of good service. You can hold young employees ten years or more by showing that you will pay them properly, appreciate them as individuals and reward them for outstanding performance.

However, as consultants approach age 40, they frequently expect a piece of the action. Some firms offer an ownership position early on, and some function as cooperatives. It is often preferable to be the sole owner of a firm for as long as possible so you can make decisions quickly on your own responsibility. The other side of the coin is that, without the possibility of profit sharing or a partnership, your people may not have the sense of participation in the business that you would like, even though they perform well and take an active interest in the firm's well being.

If you intend to offer partnerships, do so only with extreme care and good legal counsel. Your partners will be around for a long time and will have to wear well. Be sure to make them buy their way in, or they may not take their responsibilities as seriously as they should. (For more on this topic, see Chapter 3.)

Bad apples. Some employees lie, cheat, steal or make too many mistakes. Others are just lazy and pigheaded. Firing them will expose you to certain risks, as the laws are moving toward a blanket endorsement of any discharged employee's claim to damages for rape, murder, arson, theft, unfair discrimination, sexual harrassment and impolite behavior.

Part-time or full-time, written contract or no, employees have legal protections that vary from state to state. Under the common law, you used to be able to fire non-contractual employees at will, which made great business sense but was sometimes hard on the people who were fired. Now, however, the law on this subject is changing. No longer can you safely fire even a viciously delinquent ne'er-do-well without consulting your lawyer, an experienced personnel director or both. While you may object to this situation, chances are you won't be able to fight it successfully. Just bite your tongue and raise your fees.

Before you hire and fire, inquire.

The two touchiest and most controversial employment issues are:

1. *Promises.* Any representations you make to a new employee about a trial period or a minimum duration of employment may be honored by the courts even if you did not set them in writing.
2. *Discrimination.* Age discrimination laws apply to all employees age 40 and above. Laws against discrimination for reasons of sex, race and disability also apply and can have an impact on your hiring and firing as well as on your promotion decisions.

You can protect yourself against some employment problems by making—and documenting—an honest effort to salvage an employee before issuing a pink slip. Explain promptly, politely and privately what is wrong with the employee's work and how you expect these flaws to be corrected. Then set a reasonable deadline and a make a record (not a recording!) of the conversation. If things don't improve promptly, turn the matter over to a trained human resources professional—or a labor lawyer—for appropriate action. Don't risk doing something on your own that could result in a lawsuit for wrongful discharge or a complaint to some disrespectful public body.

After anyone, bad apple or not, has left your employ, be careful what you say about him. Unkind comments about a former employee may come back to haunt you. Experienced personnel directors usually disclose only the fact of employment, the dates of employment and the salary, furnishing no evaluation whatsoever of the employee.

Because even the best apples sometimes turn bad, it pays to make a careful investigation of each prospective employee *before* you add him to your staff. Check the person's references, find out everything you can about previous employment, verify educational degrees and transcripts, call or write the applicant's professional societies. It's also wise to check credit records for possible bad news. An employee with money worries is one who won't be paying full attention to the job and who may be under a dangerous temptation to steal or to accept improper bonuses from others.

DESK MANAGEMENT

Different people have different systems for managing the flood of paper, telephone calls and unplanned visits that characterizes the ordinary business day. Some prefer to make notes on odd scraps of paper, which can be folded or put into stacks. If you are going to use this method, it is best to make sure that the scraps are of uniform size and of reasonably good paper stock, preferably a light cardboard. Standard 3" x 5" index cards are excellent, as they can be shuffled repeatedly without incurring serious damage, and stuffed into a pocket or briefcase for homework sessions and out-of-town trips.

For those who prefer to develop a more organized business style, a variety of commercial desk management systems, some of them quite elaborate, can be found at your favorite office supplies store. Perhaps you will find one suited to your needs.

These days more and more professional people have come to depend on desktop, laptop and briefcase computers equipped with word processing, a list manager and a memory jogger such as MemoryMate to keep track of all the business tasks that need to be done. MemoryMate will recall any entry and its context if you can remember even one word of what you typed. It also allows you to create separate files of up to 120 lines so you can maintain in individual files, for example, a personal schedule and lists of prospects, job quotations and jobs in process and print out any of them on command. The software doesn't always work the way you may want it to, but it's a cinch to use and usually does the job. More powerful systems like Lotus Metro and Borland's Sidekick Plus are more versatile but much harder to learn.

The computer is also handy for keeping your staff and colleagues informed of your whereabouts. If your schedule isn't on the network, print it out every week or when you are about to leave town, and send photocopies to the people who are likely to be concerned. Your assistant should have a list of all the things you plan to do so he can keep track of where you are and what you are doing and can fill in for you when necessary. Lists of prospects and clients will help the receptionist to recognize important callers.

The top of your desk should have a clearly marked in-box, divided into sections to separate the wheat from the chaff. You can work out a system with your secretary that distinguishes urgent matters from merely important ones and other matters that need to be done only when you can make the time. Your out-box can be similarly divided, with compartments marked more or less as follows:

    XEROX ME
    FILE ME
    SEND ME
    PAY ME
    READ ME
    ASK/TELL THE BOSS WHAT TO DO ABOUT ME
    FORGET ME (in another receptacle under the desk)

FILES AND WORK PAPERS

As with desk management, different people have different ideas about filing. It's essential, though, to keep a file for each assignment and to identify each file with a number and a title. Such job files may be labeled according to the addresses of the properties in question, clients' names or the titles of specific reports. Files should be indexed in such a way that they can be found easily by recalling the name of the client, the location of the project or the nature of the job.

Some of your clients may deserve individual files of their own, with subfiles for specific assignments, or you may want to maintain files on various categories of assignment, such as appraisals, feasibility studies and market analyses, again with subfiles for individual jobs.

The main consideration when preparing files is to conserve the documents that must be kept and discard inessential items as promptly as possible. Think before you create a file document. Files accumulate rapidly, take up space and cost money. Set up your system so that out-of-date files can be identified and scrapped. Extraneous material not only takes up file space; it also can expose you to embarrassment, or worse if you become entangled in litigation. To prevent premature disposal of important file materials, find out from your accountants and attorneys how long to preserve job files.

Information files can be organized in a number of ways. A good one is to divide them into national and local categories; your national files might include general information on the office, the industry, housing, hotel, retail and land markets, demographic information, macroeconomics, national data sources, national organizations in which you are active and communities in which you expect to work. Local files might include the following:

> Property sales–Residential, commercial, hotels, offices, industrial, land
> Community data
> Market information–Residential, commercial, hotels, offices, industrial, land
> Legislation
> Litigation cases
> Assignments in process
> Client files
> Prospect files
> Contracts
> Invoices

You may extend and adapt this list to suit your needs. Ask your assistant to help you design your filing system. The more he has to say about it, the more attention your assistant will pay to its proper upkeep.

Work papers. Accounting, law and appraisal firms support the findings they submit to clients with work papers that are kept on file for specified periods. Maintaining files of work papers serves at least three purposes: (1) they guarantee a certain level of thoroughness; (2) they satisfy legal requirements or professional standards; and (3) they are available to successors and colleagues who may find themselves working with the same client or on the same type of problem.

The preparation of good work papers is time-consuming and tedious. Try to systematize their production and put them together as the report progresses instead of waiting until the report is finished. If you use work papers, make sure they are legible and complete. Include the names and telephone numbers of the people you have consulted in the course of your investigations. Remember, though, that work papers, like reports, are subject to subpoena in discovery proceedings and can prove to be embarrassing or annoying to the people whose names are mentioned. The facts cited in your work papers should support your conclusions, not controvert them.

Safety first in the file room.

OUTSIDE SUBCONTRACTORS

You may have occasion to hire and work with architects, engineers, contractors, demographers, market researchers, space planners, environmental scientists and other professionals whose expertise touches on real estate. When choosing these professionals, you'll want to assure yourself of their competence and their ability to sustain a relationship with you. While you won't make your choice entirely in these terms, you'll want to deal with folks who can provide valuable leads and who sometimes control important jobs.

The first concern is always the subcontractors' integrity. You must be able to count on the outside professionals you use to be honest and loyal in the clutch. You also need to be able to rely on their ability and willingness to jump in with both feet when you are in trouble and need their help. Don't choose associates who won't have the time or the desire to back you up.

Treat your subcontractors as business people. Let them know exactly what they are expected to do and when. Unless the relationship is of long standing, put them under written contract and make sure the contract specifies the tasks to be performed, the schedules to be met, the provisions for payment and other important conditions.

These contracts need not be complicated. Simple letter agreements will suffice in many cases. Ask your lawyer to draft a format you can adapt for small contracts. The essentials generally will include:

- Identification of the parties
- Description of the work
- Date of the agreement
- Completion date
- Other significant dates
- Price and terms of payment
- Special conditions and disclaimers
- Insurance coverages required
- Provision for early termination

Once the contract has been signed, put the subcontractor on your team. Encourage your people to cooperate fully in any work the subcontractor is doing. The more they do so, the more your staff will learn, and the better (usually) the subcontractor will perform.

Make it a point to pay subcontractors by the job whenever possible, not by the hour or day. They'll work better, finish the job sooner and be more eager to work for you next time. You'll also run less risk of an IRS or state challenge to their contractor status (see Chapter 8).

SUPPLIERS AND OTHER CONTRACTORS

Providers of stationery, computer services, rental cars, construction, lunch boxes, coffee and soda pop can be chosen to suit your convenience. Your main concern should be reliability, assuming the quality of the supplies or services is acceptable. Even at a lunch for your best clients, it's more important for the food to be there on time than for it to be eligible for a review in *Gourmet Magazine*.

On the other hand you don't want to use computer paper that will fall apart in the machine or an office copier that breaks down every time you have a big report to get out. Go for reliability, quality, quick service, good prices and longevity; choose a vendor who will be in business next year to look after the equipment if it breaks down. *Never* (if you can avoid it) buy any piece of equipment that must be sent out of town for repairs.

Financial strength and business viability also may be important, especially when construction is involved or when the contractor is asked to undertake a significant long-term commitment. You don't want to contract with a company that may fold before the work is completed. To protect against contracting with a potentially bankrupt company, check the company's bank and business references and have a credit report drawn. If you like contractors to be bonded, you can find out their bondable limits from their bonding companies.

Another factor to consider is insurance. When something goes wrong because of a product, service or job provided by a supplier or someone is hurt because of a supplier's action or inaction, will your insurance company provide redress, or will you be at the mercy of the contractor's lawyers and perhaps its hungry creditors? When circumstances warrant, ask for a certificate of insurance from the contractor's insurance carrier that itemizes applicable coverage. You don't have to settle for the simple statement: "We're insured." Neither do you have to apologize for insisting on specific types of coverage or high limits when your own financial health is at stake.

To keep expenses under control, you may want to set up a system that accounts for purchases and accounts payable (see Chapter 10). Such a system is particularly important if your business is large enough for an employee to steal without being promptly detected. You don't want to create a formal data bank, but you do need enough documentation to protect against easy rip-offs. Make it a practice to sign all the checks personally as long as you can; then call in your accountant to install appropriate controls.

References

ARTICLES

1. Blanchard K: Managing with style. *Today's Office* 24(8) Jan 1990, p 8.

2. Dykeman J et al: Managing creative and cost effective office services. *Modern Office Tech* 35(13) Mar 1990, p 37.

3. Edwards S: How to balance needs of workers and equipment. *Office Systems* 7(9) Aug 1990, p 22.

BOOKS

1. Barrons: *Time Management*. (New York: Barron's Business Success Series) 1992.

2. Burstiner I: *The Small Business Handbook*. (Englewood Cliffs, NJ: Prentice-Hall) 1992.

3. Carnegie D and Associates: *Managing Through People*. (New York: Simon and Schuster) 1978.

4. Drucker P: *Managing For The Future*. (New York:Viking Penguin) 1992.

5. Engstrom TW: *Managing Your Time*. (Grand Rapids, MI: Zondervan Publishing) 1988.

6. Fleury RE: *The Small Business Survival Guide*. (Naperville, IL: Sourcebook) 1992.

7. Goldstein AS: *Commercial Transactions Desk Book*. (Englewood Cliffs, NJ: IBP) 1978.

8. Handcock WA: *The Small Business Legal Adviser*. (New York: McGraw Hill) 1992.

9. Hemphill B: *Taming the Paper Tiger. Organizing the Paper in Your Office*. (New York: Dodd, Mead and Co.) 1988.

10. Peters T: *Passion For Excellence*. (NY: Warner Books) 1989.

11. Poteet GH: *Making Your Small Business A Success*. (New York: McGraw Hill) 1992. (Englewood Cliffs, NJ: Prentice-Hall) 1986.

12. Tang Thanh Trai Le: *Sales and Credit Transactions Handbook*. (New York: McGraw Hill) 1985.

PERIODICALS

1. *Business Age*, Business Trends Communications Corp., 2401 N Mayfair Rd., Milwaukee, WI 53226-1408

2. *Entrepreneur*, Entrepreneur, Inc., 2392 Morse Ave., Irvine, CA 92714

3. *Independent Business*, First Sierra Publishing, 875 South, Westlake Village, CA 91361

4. *Nations Business*, Chamber of Commerce, 1615 H St, NW, Washington, DC, 20062

5. *Office Systems 92*, Office Systems, 941 Danbury Rd., PO Box 150, Georgetown, CT 06829

6. *The Office*, Office Publications, 1600 Summer St., PO Box 120031, Stamford, CT 06912

ASSOCIATIONS

American Management Association, 135 W 50th St, New York, NY 10020

Chamber of Commerce of the US, 1615 H St, NW, Washington, DC 20062

Small Business Administration, 1441 L St, NW, Washington, DC 20416

Chapter 12

Minding the Money

BILLING AND COLLECTIONS

Most people are willing to pay for the services they receive, especially after they have been reminded once or twice. A degree of moral fortitude is appropriate when dealing with those who aren't. No amount of friendly persuasion will prevail against deadbeats with whom you should never have been doing business in the first place.

When the job is finished, send a clear, complete invoice to the party who contracted for the work. Don't add an explanatory or apologetic cover letter that may take away from the plain meaning of the invoice—the legal demand for payment. If you must communicate anything other than the invoice itself, send it under separate cover.

Send a bill as soon as the contract allows. The perceived value of your services will shrink steadily beginning on the day the job is completed. It will be harder for you to collect payment as time goes on. When possible, tender the bill along with the report, whether it is oral or written.

Such a statement should work; if it doesn't, something is wrong. The next step is to make a telephone call to find out what it is. The call itself may be enough to shake loose the payment. At a minimum it should result in a promise to pay by a specified date or on a specified schedule.

Sometimes, though, the phone call will have no effect. If the client takes your telephone call as an opportunity to find fault with your work product, you are on notice that he lacks good faith and is not to be trusted. The client should have raised complaints about your work when it was delivered, not after the statement was sent. If, on the other hand, his problem is with the amount of the bill rather than the work that was done, you may want to remain polite while you try to work out your differences in an amicable spirit.

Often a client genuinely wants to pay but cannot because he is temporarily short of funds. In such cases don't hesitate to ask for a note to cover the amount due.

This request will test the client's intentions, improve your balance sheet (a note generally is considered a better asset than a receivable) and your legal position if the client goes broke.

It pays to insist on a definite date for payment. If the client won't give you that much, you are in trouble. Blandishments may work; threats seldom do unless

Sample Invoice

JONES CONSULTING COMPANY
1111 JONES STREET
JONESVILLE, ILLINOIS 66666
INVOICE
JUNE 30, 199__

To:
Client Corporation
1111 Wall Street
Big Town, AS 12111

Att: Ms. Jane Doe, Vice President

To: Professional Services

Re: Southeastern Terminal Project, Jonesville

Professional Time: RJ Jones, 12 hours	
at $200 per hour	$2,400.00
Expenses per attached receipts	$ 84.00
Total	$2,484.00

Terms: Net 10 days

Invoice Number 111

If your invoice isn't paid on time, you can send a statement like the following:

JONES CONSULTING COMPANY
1111 JONES STREET
JONESVILLE, ILLINOIS 66666
STATEMENT
AUGUST 10, 199__

Balance due per invoice #111
dated June 30, 199__ $2,484.00

Please Remit

you can back them up. Except when the amount in question is large, litigation doesn't pay, although a letter from your lawyer may be helpful. As a last resort you can send the bill to a collection agency, which at least will annoy the client and may yield partial payment.

You conceivably may be entitled to place a mechanic's lien against the title of the deadbeat's property; however, collecting on the lien most likely will take a long time (usually not until the property is refinanced or sold). Even if you go to court for your fees and win, the judgment probably will be hard to collect. The best solution usually is to settle for any decent amount you can get, although some feel a hard line works better in the long run.

Learn to avoid clients who don't pay. Experience eventually will teach you how to identify them. Make questionable clients pay in advance or send them to somebody else. Chances are, they'll never amount to much anyway.

Bear in mind that some clients, by their nature, are not able to pay you promptly. These include many governmental bodies and institutions. If you are confident that you will be paid in the long run and are prepared to serve as the client's banker, go ahead and take the business. If not, don't waste your time with the client; look for other fish in the sea.

Danger Signs. Collection difficulties often can be anticipated. Watch out for these red flags:

1. *The client doesn't seem to care about the cost.* You're probably better off with a client who fights you tooth and nail over the amount of your bid. The client who doesn't seem to care about it may be indifferent for a reason.
2. *The client is in another state.* It's hard to collect from people outside your jurisdiction. A good policy is to insist on 100% of the money up front, even from major law firms, unless the client is a reputable institution with a long-standing record of prompt payment.
3. *The client is not reasonably well known in the industry.* Beginners and casual players are often bad risks.
4. *The client won't sign a contract.* Take offense at the client who takes offense when you propose a simple letter agreement and demand that it be signed before you undertake the work. Whether or not the client intends to stiff you, the temptation will be there.
5. *The client whose authority to make a deal isn't clear.* Sometimes an employee or junior associate who isn't empowered to obligate the firm will try to engage you without seeking proper authorization. If the firm denies liability, you're in trouble. The same thing can happen with a lawyer and his client.
6. *Bad credit.* If you have any doubts at all, make inquiries. Check the prospective client with an established credit rating service or have a report drawn. Outstanding judgments against the client or a record of slow payment should alert you to the likelihood of trouble.

Be wary of these danger signs and consider each prospective new client who exhibits any one of them as a possible credit risk. Get as much of the fee as you can in advance and provide for regular progress payments on the rest. Make it a practice to watch your receivables constantly and to follow up on slow payers. Even a prosperous corporate client sometimes loses track of an invoice and needs to be reminded.

A few last-resort letters:

> Dear Cousin Buck:
>
> Why don't you answer my calls? Is something wrong? Has Nellie run off again?
>
> Worriedly,
> Bubba

> Dear Ms. Deadbeat:
>
> Why not pay now? The consequences of further delay will be painful. On the other hand a prompt check will earn you at least our gratitude and perhaps also a modicum of good will.
>
> Still cordially,
> Jones Consulting Company
> Statement attached

> Dear Deadbeat Corporation:
>
> I note with dissatisfaction your failure to pay our December 31 invoice. We did the work properly and did it under the severe time constraints you demanded. It cost us money to do so, and we expect payment, which is now three months overdue. To date we have had neither a convincing explanation for the delay nor a firm promise of payment. Unless we hear from you by next Tuesday, the matter will be turned over to our attorneys Robham, Kilham and Burnham for aggressive action.
>
> Very sincerely,
> Jones Consulting Corporation
> Statement attached

CASH FLOW PROBLEMS?

The busiest shops run slow at times. These slack moments, troublesome as they may be in terms of cash flow, present opportunities to build for the future. Use them. Organize a seminar; invite guests and hold a series of office lunches to develop ideas about some area of the real estate business; increase your civic activities and encourage your staff people to do the same. Mount special projects. Take vacations. Send your people off for education or go back to school yourself for a time. Stir the pot; who knows what will bubble to the surface?

When things slow down, speed up.

Big jobs that can't be invoiced yet, slow-paying clients and variations in the workload can cause uncomfortable fluctuations in your cash flow. Feast-or-famine may not be the rule, but it's common. Unless your personal cash reserves or those of your company are large enough to cover the downswings, you'll need to arrange a line of credit with your friendly neighborhood banker.

A line of credit can be obtained on an unsecured basis some times; most bankers, however, want collateral. Life insurance policies, real estate and your own receivables may be used, or a third-party guarantee may be sufficient. The financial statement of your company, and perhaps your personal statement as well, will be needed for the banker's file.

You can draw funds, as needed, against this credit line, usually at interest rates one or two points over prime. Use your credit line sparingly and pay your borrowings back as promptly as you can. You may need the money again later.

The rules for maintaining good credit apply to real estate counselors as much as they do to anyone else. Pay your bills on time; take discounts when you can; maintain a good relationship with your bank. Invest idle cash in some form of interest-bearing account or in liquid short-term assets such as a money market fund or bank certificates of deposit. Your cash management techniques don't have to be as sophisticated as those of a major corporation, but a reasonable amount of attention to cash planning will make it easier for you to borrow on rainy days and to seize opportunities that require available capital.

CHARITABLE CONTRIBUTIONS

As a responsible local businessperson, you frequently will be called upon for charitable contributions of various kinds. Give, but not too much and not without careful consideration. You want to maintain both your solvency and your reputation as a thoughtful contributor to the needs of the community. If you enjoy raising funds for charity, by all means indulge yourself. Your skills in this department will elevate your status, make you a welcome member of influential boards and multiply the size of your direct benefactions.

References

ARTICLES

1. Bolton WD: Planning your insurance for success in the 90s. *Office Systems* 7(10) Oct 1990, p 133.

BOOKS

1. Anderson D and Wardell MJ: *Surviving Bankruptcy.* (Englewood Cliffs, NJ: Prentice Hall) 1992.

2. Noble SP: *301 Great Management Ideas.* (New York: Inc. Publishing) 1992.

3. Silver AD: *The Turnaround Survival Guide: Strategies for the Company in Crisis.* (New York: Dearborn) 1992.

4. Ventura J: *The Bankruptcy Kit.* (New York: Dearborn) 1992.

PERIODICALS

1. *Management Accounting,* Institute of Management Accountants, 10 Paragon Dr., Montvale, NJ 07645-1760

CHAPTER 13

Insurance and What It's for: Risk Management

Businesses face many kinds of risks. To protect against some, the only defenses are prudence and good luck. Nobody can do much to prevent an attack of the flu or gallstones, a broken leg or a check that arrives unexpectedly late. However, many risks can be deflected simply by doing good work and making a reasonable effort to mind the store properly. Counselors who fail to observe these precautions probably won't be around for long.

Cost overruns, cash shortfalls, employee defections, client betrayals and similar disasters, for example, can be controlled through sensible management. Even the most careful counselors can use insurance to reduce their risks even further.

INSURANCE

Insurance is the best defense against hazards such as fires, windstorms, floods, earthquakes, thefts, embezzlements, car accidents, liability claims, even the death of key employees. It doesn't offer complete protection, but at least the insurance company, if it is solvent and the policy was written correctly, will ease your financial woes.

Because insurance policies don't always mean what you think they say, or vice versa, your business survival may depend on your willingness to go through their language with a fine-toothed comb before you buy. The Chicago Flood of 1992 offered many examples of insurance carriers that denied liability for business interruptions and other losses not directly caused by water damage to the property of the insured even for policyholders with flood protection. Some carriers took the position that the incident was not a flood because it didn't involve the overflow of a body of water, just a leak. Upper-floor businesses that couldn't operate while power, telephone and other essential services were shut down because of water in the basements found themselves without recourse except through the courts. A strong agent can help in such situations, but the best defense is a careful reading of the fine print *before* the damage occurs.

A good policy.

Protecting against casualties. Fire and similar disasters (floods, earthquakes, volcanic eruptions) can be devastating to a business. So can burglaries and defalcations. Fortunately, even if you rent your office space, you can protect its contents against such casualties; you can cover the furnishings, equipment, file contents, computer data and leasehold improvements, through broad form insurance policies. Equipment like computers and dictating machines can be covered under floater policies against theft, damage, destruction and even loss or mysterious disappearance. You can also protect yourself against robbery, burglary, employee dishonesty and similar risks.

In discussing these types of coverage with your insurance agent, remember that it may pay for you to cover depreciable items with replacement cost coverage rather than with depreciated value, though the premium for replacement cost coverage is higher. Watch out for unreasonable exclusions, unwanted or excessive deductibles, unfair notice provisions, too-narrow geographic limitations and other fine-print hazards too numerous to list (get advice or read up on the subject). Generally speaking, it pays to go for broad-form policies instead of trying to cover all the specific hazards that may arise. Broad-form and package policies usually give better value and provide some assurance that your claims will not fall between the cracks.

The laws affecting these and other types of coverage vary from state to state, and though the subject can stand a lot of discussion, there is not enough space here to do the job. Talk to a good insurance agent, shop around for ideas and price quotations, read up on business insurance (see the References), then do what you can to protect yourself.

Workmen's compensation. The death, injury or disease of an employee can give rise to claims under state workmen's compensation laws. Find out what your obligations are and get appropriate insurance.

Liability insurance. Liability claims are particularly threatening, as they attack all your assets, not just those at the office, and can undermine your financial future. They can come from almost anywhere. Americans slip, trip and break bones, crash automobiles, eat questionable food, lose money, lose face, make bad decisions, suffer emotional traumas, and when they can find a lawyer to take the case, they will sue you if you had anything to do with their misfortune. By all means discuss possible liabilities with your lawyer as well as your insurance agent and follow their advice. It could save you and your company from disaster.

The principal liabilities you may face are of two types: those you undertake voluntarily (leases, contracts, guarantees, obligations to pay employee salaries) and those you encounter merely because there are lawyers in the world. It's this second category that makes well-planned liability coverage indispensable to any business, including yours.

Many kinds of liability policies are available. The field is changing quickly, premiums vary tremendously and states have different laws relating to liability. By all means shop around and ask questions before you decide on a policy. Does it accurately reflect the work you do and address the risks you face? Is there a deductible, and if so, can you afford it? Does the language cover only claims that arise while the policy is in force ("claims made") or will it protect you in the future for things that are happening now? Will legal fees be subtracted from the stated limits of the coverage?

Remember that your insurance should cover not only third-party claims but also claims made by your own employees and independent consultants (see Chapter 8). That means workmen's compensation coverage as well as liability insurance.

For further information about liability insurance you may find it worthwhile to consult the American Society of Real Estate Counselors and the Appraisal Institute. They should be familiar with the types of coverage that are available and can draw upon the experience of others to advise you.

Other coverage. Two of the most important additional types of coverage are policies covering any vehicles you or your people may be using on business, including rental cars, and policies covering business interruptions, which pay at least some of the costs associated with a business shutdown following a fire or other insured casualty. Another potentially valuable kind of coverage is key person life insurance, which pays your business a specified sum if the key person (such as you) should die. Health insurance, which comes in many forms, is becoming standard in professional service firms; your agent or a good human resources director can suggest the right kinds. Disability insurance also may be worthwhile, for yourself and perhaps also for important employees. Your accountant can help you assess your need for these and other coverages.

Keep your backside covered.

REDUCING YOUR LIABILITY EXPOSURE

How can you, a real estate counselor who advises people about important financial matters that can expose them to financial loss, hold your liability exposure to a minimum? There are a number of ways besides errors and omissions insurance, which some people feel actually attracts litigation.

One of them is to be especially careful in your contracts with clients to include language that will guard against professional liability arising from your counseling work (see also Chapters 20 and 21). For example, you can:

- Spell out the scope of the assignment in detail, specifying the product that will be delivered, the tasks that will and won't be performed, the factors that will and will not be considered.

- Specify the uses to which your reports can and can't be put.
- Limit the time period for which you may be responsible.
- List all fees and charges.
- Catalog the client's responsibilities as well as your own.
- Make it a policy (pun intended!) to include all the exculpatory language you can get away with ("It's not my responsibility!" "It's subject to circumstances beyond my control!" "I'm paying no attention to toxic substances, tenant credit and other important things because you said not to!"), preferably in the form of a standard statement of limiting conditions attached to the document.

Self-serving exculpatory language like this last may not be of much help when push comes to shove, though state laws concerning such language vary. You probably can't disclaim the consequences of your own negligence or that of your employees, but a carefully drawn contract will at least give you a leg to stand on if you do find yourself in court. Your attorneys, though they may be pessimistic about the value of such statements, can help you draft them.

You also should take a good look at the client and the way your work is likely to be used. Will it expose you to additional risk because it goes into a securities offering brochure? Is the client a litigious rascal, likely to sue or perhaps already in court for something else which may entangle you? How will your reports be distributed? Who else besides the client may rely on them and thus possibly have rights against you? To protect yourself against claims from such unintended users, try, in your contract language, to limit the use and distribution of your reports, denying any responsibility to third parties who may stumble across them against your stated wishes—or receive them from your faithless client.

One of the best protection you can have is a convincing report (see Chapter 24), written in plain language so clients, judges and juries can understand precisely what you meant. If no written report is called for, at least have good work papers (see Chapter 11). Standard report formats similar to those generally used in the industry offer some shelter against attacks on your methods. So do thorough checklists and your own good reputation as a professional.

File contents also are important. That's one of the reasons for carefully preparing work papers that spell out what was done, when and by whom. Your files will be the first things demanded by a plaintiff's attorneys if you are sued, and they probably will have to be turned over to them. Keep the files spare but thorough. With luck and reasonably good judgment, you will be able to use these papers to support your findings and show that you did everything a prudent counselor should have done.

Remember that you may be responsible not only for your own work but also for that of your employees and subconsultants. Watch and document what they do, making sure that they are qualified and the work is done to your standards. See to it that your people are properly trained and indoctrinated; when appropriate, consult with the National Association of Realtors about its employee training program. Read and honor the rules of your licensing bodies and professional societies and take care that your people's licenses, like yours, are kept up to date.

Perhaps the main thing is to keep your nose as clean as possible, avoiding self-dealing and conflicts of interest. A reputation for good character and quality work is invaluable in court.

CHOOSING AN INSURANCE AGENT

Insurance agents come and go. Pick one who will be around to help you when the need arises. Try to choose an agent who is knowledgeable, communicative, thorough, fair, reasonable and willing to render service later on. An agent who sells a lot of policies, especially big ones, should be able to help you more with the insurance company when the time comes to place a claim. It's also good to have an agent who will remind you faithfully about renewals, look after you promptly if one of your insurance companies sends a cancellation notice and tell you about any new coverages you should have.

There has been enough news on the subject of insurance company failures to emphasize the importance of choosing your insurance company with care. You can check the health and performance of insurance carriers through your agent or directly with A. M. Best, Moody's, Standard & Poor's or another rating service. Insurance that isn't going to be there when you need it is worthless.

HANDLING OTHER CATASTROPHES

Unavoidably, your ability to deal with adversity will be tested now and then. Things have a tendency to go wrong, especially the things you don't worry about and can't insure against. It's impossible to list all the dangers; the following are just examples.

A key employee quits. All you can do is make the best of it. Don't offer raises or try to correct the problems the employee claims are causing him to leave you in the lurch, as this will, at best, only delay the inevitable. Wish the person well and keep your curses to yourself. Otherwise there's a good chance that the rotten deserter will bad-mouth you from a safe distance at the new employer's or even sue you for slander. Anyway, you don't want clients to think that you can't get along without that "indispensable genius" who used to work at your place.

A major client makes an unreasonable demand or threatens to pull the account. Be polite, but stand firm on your principles. If you cave in to keep an account, the client will think less of you and probably will share his low opinion with others. Firmness in this situation may demonstrate to a client that you can pass a character test, and may lead to a stronger relationship. Even if you do lose the account, the story will get around—possibly to your benefit.

An important document is lost. It happens. Do the best you can to find it, recreate the document if possible, and/or show any parties concerned that you are trying to undo the damage. As a last resort you can volunteer to nail yourself to the wall and bleed to death. That usually makes them feel better.

Your partner (or long-time associate) commits a gross indiscretion or stops working and won't retire. Keep your temper under control. Speak, reason, offer to help. If all else fails, put up with the situation but don't make it too comfortable. Sooner or later the person will move on; meanwhile, you are giving back only a part of the benefits that person contributed to the business.

You are sued. Don't panic. It has happened to others and may happen again to you. Don't waste time, either. Pick up the phone immediately and call your lawyer, your public relations counsel if the matter is sensitive and your insurer if you have one. They will help you decide how to respond. Be sure to level with your advisors, especially your attorney, as any attempt to conceal information from your own counsel is foolish and can prove to be catastrophic. If you don't think your usual advisors can handle the job, say so and ask for their help in finding appropriate co-counsel (see Chapters 10 and 12).

You suffer a stroke (a heart attack, a crippling accident, a financial disaster) and can't carry on. Face up to it. Do what you must to dispose of the business or wind it down; get whatever help you need; recognize that this will cost you but the cost can't be avoided. Your partners, employees, lawyer, accountant, family and friends, if you have treated them right, should be willing to step into the breach.

References

ARTICLE

Bolton WD: Planning your insurance for success in the 90s. *Office Systems* 7(10) Oct 1990, p 113.

BOOKS

1. Anderson D and Wardell MJ: *Surviving Bankruptcy.* (Englewood Cliffs, NJ: Prentice Hall) 1992.

2. Noble SP: *301 Great Management Ideas.* (New York: Inc. Publishing) 1992.

3. Silver AD: *The Turnaround Survival Guide: Strategies for the Company in Crisis.* (New York: Dearborn) 1992.

4. Sundheim Finn A: *How to insure a Business: Solving the Business Insurance Puzzle.* (Santa Barbara, CA: Venture Publications) 1988.

5. Ventura J: *The Bankruptcy Kit.* (New York: Dearborn) 1992.

PERIODICAL

Management Accounting, Institute of Management Accountants, 10 Paragon Dr., Montvale, NJ 07645-1760

Part IV

Marketing

CHAPTER 14

Where Work Comes From

Sources of business are many and diverse. Your family or former classmates may help you to get you started in business, but most likely it will be your everyday contacts and the friends you make at business and professional gatherings who will open the door to new work. Different counselors, of course, depend on different sources, but most counselors find work in the following areas:

Who needs you — and has the money?

Law firms. Many counselors draw most of their practice from law firms. Especially if you are a reliable performer on the witness stand, you may find that a large share of your business inquiries comes from litigators or through them. If that's the case, by all means spend time with members of key firms and try to arrange speaking engagements at the local bar association. Look for opportunities to participate in the meetings where attorneys gather to fight over a case. If you can make your presence felt at such a meeting, additional work is likely to result.

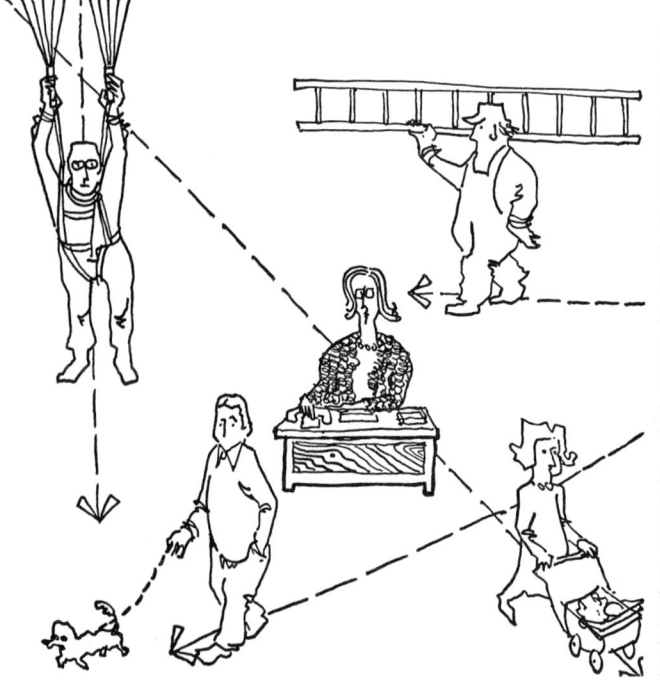

Banks. Another major source of work and referrals is your local bank, which may control a good deal of trust and mortgage loan business that generates counseling work. Depositors and other customers look to the banks for advice in selecting other professionals, which makes the banks good sources of referral business as well. Banks also may participate in mergers and acquisitions, serve as general business advisors and have real estate holdings of their own that require outside attention. FIRREA, the federal law that created the Resolution Trust Corporation and set demanding new regulatory standards for banks and thrifts, has intensified the need for banking institutions to retain quality appraisal and counseling services. In most cities one or two banks dominate the local real estate field. Make it your business to get to know their key people.

Mortgage bankers and brokers. Mortgage professionals control considerable amounts of real estate appraisal work and may need counseling services as well. In recent years investment bankers also have become sources of counseling work, such as due diligence in connection with mergers, acquisitions, reorganizations and workouts.

Local and state governments. Government agencies are extensively involved in real estate. Highway planning and right-of-way acquisition, facilities management, land use planning, housing finance, community development, ad valorem taxation and a host of other programs require professional real estate services. Some of this work may be allocated politically, but more of it depends upon professional competence and reputation. Make yourself known to the governmental agencies that interest you, present your qualifications and expect that at least some business will come your way.

Federal government. The same principles apply to the federal government. The General Services Administration, the Postal Service, the Department of Housing and Urban Development, the Internal Revenue Service, the Resolution Trust Corporation and other federal agencies frequently need appraisal and counseling services. Submit your qualifications and try to make friends with agency officials if you are interested in this kind of work. Make sure, though, that the agency is willing and able to pay its bills in a timely manner—unless you don't mind waiting for your money.

Pension funds, pension fund advisors, and insurance companies. Insurers and pension funds can be extremely worthwhile sources of counseling business. They generally have in-house staff, often of high quality, to look after their investments, but they may need outside help with their real estate. More and more of them have been seeking outside assistance, in fact, since the real estate crash of 1990. Most of these organizations are astute buyers of advisory services, so don't expect bonanzas—just a good flow of work.

Corporations. Probably the least exploited sources of counseling business are the large corporations. Real estate often accounts for 25% or more of their asset value, and much of this real estate contributes less than it should to corporate earnings. Your services as an asset management advisor can add substantially to a company's net worth if you can convince the chief financial officer that its real estate is worth thinking about. A program of corporate real estate analysis that leads to improvement at the bottom line can open the door to large amounts of business.

Other marketing targets. Small businesses, property owners and investors (especially those with large portfolios), and other people involved in real estate such as accountants, architects, contractors, developers, brokers and managers may not need counseling services often, and may not expect to pay much for them when they do, but sometimes they are the only clients available, especially in a small town or city. They can be sources of valuable referrals as well as occasional jobs, and with enough such people on your string, you can enjoy a varied practice without having to cope with impersonal big clients. By and large, though, your marketing and professional time will be better spent seeking out and developing relationships with deep-pocketed institutions, governments and corporations.

In directing your marketing efforts, bear in mind your own qualifications and personality. Will your rough-and-ready nature appeal to corporate clients, for example, or do your dark suits and graduate degrees make you more attractive to institutional investors? As Polonius said: "To thine own self be true." You won't do much business in Boston if you insist on wearing blue suede shoes or with corporate middle management if you picked up your accent at Choate.

Bear in mind, too, that your marketing time is precious. Don't waste it on prospects who aren't serious or don't have much business to offer. Qualify your prospects early: Find out who they are, what they control, where they have been getting their work done, how much business they represent and whether they pay their bills on time. The information you gather can be used later, when the time comes to make the sale (see Chapters 18-19).

HOW CLIENTS FIND COUNSELORS

Clients are likely to seek out real estate counselors in the same way they, or you, would seek out a doctor or lawyer: by consulting their colleagues, business connections and friends. Some clients will look to the local real estate board, chamber of commerce or bar association for recommendations. Others will contact the American Society of Real Estate Counselors or another industry group. Often they will ask their lawyers or a respected real estate person or firm for a referral; rarely, they will check the *Yellow Pages*.

Like other people, prospective clients are susceptible to the allure of fame. If you are well known to the media through your speaking, writing and civic activities, your name eventually will be remembered by prospects and referral sources. Even bad publicity, cynics say, is better than none.

The most reliable source of new clients is word of mouth. It pays to take good care of your existing clients if only so they will speak well of you when asked. Do your best to maintain high professional standards and deliver good service. It'll be noticed and you will benefit.

THE MARKETING PLAN

Whether or not you are going to advertise, you have to let the world know you're in business and find ways to reach prospective clients. This will require that you position yourself correctly in your natural marketplaces, develop a professional image and facilities consistent with your market position, identify likely referral sources and prospects and communicate with them. In doing this you will find it worthwhile to engage in a variety of reputation-building activities: public relations programs, civic and professional activities, speeches, articles, contacts with opinion leaders. You probably also will want to use professionally prepared brochures and other materials such as private publications, slide shows and videotapes to get your message across.

The time to engage in marketing is not necessarily the time when you have nothing better to do. There is a lag between the client's discovery that you are available for business and its decision to find out whether you are willing and able to accept a job. This lag, which can run six months or longer, has to be taken into account when planning your marketing campaigns. The best rule is to *market all the time*, starting from Day One and continuing even during busy periods. We all tend to stop worrying about the future when things are going well. The trouble is that too much concentration on the job at hand can keep you from doing what is necessary to assure a good flow of new work when things slow down.

Marketing: a full-time concern.

Use your marketing plan to identify in advance the individuals and groups you should try to reach, what you should tell them and how you will win them to your cause. If you aren't marketing-oriented, or have trouble figuring out what to do, help is available from books (see References) and from marketing and business consultants. For guidance and names talk to successful counselors, local public relations firms or one of the marketing professors at your local school of business.

The marketing plan has a number of components. It describes the image you want to project, identifies the markets you want to serve, pinpoints your primary targets, sets goals, lists priorities and schedules a program of activities such as advertising, news releases, speeches and sales calls. Almost certainly it will call for an initial announcement—possibly accompanied by a party for clients and friends—to let the world know you have entered the business, followed by a series of media events and news releases to reinforce the message.

Make sure to remind people at frequent intervals that you are working, doing useful things and interested in hearing from them. This can be accomplished with greeting cards, tombstone ads and announcements, newsletters, press mentions of your name, TV and radio interviews and mailings. Failing to engage in these strategies invites trouble, as even your best clients will forget you exist if you neglect them.

FINDING YOUR NATURAL MARKETS

Where do you and your organization fit into the scheme of things? Are you a department store, a bargain basement, a luxury boutique? Look at yourself realistically and try to assess who you are and how you impress other people. One way to do this is to think in terms of automobiles: Rolls-Royce? Maserati? Dodge? Suzuki? Minivan? Trailer truck? Who needs your particular brand of wheels?

The considerations here aren't merely psychological; they also reflect the marketplace. What kind of service do your clients expect? Where are your

Your natural clients: those who recognize your value to them.

opportunities for growth and profit? Can you compete as a general store against the giants in the business, or should you limit yourself to selling high-markup designer shirts and ties?

It may be worthwhile to perform a systematic market assessment for your own use and that of your fellow rainmakers. Such a study may explore the universe of prospective clients, evaluate the competition, review your existing client base and assess your ability to serve and develop your natural markets. Translated into a business plan that is aggressively pursued, such research can lead to rapid growth and improved profitability. On the other hand, if your present pace makes you happy and yields satisfactory results there's no point in spending time or money on high-powered marketing efforts.

Try to find and develop your natural clients. Formal people who are detail-oriented and perfectionistic may be better adapted to serving a clientele of institutional investors than one of developers and go-getting entrepreneurs. If you are a diamond in the rough, you may be better off focusing your efforts on others of similar cut, i.e., valuable but unpolished. Even the uncut diamond can be appreciated by an insurance company in trouble, but most of the time it will prefer to deal with somebody in pin-stripes who wears bifocals and has a full head of gray or graying hair.

HOW CLIENTS CHOOSE COUNSELORS

Clients will select you on the basis of one or more of the following factors:

1. *Reputation.* Clients will seek you out if they've been told you may be a good person for the job (see Chapter 15 for advice on how to encourage this sort of thing).

2. *Name recognition.* This is not quite the same thing as reputation, but it's close. Certain assignments will be given to counselors because their names or the names of their firm are familiar to a banker in a distant city. If your practice is entirely local, chances are you won't be chosen in such cases, even though your standing is very high in your community. It is in this area that big international firms have a real advantage.

3. *Track record.* Clients like to know that their counselor has successfully completed a number of similar projects. If you are known for your feasibility studies, business of that type will gravitate to you.

4. *Familiarity with the property type.* In every metropolitan center there are people who know a great deal about, say, shopping centers. Clients with shopping center problems will find them.

5. *Attitude.* A counselor who seems likable and willing to serve will often be preferred over a crustier or more difficult person. Being nice won't get you the job, but at least it will stop you from losing it to someone else on personality grounds.

6. *Networks.* Clients like to know that their advisors are well connected. Do you belong to a respected professional society? Are you known to local leaders? Will important people answer your telephone calls? Can you get the facts?

7. *Tact.* Clients need to be sure you will not get them in trouble by stepping on someone's toes.

8. *Discretion.* Nobody likes a leaker. Your tendencies to brag about work in process, thus relaying client confidences to others, will be noticed and can be costly.

9. *Competence.* Intelligent clients can recognize intelligence in their advisors. They may hire someone who is less competent than they are, but only for limited purposes. On the other hand they may be rightly suspicious of someone who is a lot smarter than the job requires.

10. *Availability.* Can you take on the assignment now? Do you have the time to do it promptly or at least by the deadline? Will conflicts of interest interfere with your objectivity or prevent you from accepting the assignment?

11. *Reliability.* Based on their own experience and that of others, clients will judge you by your ability to deliver work as promised, on time and in good order.

12. *Location.* Clients like you to be nearby so they can check up on you occasionally, but they don't usually insist on proximity. Still, most counselors find that it pays to be centrally located in a major city where much real estate business is done. If nothing else, your chances of being seen by the client on the street or at lunch are greatly improved if your office is in the neighborhood.

13. *Office environment.* People like to do business with an office that seems lively, cheerful and engaged in work. The too-quiet office suggests the business has too few customers; the too-noisy one suggests that nobody will have time to tend to the client's needs. Most clients also like to see reasonable amounts of modern equipment, youngish people and lots of work in progress.

14. *Credentials.* The CRE and MAI designations add value to your name. So, at least in some cases, do the CPM and other real estate credentials. Also worth having are the CPA, a law degree and the MBA or some other relevant academic certificate.

15. *Price.* This may come last, but it *is* a consideration. If you're too far out of line, the client may still hire you in a pinch, but he will keep looking for someone whose charges are more reasonable.

CREATING THE RIGHT IMAGE

Your effectiveness, like that of the physician, depends to a large extent on your clients' willingness to trust you and accept you as an authority. You don't have to project any particular style to gain their trust and acceptance, but the style you do project should be consistent with the importance of the work you do and with your concern for the client's interests. (See Chapter 22 for ways to convert customers into true clients.)

Your image needs to be consistent and professional.

The key is to have and sustain a professional attitude—one that projects competence, confidence, objectivity, self respect and concern for the client. This calls for appropriate clothing and office furnishings as well as appropriate behavior. There's no need to be overly conservative; a dash of personality takes nothing away from your professionalism and increases your appeal to clients who are uncomfortable dealing with stuffed shirts and poker faces. Don't hesitate to be spontaneous on occasion and to share at least some of your wit and worries with the client.

The image you want to project—in meetings, in speeches, in brochures and advertising, in your correspondence and reports—is one of unquestioned professionalism. Prospects want to believe that *you are exactly the right person to deal with the problem*—a person whose attitude, skills and experience practically guarantee success. The people and things around you should respect that hope. Your accoutrements don't need to be expensive, but they should exhibit good taste and an attention to detail. If yours is an old-shoe community, you don't want to appear to be fussy or overconcerned with style, but if you're located in a sophisticated big-city, a bit of style may not hurt.

Consider engaging a designer to help you choose stationery, cards, report covers and similar items. Make sure the graphics associated with your office are consistent and that your name or your company name is presented consistently in all your printed materials.

Tone. There is no one right way to present yourself and your office. You may want to project friendliness, warmth and confidence, or you may choose a more reserved approach. Some offices prefer a trendy image, using up-to-the-minute graphics and eye-catching colors. Select a tone that is suited to your personality and the markets you serve in the same way you may select a dark tie and white shirt for a meeting with your banker while preferring an open collar and sweater for an informal session with your partners.

A pompous manner used to be traditional in counseling, medicine and banking. Everyone wore dark suits, quiet neckties, uncomfortable collars, gold-framed spectacles and severe expressions. This manner is effective mainly with fearful, supercautious people, many of whom work for financial institutions. It is less effective with developers, entrepreneurs, politicians and ordinary folks. Be guided by your experience with your own clients. How do they want to see you? What kind of style will make them—and you—most comfortable? Strike the balance that you think will work best for you over the long run.

Decor. Your office should manifest the same kind of image you put forward in your choices of clothing, stationery and conversation. It can be light, airy and relaxed or mahogany-paneled, subdued and soothing. No matter what type of decor you choose, your objective should be to reduce the client's anxieties so he can discuss problems openly and calmly. That is, unless you enjoy intimidating your clients—in which case you'll want to have an enormous desk placed on a Sam Goldwyn dais at the far end of an immense office, surround yourself with symbols of power and in general do whatever you can to make the client feel small and unimportant.

Remember that most clients are cost-conscious and like to see people actually working in the offices they visit. Organize your space rationally and arrange it so busy people can be found in practically every area. This setup will reassure the economy-minded and may improve your bottom line.

MARKETING ALLIANCES

Few firms are equipped to take care of every client need or to do every job. One way to expand the scope of the problems you handle is to form occasional or permanent alliances with other firms for promotions, bids and jobs, on the principle that one and one often add up to more than two. Big corporations do it (soda pop and sneakers, airlines and resorts, many others); why not you?

A common type of alliance is one with another counselor whose specialty complements your own. If what you know best is housing and the client is contemplating a mixed use development with apartments and offices, you may want to join forces with an office specialist. Usually all you'll need is a temporary joint venture with a specialist, though it may be convenient for frequent allies to have nearby offices or even to combine their practices.

You may find it advantageous to work out similar arrangements with lawyers, accountants, architects, cost estimators, appraisers, traffic engineers, environmental scientists and other kinds of professionals. The firm you ally with doesn't have to be the same size as yours; often large and small firms get along well together as co-venturers. Just make sure before you form the alliance that the other firm is a good one that you can work with and won't disgrace or betray you on the job.

Collaborate to add value.

REFERRAL SOURCES

Much of your work will come from people—individuals, not organizations—who have obtained your name from satisfied clients. Those clients are among your key referral sources. So are the professionals, investors, developers, bankers, government officials and others who in one way or another have become aware of you and your work. Also important are the executive directors of your trade and professional groups.

You must take care of such people. Thank them for suggesting your name; let them know that you will care for the clients they refer; put them on your list for small courtesies and occasional lunch invitations. If you can find ethical ways of returning their favors, do so. Even the most influential referral sources will appreciate your appreciation.

USING THE LEMMING EFFECT

Have you ever watched a flock of gulls deciding to take off, land or change direction? One or two individuals take the lead, often for indiscernible reasons, and the others follow—not all at once, but gradually as they get the idea and decide to go along with it. A few stragglers usually lag behind, waiting to make sure that it's the right thing to do before they chase after the flock.

The lemming, which doesn't fly, is an extreme case of this phenomenon. A flock will go where its leaders go, anywhere, marching over the edge of a high cliff if that's the order of the day. The flock's willingness to sacrifice its life to the follow-the-leader principle, well known to the business community, has been a long-standing inspiration in the world of middle management, where nobody ever got fired for doing what everybody else did.

This principle is one of the reasons most fleet cars look alike. It's also the reason a few of the biggest real estate and management consulting firms get most of the corporate and government business. To find somebody new, who isn't known as a regular player in that league, is to violate the Law of the Lemming.

If you're well established in counseling or belong to a dominant firm, you can use the lemming principle to sell corporate and government business. Talk about the other companies and agencies you work for; point to your long history of involvement with them; make it clear that you assume your listeners will do what their peers do when facing the unknown. They will march.

References

BOOKS

1. Chajet C: *Image by Design*. (Reading, MA: Addison-Wesley Publishing) 1991.

2. Cohen WA: *Developing a Winning Marketing Plan*. (New York: John Wiley and Sons) 1987.

3. Davidson JP: *The Marketing Sourcebook*. (New York: John Wiley and Sons) 1992.

4. Engel JF: *Promotional Strategy: Managing the Marketing Communication Process*. (Homewood, IL: Dow Jones-Irwin) 1987.

5. Hearn EE: *Handbook on Government Contracts Administration*. (Los Altos, CA: Hearn Associates) 1987.

6. McVay BL: *Getting Started in Federal Contracting*. (Woodbridge, VA: Panoptic Enterprises) 1984.

7. McVay BL: *Proposals that Win Federal Contracts*. (Woodbridge, VA: Panoptic Enterprises) 1989.

8. Weitz BA: *Strategic Marketing: Planning, Implementation, Control*. (Boston: Kent Publishing) 1984.

PERIODICAL

Business Marketing, Crain Communications, 740 N. Rush Street, Chicago, IL 60611

ASSOCIATIONS

American Association of Advertising Agencies, 200 Park Ave., New York, NY 10017

American Marketing Association, 250 Wacker Drive, Chicago, IL 60606

International Association of Business Communicators, 870 Market St., San Francisco, CA 94102

Chapter 15

Marketing Tools

The classic ways to get new business—inheritance, marriage, political connections and bribery—are still the most effective, though are not necessarily recommended. This chapter deals with other ways of attracting business, for the benefit of those counselors whose bad luck, bad timing, good taste or personal scruples make such reading necessary. Use these strategies well, and good things happen. "If we build it, they will come."

They can take many forms. All of them depend on communicating, directly or indirectly, with prospective customers. Resumes, advertising, publicity, public service, professional society work, speeches, seminars, writing, brochures, reminders and sales calls, are all effective tools for making yourself known and attractive to prospective customers.

THE RESUME

Because resumes serve a number of purposes, you may want to have several in your tool kit—one for applying for a job, one for preparing a presentation and one for submitting to a particular client. Counselors who have been in practice for some time often engage in so many activities that no single resume can do justice to their backgrounds without running an unreasonable length. Separate resumes not only simplify your work history into a series of manageable documents, but also highlight specific, relevant qualifications.

Some people, particularly academics, develop resume writing to a high art, padding their biographies with long lists of publications, courses and conferences, speeches, clients and organizations. This type of resume is not necessary for most counselors, and may actually create the wrong impression. The counselor's basic resume should be simple, straightforward and unpretentious, which is not to say unimpressive.

Short and to the point.

All you should want is a one-page summary of your credentials and accomplishments, backed up as needed by other materials, to create a comprehensive picture of the qualifications you can bring to an assignment. Here is an example of a basic counseling resume:

Professional Qualifications of John Smith

BUSINESS AFFILIATION: President, Smith Consulting Associates, Inc., Blanktown, Any State

PROFESSIONAL MEMBERSHIPS: American Society of Real Estate Counselors (designation CRE), Appraisal Institute (designation MAI), Blanktown Board of Realtors

EDUCATION: MBA, Blanktown University, 1967; BA, Blanktown College, 1965

HONORS: Honored by the Blanktown Chamber of Commerce as Realtor of the Year, 1974. Member, Lambda Alpha, an honorary society of real estate economists and professionals.

CIVIC: Chairman, 1986 United Way Fund Drive. Member, Planning Committee, Blanktown Chamber of Commerce.

PUBLICATIONS:

"The Blanktown Property Market," *Blanktown Magazine*, July 1982

"Blanktown Real Estate Investment Opportunities," *Blanktown Business News*, September 12, 1984

"Measuring Damage to the Remainder," Journal of the Any State Condemnation Society, January 1991

In addition to the basic resume, you may find it useful to keep on hand supplementary lists of publications, major studies, experience with specific property types, market and feasibility analyses, appraisals of important properties and experience in specific communities. Any or all of these supplements may be added, as necessary, to the basic resume or inserted with your resume in a company brochure.

ADVERTISING

Paid advertising is probably the least effective and certainly the most expensive of the available marketing techniques for counselors. It is best done, if at all, at the institutional level. Large firms, whether devoted exclusively to real estate counseling or active in other fields as well, have advertising policies and plans you can piggyback on to take advantage of the name recognition and goodwill they generate. Work with the ad agency and the firm's corporate officers to integrate your objectives with those of the firm.

Sole practitioners and small firms generally find advertising impractical. It costs money, often generates mainly useless inquiries and does little to strengthen your opinion of yourself as a person to whom business should gravitate without prompting. If they do advertise, small firms generally do so modestly, publishing simple business-card notices in local newspapers to keep their names before the public. At most they may want to add to those notices a short slogan or a few adjectives (honest, knowledgeable, independent) to enhance the resonance of the company's name and the power of its reputation.

Promotion can be cheaper and more effective.

Mailings. Direct mailings of the usual kind ("Our advice is good and cheap.") don't generate much worthwhile counseling business. You nevertheless may want to write to existing clients and prospects to let them know about a new service or remind them that you are interested in their work. A new brochure, a change in the tax laws or some local event affecting real estate can serve as a reason to send out such a mailing.

Counselors who enjoy writing will find it useful to publish an informal newsletter recounting some of their activities over the preceding months. A newsletter, which should be sent to clients, referral sources, news media, and anyone who requests it, serves a number of purposes. It can remind people of your existence, suggest ways you may be of use to them, impress some readers with the range and depth of your capabilities and help shore up your sometimes sagging confidence in the value of what you do. In time the newsletter will lead to other assignments and build the reputation of your firm.

PUBLICITY AND PUBLIC RELATIONS

Some counselors use professional public relations advisors, most of whom will require a retainer of several thousand dollars a month and a considerable amount of your time to learn about your business before they can do you any good. A better policy for small firms is to engage a PR advisor on an hourly basis. Read an article or two about the uses and methods of PR, spend a couple of hours with the advisor to learn what it's all about and then do the work yourself or have a suitable staff person look after it. The effectiveness of your subsequent efforts will be multiplied.

You can do your own public relations, with a little help.

The secret of public relations is to do good things and then tell the world about them. The good things can come from your counseling work or the larger arenas of business and public life. Your clients' successes, your own technical innovations, your contributions to the political and social debates of your community and your willingness to support your local charities are all good things worthy of promotion. Probably the best things to promote are those directly associated with your primary business activity, which is the furnishing of real estate advice and guidance for a fee. A well-told story growing out of a successful counseling assignment can do more for your reputation than a report of your attendance at a charity ball, even when accompanied by flattering photographs of you and your companion.

You don't have to be shy about communicating such stories to the media. Prepare a simple news release telling the story and inviting the reporter to call you for further information. Better yet, take the reporter to lunch to learn which story ideas are worth exploring. Perhaps you can hook into something bigger that will lead to a series of stories. If not, you at least have the chance to make a friend who may stand you in good stead over the years.

Try to make yourself available to reporters who call to check a fact or get a lead for a story. Don't panic when a reporter calls; look upon it as an opportunity. The interruption is worth tolerating for the sake of your long-term press relations. Obviously you won't want to betray client confidences or give off-the-cuff opinions that may compromise your reputation. Often you can provide background information during the investigative stages of a story and benefit by being quoted in the story, by enhancing your reputation with the reporter and by increasing your exposure as a source of wisdom and factual knowledge. But beware of formal or extended interviews (see the discussion later in this chapter), and never let down your guard completely.

Over time your willingness to answer questions will build your reputation as an authority and lead to a steady flow of media queries. This is the ideal public-relations position for a real estate counselor: to be asked regularly for his opinion on matters of importance to real estate. If you are willing to answer the phone, have access to interesting facts and know how to articulate a quotable phrase on occasion, you will get the calls, and your fame will grow.

PR goals and strategies. In all your public relations activities, have a plan in mind. You won't be doing PR for the glory but to try to reach potential clients, referral sources and opinion molders with a specific message: that you are a high-quality professional who is known for doing a good job, being well informed and caring about the public interest. If your PR activity promotes that goal, it's worth doing; if not, it's not.

Related messages that are worth promulgating include the following (use only when true and applicable!):

- The counselor is prominent and influential.
- The counselor is knowledgeable about important matters.
- The counselor has prominent clients.
- The counselor handles major assignments.
- The counselor is respected by his peers.
- The counselor is creative.
- The counselor is concerned about the community.

These messages usually can't be said in so many words, but readers will understand them when, for example, your opinion on an important public policy issue affecting real estate is solicited and printed in the morning newspaper or when you are interviewed for television.

News releases. Depending upon who you are, what you do, what your clients think and how you relate to the media, you may want to embark upon a program of periodic news releases to keep the pot boiling. Some people like to maintain a constant flow of news releases in the hope that a reasonable share of them will be picked up and reprinted. This often works, leading to large numbers of stories in neighborhood and small-community publications. As a real estate counselor you are probably more interested in getting a few small stories in major financial and metropolitan newspapers than getting many stories in neighborhood throwaways. You'll find that the reporters and editors in large metropolitan papers who are of greatest value will not print your blurbs verbatim. If a news release is of interest to them, they will call to get information that will let them make the story their own.

Many people feel, however, that news releases should be issued rarely, if ever. The more news you make, the more business inquiries you are likely to attract, but a high profile also invites trouble. Assess your own situation and make your choice accordingly.

FOR RELEASE MARCH 22, 199_

FROM: Smith Consulting Associates

SUBJECT: Local Office Market Turnaround

The Blanktown office market, long believed to be in an unhealthy condition, is on the verge of a major upturn, according to prominent local real estate counselor John Smith of Smith Consulting Associates.

"What's happening," said Smith yesterday to the annual meeting of the Blanktown Turtles Club, "is that fresh capital injections and new leadership have strengthened the Blanktown Bank to such an extent that business is rapidly returning to Blanktown. Office tenants are growing again and new ones are turning up almost daily."

Coupled with the recent office construction slowdown, which has cut the number of new buildings in the pipeline to one, this means declining vacancy rates for the foreseeable future, said Smith. "There is no sign of anything on the horizon to prevent office rents from rising," he said. "We are going to be getting stronger for the foreseeable future. Our studies show that the amount of space absorbed in the past six months is 300,000 square feet, and we think that things are going to get even better."

According to Smith, current vacant space amounts to a three-year supply. "This is the smallest overhang we have seen since 1989," said Smith. "The space inventory will have to start growing again within the next couple of years."

Smith, who holds the CRE designation of the respected American Society of Real Estate Counselors, has served on the Blanktown Planning Commission since 1982. He is recognized as an authority on the office space market and keeps track of all significant space offerings and buildings in the Blanktown central area. Smith's firm recently performed an office market study for the Blanktown Insurance Group, and it regularly appraises office buildings here.

30 - 30 - 30

FOR FURTHER INFORMATION: JOHN SMITH, 333-3333

DATE: 3/12/199_

When you do issue a news release, pick a subject or an angle that is newsworthy. Otherwise, the release will go straight into the round file. To encourage a favorable reception, type it double-spaced on one side of the paper and put it into the form that has become standard in the news industry. The reporter who is handed your release may call to ask questions, so be prepared with a few good answers.

A release like this probably will catch the attention of the Blanktown papers, and it also may reach real estate and financial publications in Blanktown and elsewhere. Note the following points:

- The release gets to the point right away: The Blanktown office market is in good shape. To many in Blanktown, that's news—unless others have been saying so for a while.
- It identifies John Smith as a prominent counselor in the first sentence.
- It provides enough background information to support the opening statement without going into excessive detail.
- It reinforces the credentials of John Smith and his firm and reminds the world that they are in business—and probably available for other work.
- Its style is simple, direct and doesn't try to be cute. It leaves personal touches to the reporters.
- It makes extensive use of direct quotation. This helps to personalize the release and to emphasize that a qualified person has announced reassuring news on an important subject.
- The end is marked with the journalist's traditional "30."
- The release is dated and has a specified release date. This is intended to prevent dilution of its impact by premature publication.
- It provides the name and telephone number of a contact source who will answer any questions the reader may have.

Surveys. There's more than one way to use a good survey. The knowledge it provides can be a valuable promotional vehicle. Use the information to guide your prospecting efforts; find stories in it for your reporter friends; announce the survey and its findings with a news release. If none of these appeals to you, try writing an article based on the survey. It may open the door to a new prospect or referral source.

Interviews. Be careful of reporters who want to interview you, whether it's for television, radio or the print media. It's almost impossible to protect yourself against editing that will make you look bad, as many trusting interviewees have discovered much too late.

Paul Johnson, the British historian and journalist, has written astutely on this topic using former prime minister Margaret Thatcher as an example ("The Perils of Vanity Fair," *The Spectator*, June 1, 1991). When approached for an interview for *Vanity Fair*, says Mr. Johnson, Mrs. Thatcher "should have flatly refused." Told that this would be "a sympathetic piece," says Mr. Johnson, "she should have become doubly suspicious. She should have asked herself: What is in it for *Vanity Fair* to publish a 'sympathetic' interview with Margaret Thatcher? The answer: nothing."

Mr. Johnson recommends insisting on the right to see and approve a transcript of the article that will be published or broadcast. Even this, as he points out, will not always save you from embarrassment, as the reporter can't prevent someone else from leading into the story with a hostile headline or introduction.

> If you have something to say, make a speech, put it in a press release, best of all write an article. But, if you are asked to give an interview, remember you are accepting a collaborator you may not be able to control and, behind him or her, other collaborators he or she cannot control. In short, dear celebrity, you are gambling in the media casino.

Public life at the level of the ordinary real estate counselor may be less dangerous than Mrs. Thatcher's. All the same, these Johnsonian cautions should be taken seriously. Unless you have much to gain, and good reason to trust not only the interviewer but also the organization that will run the interview, take a pass. That shouldn't prevent you from uttering a few carefully chosen remarks that do you no harm, and perhaps some good, even when taken out of context.

Additional words of caution. Some clients will resent any media attention that comes your way. They may be jealous or feel, rightly or wrongly, that attention paid to you will somehow work against their best interests. Talk things over with them; find out exactly where the problem lies. You may be able to show that your value to them, as to your other clients, will increase as a result of public recognition of your abilities.

Remember, too, that it can be dangerous to take a public stance on a controversial issue or one that might become so. You may find yourself on the wrong side of the issue.

If you are attacked in the media. Defend yourself. Get competent legal and public relations advice. Sometimes the situation will demand that you lie low for a while to let the issue cool down. More often some sort of positive public relations effort should be made. You can gather supportive statements by people who are on your side, provide a good-humored refutation, make a direct counterattack that gives the lie to your accusers or release a series of stories about the important contributions you are making in other areas. Experienced lawyers and public relations people generally have excellent antennae and know what to do, although not every problem of this nature can be solved completely. It helps to have friends in business and the media who will rally to your support. Best, of course, is always to do the right thing and never make a mistake.

PUBLIC SERVICE

As a counselor you will be asked to participate in many kinds of civic and professional activities. People who respect your counseling abilities will assume that those abilities can be tapped for other purposes. You may be called upon to lead a cause, head an agency, chair a commission or advise a civic group. At a minimum you will be asked to serve on committees and help local service organizations deal with their real estate problems.

Look before your leap.

Accept these leadership responsibilities good naturedly. They will help you grow, add enjoyment to your work and build your reputation. Be a good citizen, a good colleague, a good professional; put a coin in the jukebox now and then, if only for the sake of the music.

Watch out, though. Some situations are potentially dangerous and should be avoided. Try not to climb onto a sinking ship; don't make enemies or lend your name to a highly controversial undertaking unless you are certain you will be in a satisfactory position at its outcome. On the other hand, a willingness to stand up and be counted on important civic issues will be admired by many and cause your name to be remembered. It also will make you a larger person than the individual who always remains quiet for fear of offending.

Probably the best kinds of civic activities for you, from the viewpoint of marketing, are those connected in one way or another with your primary field of activity. Your opinion on zoning law changes, local tax reforms, planning issues and economic development policy will carry special weight. Make your presence felt in such areas, and your expertise will be appreciated. Step forward as a leader on some issue of real importance to the community, and your reputation is almost assured.

PROFESSIONAL AND BUSINESS GROUPS

The magic word is "participation." Take an active part, make a contribution, let people know you are there. The greater your willingness and ability to contribute to the workings of your professional and business groups, the faster your reputation will spread.

After joining an organization, find a committee that interests you and volunteer. Drop in on other committee meetings to see how things go and find out whether you have a contribution to make. Get to know the organization's leaders and the members who have interests that are similar to yours.

The importance of organizational work to the building of a reputation may be obvious, but such work is useful even to those who don't need or want to become better known. The friends you make while participating in a group's activities can form an important part of your network of information sources and business contacts. They also can broaden your horizons, expand your reach, develop your social skills and make your professional life more rewarding.

MEETINGS

There are many types of meetings. The role of the counselor differs according to their nature and purpose.

The informational meeting. People are often convened just to let them know what's going on or to provide other interesting information. Such meetings are nonconfrontational; their only purpose is to communicate useful knowledge. No decisions need to be made, and no particular action is necessary.

The business meeting. Here the group is expected to identify and focus on problems, contribute facts, exchange views, reach decisions and agree upon a course of action. Participation is obviously important and must be encouraged by the meeting leaders. Such meetings work better if someone serves as facilitator, helping to move things along and to smooth over ruffled feelings. The counselor often is a natural for the job.

The rally. The purpose is to warm up the troops and set them marching. A good harangue may be all that's necessary. The troops, on their part, have only to listen, stamp their feet, cheer and follow orders.

Of these three the counselor is most likely to concentrate on types 1 and 2, leaving type 3 to others. The following comments make no attempt to provide instruction in the art of mounting a good rally. For other kinds of meetings they assume that the counselor at least has something to say about the place, time, arrangement, composition, conduct and length of the event.

Place. When you have the choice, pick a location that's appropriate as well as convenient. Don't convene a group to discuss the problems of the homeless at the fanciest hotel in town or assemble a conventicle of bankers at the neighborhood motel—at least not without good reason. And remember that many public figures won't attend a meeting in a nonunion hotel or restaurant.

Pay particular attention to the room: Is it the right size? The right shape? Suitably equipped? Close enough to the washrooms? Are the acoustics (or the public address system) right for your purposes? Pick a lively room to encourage participation, a dull one (with thick carpeting and draperies) to keep the proceedings calm and orderly while you quietly explain what needs to be done.

Time. How long do you plan to continue the meeting? If it's all day, obviously you'll want an early start; if you'd like to keep things short, you may prefer late afternoon, when people are eager to get home to their armchairs and TV. If you want people to be particularly alert, schedule the meeting in the morning, not after a heavy lunch or dinner. If the opposite is the case, plan accordingly.

Arrangement. A strong leader can lead from almost any point in the room, but the person at the head of the table has a clear advantage: He can see everyone, and everyone can see him. Another good vantage point is at the foot of the table, particularly if you intend to oppose or upset a proposal being made from the table's head. For those who are not accustomed to these games, the head of the table usually is at the end farthest from the main entrance to the room, where the bosses are least likely to be disturbed by passing underlings.

If your intention is to encourage maximum participation, sit in the middle of the table along one of the sides. This position will minimize the intimidation factor, reduce the general anxiety level and reassure the shy that you won't bite.

Composition. Try not to outnumber the other side, particularly if they represent the client. A precise match is unnecessary, but it's wise to have a somewhat smaller team of roughly similar age and experience. If you also can show versatility, intelligence and judgment, so much the better.

For civic meetings and other nonbusiness events, try to assemble people who will help to accomplish the purpose of the meeting, whether it is to inform, to decide or to mobilize. A diverse group usually will produce a more stimulating discussion and may be necessary to represent the interests of all concerned. If what you want is unanimity, choose people who think alike.

There are limits to the number of people who can be assembled for a useful purpose. An informational or inspirational meeting can be quite large, limited chiefly by the acoustics of the room. It even can be held outdoors if the speaker has a big voice, a PA system or a good megaphone. Business meetings may have to be large, too, but work better when held to 12-15 people, usually the largest number that will permit a general conversation.

Conduct. Meetings, like stories and speeches, should have a beginning, a middle and an end. The best beginning is usually a statement of purpose, followed by a brief outline of the program: Why are we here? What can we expect to accomplish? How will we go about it? What are the ground rules?

The middle explores the subject matter, allows people to make their contributions and leads the group toward a consensus. The leader then summarizes the consensus, watching others carefully to make sure they are completely on board and asking apparent doubters about their feelings before taking any necessary votes and closing the meeting.

Meeting leaders are responsible for directing the meeting and, to some extent, its outcome. They also may be responsible for entertaining the participants. The rule of leaders should be similar to the purposes of art: to teach, inspire and delight. This allows you to use and encourage humor and reminds you that good manners, care in presentation and respect for the abilities and patience of others are appropriate behaviors.

Length. Not too long, not too short. Diplomats, labor leaders and political organizers know how to use time to their best advantage, stretching meetings out when that strategy will drive opponents away and weaken the determination of the individuals who remain. Foes who are wise to this tactic will insist on a fixed closing time and provide a good reason for it, such as the last flight to Philadelphia or a pending shutdown of the air conditioning system. Failing that, a sudden heart spasm will do.

Most people have predictable attention spans which should be respected if your purpose is to instruct or lead. No individual should hold the floor for more than about 45 minutes, barring exceptional circumstances, and no meeting should last longer than about two hours unless it is broken up into segments of an hour and a half—or unless you hope to force agreement with the help of the audience's growing discomfort.

References

BOOKS

1. Benn A: *The 27 Most Common Mistakes in Advertising.* (New York: Amacom) 1978.

2. Boettinger HM: *Moving Mountains.* (New York: Collier) 1969.

3. Bruneau EA: *Rx for Advertising. A Common Sense Cure for Business Owners and Managers.* (Spokane, WA: Boston Books) 1986.

4. Burdette E: *Resume Writing.* (New York: John Wiley and Sons) 1990.

5. Cohen W: *The Entrepreneur & Small Business Marketing Problem Solver.* (New York: John Wiley & Sons) 1990.

6. Corrado FM: *Media for Managers.* (Englewood Cliffs, NJ: Prentice-Hall) 1984.

7. Dean SL: *How To Advertise. A Handbook for Small Business.* (Wilmington, DE: Enterprise Publishing) 1980.

8. Elam H, Paley N: *Marketing for Nonmarketers* (New York: Amacom) 1992.

9. Gordon M: *How To Plan and Conduct a Successful Meeting.* (New York: Sterling Publishing Co.) 1985.

10. Hart N: *Practical Advertising and Publicity.* (New York: McGraw-Hill) 1988.

11. Jackson T: *The Perfect Resume for the 90s.* (New York: Doubleday) 1989.

12. Koehler and Sisco: *Public Communications in Business and the Professions.* (St. Paul: West Publishing Co.) 1981.

13. Miller M: *Business Guide to Print Promotion.* (Laguna Beach, CA: Iris Communication Group) 1988.

PERIODICALS

1. *Direct Marketing,* Hoke Communications, 224 7th Street, Garden City, NY 11530

2. *Marketing News,* American Marketing Association, 250 S. Wacker Drive, Chicago, IL 60606

3. *Standard Directory of Advertising Agencies,* The National Register Publishing Co., 3004 Glenview Rd, Wilmette, IL 60091

4. *Target Marketing,* North American Publishing Co., 401 N. Broad Street, Philadelphia, PA 19108

Chapter 16

Making the Presentation

There is an art to making presentations, whether it's to a friend, a client, a group of colleagues, a review board, a civic committee, a jury or any other gathering that is charged with passing judgment on what you have to propose. It's the art of persuasion. The presenter's job is to show something to the group and obtain its endorsement. That takes a combination of things: an idea that's of interest to the audience, a convincing story, a reasonable approach and enough showmanship to bring the group around to your point of view.

A key to effective presentation is the use of exhibits: pictures, maps, charts, tapes, films. Another is a logical sequence that takes the audience from a starting point, usually an acknowledged problem about which audience members share certain assumptions with you, down a line of believable reasoning to the desired conclusion. If what you have to propose is something the group doesn't want or need, you won't find the presentation easy. Your chances are better with a group that's hungry for a solution to a problem you know how to solve—like your counseling clients.

The art of the presentation is the art of persuasion.

You won't get far with your presentation if you don't deal with the emotions of the audience members as well as their intellects. Persuasion is as much a matter of feelings as it is of logic, so if their feelings aren't with you, chances are you haven't done your job. How to mobilize those feelings is a question that has many answers, some familiar to everyone: "Laugh and the world laughs with you...." Others are less familiar and harder to use.

For help you can try paying attention to successful presenters, watching how they approach their topics to enlist the support of the group, or take a course in meetings and presentations. If you don't have time for such things, there are excellent books on the subject. My own favorite is *Moving Mountains* (see the References), but others may work better for you.

SPEECHES

There is no quicker way to gain recognition in your community and your profession than by becoming known as an interesting, informative public speaker.

Say your piece, but remember your audience.

A good public speaker is remembered; even a mediocre one usually is respected as something of an authority. Audiences assume that anyone who has been asked to speak knows a good deal about the topic. Unless the speaker is so incompetent as to dispel that illusion, his speech will strengthen it.

If you can manage to amuse your audience, don't hesitate to do so, but keep in mind that your fundamental purpose as a speaker is serious: to inform, enlighten, persuade and, if possible, make a good impression. Your listeners don't come to hear a new comedian. They come for information and ideas and perhaps to judge you as a source of counseling help.

Many books and teachers are available to assist you. The best advice generally goes something like this:

- Prepare your talk. You may not need notes, but you should think about what you're going to say and how you're going to say it.
- Have a clear idea of what you want to accomplish. Is your objective to inform, explain, make a point, teach a lesson, refute an argument, win a battle—or just to entertain and make friends?
- Recognize that you probably know more about the subject than anyone else in the room. That's why you're the speaker.
- Assume that members of the audience are at least as intelligent as you are but know less than you do about the subject or they wouldn't be sitting there so expectantly.
- Show the audience that you have something worthwhile to offer and that you care more about communicating it than about making a good impression. They will appreciate your efforts to help them, and you will avoid the self-consciousness that spoils many speeches.
- Speak loudly enough to be heard from the back of the room. Don't talk to the floor or the lectern. Watch the faces of the audience to make sure you're getting through.
- Know your stuff. There are few substitutes for actual knowledge. If you don't know enough about the subject, spend the time necessary to dig out the facts and put your thoughts together.
- Enjoy yourself. The kid in us enjoys attention and applause, and you're entitled to both as a public speaker. Feel free to wave your arms, jump up and down, make faces and crack jokes; use all the gimmicks and stage tricks you please. Audiences like a speaker

who's having fun. It lets them have fun, too. But don't abandon your self-respect altogether; after all, at bottom you are a serious professional.

Most important of all, share your enthusiasm—for the audience, the occasion, the topic, your own ideas. It's likely to prove infectious.

Where to speak? Opportunities arise from time to time, more often as you gain recognition. If you aren't getting invitations, volunteer. Look up the program chairman or executive director of an organization of interest to you and let that person know you are able and available. Organizations are constantly on the alert for new speakers and should welcome your approach.

Honoraria and expenses. Not everybody wants to pay for a speech, and not every speaker is worth an honorarium. Still, it doesn't hurt to ask. In addition to the honorarium you often are entitled to reimbursement for travel, lodging and meals. If you think you can get them, insist upon first-class accommodations all the way. Otherwise you may find yourself on the cheapest coach transportation available, wedged in between squalling babies.

Topics. The person who invites you to speak has a general idea of the subject the group wants to hear about, but usually is quite flexible as to the specifics and may ask you to create your own speech title. You can take advantage of this freedom to make your own points and enjoy yourself. Some of the possibilities:

- What's happening in (fill in the name of your town)
- Popular real estate scams and dodges
- The coming boom in (fill in the kind of real estate that interests you)
- The coming crash in (ditto)
- How to make your first million without cash or skills

Think seriously about what you are trying to accomplish with your speech. Is the idea to entertain your clients, educate your peers, impress the media or change the world? Plan the event and choose the topic accordingly, with due respect to what people are actually interested in hearing. Lectures on the fine points of discounted cash flow analysis may be saleble, but you will have to pick your audience with care.

HINTS FOR SPEAKERS

1. Have a brief but impressive or modestly witty biographical statement and a recent photograph ready and take a few sets along with you for the media and the person who will be making the introductions.

2. Prepare a press release, accompanied by a current photograph, to give to reporters who may be present.

3. Don't ask the person who introduces you to cut the introduction too short. A reasonably detailed explanation of why you were invited to

speak provides an excellent launching pad for your talk. It may also increase your confidence.

4. Don't apologize. This applies to your hand-out materials, your clothing and the content of your talk as well as to your mediocre speaking skills and physical appearance. What you want to project is not modesty, humility or guilt but a healthy confidence in your knowledge—and in your ability to convey it to an interested audience.

5. Remember that any speech worth making can be turned into a publishable article. If you don't have the time or the ability to do so, there are others who can work with you to develop your ideas. Either way, a good set of speech notes is an excellent beginning.

Stage fright. Inexperienced speakers often enter the hall as though it were filled with enemies. The audience, they feel, is looking for an excuse to despise anyone foolish enough to stand up and talk.

In real life there seldom are many such people in the room. Audiences are extraordinarily tolerant of almost any speaker who appears to mean well—they are not merely uncritical but positively kind. They invited you to come, they want you to succeed and most of them are actively rooting for you.

Don't agitate yourself with needless worries. Instead, concentrate on the folks who are waiting patiently to learn what you have to say. They deserve the courtesy of your full attention, so focus on what they want, not your own fears. Show them respect by treating them as intelligent human beings who value their time and are worthy of your best efforts. The more you devote yourself to the job of communicating your message, the less psychic energy will be left to fuel your self-consciousness.

Format. A good speech starts well and ends well. After you have assumed your position and made your opening remarks, tell the audience what you're going to talk about, why it's important and how it bears on their concerns. Sketch out the main points and then expand on them, relating each point to your underlying theme. To close, restate the theme and the essentials of your talk in such a way as to throw new light on the subject, perhaps by showing how it relates to some broader concern: the future, the survival of the community, the stature of the group. Try to leave the audience laughing, thoughtful or emotionally moved.

Shorter is usually sweeter.

How long? Speakers should learn to stop when finished, if not sooner. It's preferable to leave the audience wanting more, not wishing it had received less. Take enough time, though, to get your main points across, even if the moderator is signaling that your time's up.

A speech with a time limit of 10 to 15 minutes will be livelier than one of an hour and a half. When you're the only speaker at an informal affair, this short jolt should be enough; it leaves plenty of time for questions—or an early retreat to the office. Speeches at more formal events require more time, usually 45 to 50 minutes. After the first hour, the audience will start to become restless.

The outer limit for any speaker or panel is usually 90 minutes, including a question-and-answer period. All-day programs can be constructed in 90-minute segments (two in the morning, one or two in the afternoon) with a coffee or stretch break after each segment. Don't let any program chairman persuade you to speak longer.

Questions. Some program chairmen like to save the question-and-answer period for the end of the program, after all the speakers have finished. This arrangement has three drawbacks: (1) it omits the "participation breaks" many listeners look forward to; (2) it causes people to pay less attention than they would if they were mentally preparing to challenge the speaker in a few minutes with a penetrating question; and (3) it causes people to forget a lot of good questions. A better setup is to let questioners jump in after each talk or at designated points during a long presentation. In small informal groups you can allow questions at any point so you can clarify quickly things questioners don't understand.

Program leaders may opt for written questions when the audience for a talk is too large for oral ones to be practical. Even in a big room, though, oral questions can be handled if the speaker or moderator repeats each question from the podium so that the entire group can hear it. The danger is that a few long-winded or stupid questions will turn off the audience, effectively putting an end to the session. This situation can be avoided by asking questioners to write down their questions or by using a moderator who knows how to deflate windbags politely.

Whatever policy is adopted, the moderator, or if necessary the speaker, should announce it at the beginning of the speech. Then, if someone chimes in at the wrong time, you can either appeal to the rules or graciously allow the diversion.

Your attitude toward questioners, however hostile they may seem, should be positive and as cheerful as you can manage. Before almost any business audience, the speaker who remains friendly in the face of an unfriendly challenge wins; the one who shows anger or contempt doesn't.

Gauging the room. These days most halls and meeting rooms are centrally air conditioned and heated. That doesn't mean the equipment will be working when you give your talk or that you will be able to adjust the thermostat without using a licensed union engineer. Make sure in advance that the system is in operation and that it is set properly for the size of the audience. If it isn't, do what you can to make things right: open and close windows, turn on fans and invite the audience to put on or take off their coats.

A lively room—one in which sound bounces readily—is easy to recognize. Your voice will resonate, your words will carry and the audience will feel more energized than it will in an acoustically dead room, the kind with thick carpets, heavy wall coverings and acoustical ceilings. Unless the room is too large or noisy you can take advantage of its liveliness by abandoning the podium and speaking directly to the audience. This ploy is always more effective than standing behind an obstacle that conceals your body and inhibits your movements. Bear in mind that even very lively rooms quiet down in the presence of silent people (not noisy ones!) because their clothing absorbs sound.

Large rooms may require you to change the manner of your presentation. They invite you to raise your voice a notch, slow your phrasing, pause for effect and use more emphasis than you would in a smaller room. The people in the back are at a considerable distance, psychologically as well as physically; they will be hard to reach unless you make a special effort.

Getting and holding audience attention. Some people advise carrying a large revolver, setting off fireworks or entering the room with a chicken on your head. These are all effective attention-getters but so is a confident entrance followed by a good opening line. Walk right in, step right up, take possession of the room and the audience. Wake them up with a striking or funny remark about your topic or the occasion. After that, all you have to do is communicate your ideas and the essential facts in a clear, friendly and cheerful manner or, when the situation demands it, firmly and emotionally. Don't waste time on lengthy stories or extended compliments; get on with the show.

Attitude and demeanor. Certain subjects require a serious approach; others allow levity. You wouldn't want to joke about the Holocaust or be too serious about the subject of pornography in shopping centers. The occasion as well as the subject can influence your approach. Are you speaking in the morning on a technical topic to an audience of professionals or after cocktails and dinner to a relaxed group of conventioneers? The content of your talk, not to mention the way you give it, will differ accordingly.

Unless you are in a working session with a relatively small group or having lunch with friends, by all means stand up to speak. It puts you in a position of authority, makes you easy to watch and gives your audience a better chance to hear what you have to say. It also frees up your body so you can gesture naturally while giving your lungs and diaphragm room to project your voice.

Unless you are Johnny Carson, don't put your hands in your pockets. It makes most speakers look constricted and timid. Keep your hands free to describe a curve, challenge a misconception or drive home a point. You don't have to wave your arms about, but a reasonable amount of movement adds liveliness.

Look healthy.

Another no-no: Don't shuffle about, shift from foot to foot or lean on things. A relaxed grip on the podium is allowed; a hand on the table is not, unless you are leaning forward. There's no need to stand at attention, but you are trying to project confidence, and you can't do that from a weak position. It generally pays to stand tall and look healthy, even if you are communicating bad news.

Audiences are readily distracted by speech mannerisms and twitches. Speak normally but avoid cliches and tics—you know, like ("he was, like, you know, all set to go for it"), sorta, at this point in time, it goes without saying, to be honest.

Many speakers unconsciously discourage the audience's attention by speaking too slowly, allowing long pauses at inappropriate moments and using fillers ("uh," "well..."). These, like obvious errors of grammar and vocabulary, tell the audience that your thinking is sloppy, your command of the language is poor and your own attention is not fully devoted to the task at hand. Repetitions, redundancies and other signs of carelessness greatly reduce the effectiveness of any presentation.

Depending on the occasion, the subject, the size of the group and other factors, you may choose to come across as energetic and creative, calm and thoughtful, direct and plain-spoken or some other recognizable personality type. But don't forget that, as a real estate counselor, you want to project a certain maturity and professional authority. Don't let yourself be carried away by your own enthusiasm or anger, though it is usually all right to let them be seen. Use sarcasm sparingly, if at all; avoid unjustified criticism and negativism and try to project fairness and good judgment.

If stories are appropriate and you tell them reasonably well, by all means include them in your presentation. Be sure, though, to choose stories that relate to your topic, or at least to your audience, and tie them in. "Our topic today brings up the experience of Pat and Mike... What happened to Mike, of course, is what will happen to you unless..." If you don't or can't tell stories well, don't try. Most business audiences prefer a witty sally now and then to canned jokes, even if they're listening to a presentation after dinner and have had a few drinks. They certainly would rather listen to the substance of your talk than to bad stories poorly told.

Clothing. Wear clean and well pressed clothes and opt for your standard business attire unless the occasion is informal and the audience is in sports clothes. Even at these times a coat and tie will show that you take the group and your talk seriously. You'll be most confident and appealing in clothes that are familiar.

As to tie color and other fetishes of the speech consulting industry, they don't matter much and can be ignored safely. Just don't be surprised if you find that the other speakers all sport dark suits and red cravats.

Aiming your shots. Is your audience the group of people in front of you, the one on the other side of a TV camera or both? The location of your principal audience will make a difference in your presentation. If you are speaking directly to people in the room, look at them; as your speech proceeds, check their faces frequently to make sure they understand what you are saying and are responding to it. If they look sleepy or bored, change the subject, speed things up or inject a note of humor when you can; if they are alert and nod agreement, by all means keep doing whatever is making them respond so positively.

If on the other hand the proceedings are being televised, you must decide whether the reactions of the audience in the room or those of the video audience are more important. If the latter, you'll need to focus more on the camera, as the tennis-watching head turning used by group-oriented speakers looks a little peculiar on television and is far less effective than speaking directly to the viewer inside the black box.

If you follow a series of dull speakers, make it a point to liven things up with a quick series of witticisms, an unexpected approach or a faster and livelier delivery. If on the other hand you follow an exceptionally humorous and energizing speaker, you may prefer not to compete as an entertainer but simply to deliver a quiet, thoughtful talk.

Where you are in the room influences what you have to say and how the audience receives it. Speakers are expected to be at the front where everybody can see and hear them. What happens if you move to the middle? The rear? If you move around while speaking? Obviously some topics should be addressed straight on in the conventional manner from front and center; others may call for more mobility or a different position. It is often effective to begin your talk from the usual place and then move into the audience to answer questions or add a few personal thoughts.

Whatever you do, remember that the reach of your voice will change as you move about the room. For maximum sound projection speak with a wall behind you; for intimacy get closer to the audience.

Notes and visuals. Use notes if they make you feel more comfortable but *never* read a speech unless you are a leader in a crisis and care more about precision than audience impact. You usually will get the best results when you carry only a few notes to the podium. A list of key words and topics should be sufficient, if you know your subject. Detailed notes do have one important advantage: They can be turned into an article easily. Often the organizations that invite you to speak have journals which will be glad to include your remarks.

If you must use a lot of notes, ask for a podium so you have a place to put them. A podium also is useful if you're feeling insecure and need something to hang onto. Otherwise feel free to come out from behind the obstacles and let yourself be seen. Members of the audience will appreciate the fact that you don't need to keep a barrier between you and them, and you will appreciate your greater freedom of gesture and expression. If you do use a podium, try not to cling to it like a drowning person; keep your arms relaxed and use them at least occasionally for gestures, as well as to turn pages, scratch yourself and fuss with the mike.

Slides, films, audiovisuals. Use audiovisual aids only to keep the facts in front of the audience or when the presentation absolutely demands them. Visuals reduce the impact of your personality and your talk by distracting the audience from your face, which is what people should be looking at even when it is ugly.

Slides may be necessary to reinforce key concepts or to display relevant pictures, ideas or figures. The trouble with slides is they force you to darken the room so the audience can't see you properly. Besides, the machinery tends to be distracting—especially when it doesn't work. Factual material and calculations can be displayed on an easel, but usually they are best presented in printed form rather than on a screen so the audience can take them home and won't be distracted by note-taking.

On the other hand a well-prepared multi-projector slide show, when everything goes right, can have a strong impact. Don't hesitate to use this format if your message is largely visual and emotional. Use a pointer, if it helps, but don't wave it about or use it like a sword. Overhead projectors should be used only when absolutely necessary, never as a crutch.

Use audiovisuals only with caution.

Trickiest of all is a film or video with sound. These throw the audience into a passive mood like the one they experience when watching TV. If you must show such a production, do it at the end of your talk, not in the middle or at the beginning when it will interfere with the rest of your presentation. When the lights go down, the audience tends to get sleepy. What you want, of course, is for the audience to be wide awake and 100% attentive to you.

Voice, microphones, etc. The near-universal availability of microphones has encouraged naturally timid speakers to lower their voices out of modesty rather than try to reach the back of the room. Take a look around you and gauge the distance your voice will have to cover. Project your voice to the people in the far corners unless the microphone will intensify the sound too much. If you can't hear a little resonance from the farthest walls, chances are you aren't speaking loudly enough for maximum impact. (This doesn't mean you can't lower your voice to quiet the room or for dramatic effect.)

Check beforehand to make sure the microphones work. If you can get along without them, do so. Adjust them, if you must, but don't fiddle with them for long unless you are a technician, comedian or rock star.

If you tend to swallow or garble your words and people often ask you to speak up or repeat yourself, consider paying a few visits to a speech coach. Competent speakers can cover considerable distances without shouting; so can you, with a little instruction. The speech coach also can help you with articulation, phrasing and gestures.

Handouts. People like to take something home from a public event. You can oblige them and promote your own professional activities at the same time. Leave something behind, if only a map or photograph with your name and address on it.

A useful handout is a summary of the facts covered in your talk. This can be as simple as a typewritten information sheet or as elaborate as a four-color, custom-crafted brochure. A particularly nice leave-behind is a folder or binder with maps, charts, photographs and factual materials.

Don't let the distribution of your materials distract from your talk. If you are speaking after a meal, distribute the handouts before the food is served. This will allow the audience to shuffle the papers before you speak and give them time to figure out where to put them (on the chair? under the table?) while eating. If you think this will take away too much from the impact of your talk, you can distribute the materials later as the audience exits. Whatever you do, don't encourage your listeners to page through your handouts while you are trying to hold their attention from the podium. You won't like trying to compete with the sound of rattling paper.

References

BOOKS

1. Boettinger HM: *Moving Mountains.* (New York: Collier) 1969.
2. Fletcher L: *Speaking to Succeed.* (New York: Harper and Row) 1988.
3. Gordon M: *How to Plan and Conduct a Successful Meeting.* (New York: Sterling Publishing Co.) 1985.
4. Kaumeyer RA: *How to Write and Speak in Business.* (New York: Van Nostrand Reinhold) 1985.
5. Leech T: *How to Prepare, Stage and Deliver Winning Presentations.* (New York: Amacom) 1982.
6. Vardman GT: *Making Successful Presentations.* (New York: Amacom) 1981.

Chapter 17

Other Marketing Ideas

SEMINARS

Occasionally you may have the opportunity to mount a special program on a real estate subject of current interest. You can offer such programs privately to a few clients and friends or present them to a broader audience, usually (though not necessarily) under the aegis of a professional society or civic group. Seminars can be valuable and stimulating to participants, bringing fresh information and insights to their attention, introducing new personalities and allowing audience members to express their own ideas. Properly organized and promoted, they will draw a motivated audience whose members are willing to cover their share of the costs. They also will bring credit to sponsors and speakers, including you.

Association executives and their officers are aware of these benefits. That's why they are often eager to work with you, making their membership lists and promotional facilities available without charge. What they hope to get in return is a worthwhile service for their members, the chance to call favorable attention to their association and possibly a share of the profits.

When planning the event, focus on the underlying purposes of the seminar; then choose your topic, speakers, venue, dates and marketing approach accordingly. The people who are most likely to attend will be those who have a strong interest in the subject and a readiness to accept your presentation of it. If people don't care about the topic, don't think your speakers know enough about it, don't find the location convenient or are busy with their own work or another event, your program will flop no

What do you want to accomplish?

matter how well you promote it. But don't let these potential drawbacks stop you from using all your marketing skills. Even when everything else is right, the best-conceived seminar may die if it isn't served up in the right way.

Your choice of topic is particularly important. A program that offers valuable information about a current worry or a promising new opportunity will draw a good crowd as long as the speakers are well chosen. But remember: Subjects that seem quite interesting to you may hold little appeal to the audiences you are trying to reach, especially if they already have been beaten to death by other seminar sponsors or people are distracted by more urgent concerns.

The plan. The seminar plan may look something like this:

TOPIC: Retail Markets in Blanktown
DATE: March 15, 199_ (beware of possible conflicts)
LOCATION: Greenback Room, Blanktown Hotel
PRICE: $125
SPONSORS: Blanktown Realtor Board and Blanktown Realty Counselors, Inc.
PROGRAM: 7:30- 8:00 Registration and coffee
               8:00- 8:30 Welcome and introductions
               8:30-10:00 The Blanktown market background: Joe Counselor, Jr.
              10:00-10:30 Coffee break
              10:30-12:00 New projects in Blanktown:
                       Dave Developer
                       Paul Promoter
                       Bernice Banker
              12:00- 1:00 Luncheon
               1:00- 1:45 Luncheon speaker: Samuel Stranger
               2:00- 3:30 New technology and what it is doing to the
                        Blanktown market:
                       Hy Techman
                       Sally Anything
                       Abel Vender
               3:30- 4:30 Audience discussion

AUDIENCE: Board members, Blanktown Realty Counselors, Inc. clients, building owners, brokers, architects and store planners, developers, contractors, retailers, planners, appraisers, market analysts

BUDGET: Revenues: 100 paid admissions at $125 $12,500
               Costs:
                      Hall $1,500
                      Coffee   100
                      Lunch   1,500
                      Honoraria   1,000

Speaker expenses	400	
Printing	1,500	
Mailing	500	
Promotion	2,000	$8,500
Estimated profit:		$4,000

(Don't trust these figures, even if you are the one who put them together. But you get the idea.)

You can mount ambitious programs with the help of an organization's program committee or a committee you put together for the purpose. If the topic is important enough, you may be able to find financial guarantors who will contribute seed money, buy the popcorn and cover any deficit. In exchange for this you can extend appropriate thanks to the guarantors during the program, on your printed materials and in news releases. Modest programs can be presented in a hotel meeting room or your own conference room, with or without charging invited guests for a share of the expenses.

Ask your speakers to specify well in advance any audiovisual equipment they will need and encourage them to provide handout materials. You may want to provide such materials yourself. Good giveaways can be obtained from local, state and federal government agencies, universities, Realtor organizations, the chamber of commerce and other groups. Display them along with your firm's literature on a table at the back of the meeting room.

If you can get the job and handle the role, act as moderator of a seminar program at least occasionally. It adds authority to your image and will build your confidence as a leader. Don't try it, though, if you lack diplomacy and have a tendency to fly off the handle. The moderator's job is to keep things moving comfortably under reasonable control, which is hard to do when you're hot under the collar. A sense of humor, if you have one, will make it easier and add to audience enjoyment.

ARTICLES AND BOOKS

You can use your writing to develop specific market niches and build your reputation. Write about subjects you think offer worthwhile professional opportunities for you and your firm, not just about currently popular topics. Encourage your associates to write too, for their own sake as well as the firm's. Just don't forget that what you—or they—say can and probably will be used against you sooner or later in a court of law and at the country club.

In your own community you can emphasize important local issues such as those relating to the downtown area or the town's leading industry. In doing so you show that you are interested in your city's vitality, that you know and care about it. Related articles on real estate development and markets can stimulate demand for your services as an expert in these areas, both professionally and as an unpaid advisor to the media.

When choosing your topic, think about whom you want to reach and what you want to say to them. If your targets are shopping center owners, write about shopping centers from an angle that will interest them: What the centers are selling for, who the buyers are, how the deals are being financed, what is happening in retail space markets, what the newest centers look like and how they work, where new development is occurring and why, how toxic-substance problems and tenant defaults are being handled. Don't waste time writing a shopping center primer for housing brokers unless you seriously expect them to bring you shopping center business, or want to do it as a courtesy to their trade groups.

Try to write about subjects you know well. This saves research time and lends authority to what you say. Try also to write about subjects that are likely to interest readers who have current real estate problems. They will gravitate to your articles, even if they don't like your style.

Structure and content. In your writing as in speaking it's usually a good idea to follow the rule of threes: a three-part structure and three main ideas. The three-part structure naturally involves a beginning, a middle and an end. The beginning should state what you are going to say and why you think it needs saying; the middle should develop your three main ideas; the end should restate what you have already said and discuss its implications for the reader.

Other structures are possible, of course, and may work better for you. Sometimes a chatty approach is more appropriate to the topic or better suited to the publication. Your topic may demand more than three major points. Most articles, though, do better with a maximum of three.

Fresh perspectives and humor will brighten your style.

Like your speeches, your articles will be more interesting if you give the reader a fresh and personal view of the subject matter. Show originality, feeling and humor whenever possible. People won't be reading you primarily for laughs, but they will appreciate your ability to liven up their reading experience.

Your objective as a writer may not be merely to inform, entertain and promote your firm. You also may want to inspire action; if not now, perhaps sometime in the future. To be effective in this sense your articles must be memorable. You can make them so by opening up for the reader an important new perspective, showing how to solve a frequently encountered problem or stirring up buried feelings about an urgent issue. Winston Churchill was among the most effective writers and speakers of this century because he knew how to mobilize the anger, pride and courage of his beleaguered people during World War II. You may not have the same opportunities or skills, but you can learn much by remembering his example.

Charts, photographs and drawings can add sparkle to your articles and books as well as to your counseling reports. If they help make your points, use them freely; the reader will be grateful. But don't allow graphics to intrude on the text and interfere with its meaning.

Style. Articles in professional journals usually are written in clumsy, formal English you won't find anywhere else except in government reports, academic publications and the speech of small-time bureaucrats. You don't have to emulate this style; you can use any style that accomplishes your goal, which is not to be stuffy or ponderous but readable.

Write correctly and thoughtfully but as naturally and clearly as you can. Avoid long words and abstractions. Use a high percentage of words with Anglo-Saxon and Viking roots. Hold your sentences to a reasonable length and express your thoughts as plainly as you dare. Long words, long sentences and verbal complications should be used only when you don't want to communicate but to conceal.

Well-chosen imagery, contrary to what some people may expect, adds an important dimension to your writing. Use it for impact or to present a familiar idea from a new angle. Too many business writers only use cliches, as though fresh insights and expressions were somehow unbusinesslike. They aren't; on the contrary they add value to your work and improve its readability.

If you need a guide, Strunk & White's *Elements of English Style* is still among the best. It also helps to read good stylists: Hazlitt, Addison, Mark Twain and Garrison Keillor will put you on the right path.

Getting published. The most willing market for your writing is your own professional society. Chances are excellent that it publishes at least one journal, magazine or newsletter. Talk about your projects with the editor, who can suggest topics that will interest the readership.

Other organizations also may be interested in what you have to say. Read their magazines to see what kinds of articles they publish. Then send the editor a draft or an outline accompanied by a sample page or two to show your writing ability. Chances are good that you will be asked to follow through with finished copy.

In choosing and soliciting outlets for your articles, consider not only the number of readers you are likely to reach but also the prestige of the publication. An article in *Real Estate Issues* or the *Appraisal Journal* may not be read by as many brokers and syndicators as one in the *National Real Estate Investor*, but it probably will do more for your professional reputation.

For love or money? Most of the time, you'll be grateful to see your work in print at any price, especially if it's in a publication that reaches reasonable numbers of active or potential clients. The resulting exposure will be worth more than the small fee you are likely to get, if you get anything.

Sometimes, though, what you have written can be worth more than a trivial sum to a publication that really wants it. Take full advantage of such opportunities. There's nothing unprofessional about being paid for your writing, so you don't have to be bashful about it. If the stakes are high enough, consult an author's attorney or agent to make sure you'll get what's coming to you. These professionals know how to counsel you, just as you know how to counsel others.

BROCHURES

A good brochure serves several purposes. As a statement of your organization's nature, functions and style, it tells the world who you are, what you do and how you serve your clients. This helps prospects evaluate your suitability and your staff. It can also give valuable information to your clients about matters of direct concern to them.

Brochures should be well designed, nicely executed, appropriate to your firm's image and suited for the uses to which they will be put. They should be cautious about promoting services you can't actually deliver.

A brochure will not get you a job by itself. Even the fanciest ones won't impress most prospects. A good one does reinforce your other marketing approaches and add credibility to your sales calls, proposals, speeches and presentations.

In the pocket? On the table?

Different situations may demand different brochure formats. Here are some of the most common situations:

Something to leave with a prospect. Since your brochure will be the only one left on the table, it doesn't have to grab attention. The objective is to communicate information, not to wow the client. A tasteful and informative brochure in a size that fits easily into the client's file is what you want. The contents should include a statement of your firm's background and experience, qualification sheets describing the people who will be working on the assignment, a current list of references (with names of individuals and their telephone numbers), a statement of the services offered and perhaps a few good reasons for preferring you to other counselors.

An acceptable format for this type of brochure is a 9" x 12" folder with a pocket into which you can insert biographical sheets, references, a cover letter and perhaps a formal proposal. The cover should be simple, well executed and reasonably dignified.

Something to attach to your proposals. The same comments apply. Again, the idea is to communicate necessary information, not to dazzle the eye or overload the mind.

Something to leave on the exhibit table at conventions and conferences. Here, you must make a special effort to stand out from the crowd. This may require an oversized brochure or one in a distinctive format or color combination. While unusual shapes and sizes may be eye-catching, remember that they may be hard to file and use—and may not be appropriate to the image you are otherwise trying to project.

Something to attach to your letters and invoices. This calls for a simple brochure that will fit into a number 10 envelope, roughly 3" x 9". It can take the form of a letter-size sheet of paper folded in threes or a stapled booklet. Again, the idea is to communicate: Who you are, what you do, how you can help. A simple and direct statement is usually best. Brochures of this type also can be used as handouts at conventions and left on the table in your reception area for visitors to take.

Order plenty of brochures. The additional copies won't cost much, and sooner or later you will use them up as long as you can update them by adding inserts or stick-on labels. A few hundred at a time can disappear at conventions; a few thousand can disappear in mailings to fellow members of your professional and business organizations. For best results add a personalized cover letter inviting inquiries.

Reminders. Because people forget, it's wise to remind them now and then about what you do and where you can be found. Among the many ways to do this:

- Thank-you notes
- News clippings and article reprints
- Holiday and birthday greetings
- Newsletters
- Announcements of moves, hires and promotions
- Television and radio appearances
- Business gifts

For more, see Chapter 15.

Getting on the lists. Banks, insurance companies and other frequent purchasers of real estate counseling services maintain lists of qualified experts for their own use and for the benefit of their clients and customers. Find out what it takes to get on these lists and submit the required information. Usually this consists of biographical statements covering your account people, a list of references with names and telephone numbers, a summary of recent jobs with enough specific information to help the client evaluate your capabilities, and a sample report or two. Be sure, before presenting someone else's report to a new client, that you have obtained clearance from the party who paid for it. Often clearance will be given only on the condition that you sanitize the report by eliminating the client's name, any conclusions about value and perhaps the identification of the property.

References:

BOOKS

1. Bly RW: *Create the Perfect Sales Piece.* (New York: John Wiley and Sons) 1985.
2. Cohen W: *The Entrepreneur & Small Business Marketing Problem Solver.* (New York: John Wiley & Sons) 1990.
3. Elam H, Paley N: *Marketing for Nonmarketers,* (New York, Amacom) 1992.
4. Kaumeyer RA: *How to Write and Speak in Business.* (New York: Van Nostrand Reinhold) 1985.
5. Lewis D: *Secrets of Successful Writing, Speaking, and Listening.* (New York: Amacom) 1982.
6. Strunk W, White EB: *The Elements of Style.* (New York: Macmillan) 1972.

PERIODICALS

1. *Business Publishing,* Hitchcock Publishing Co., 191 S. Gary Ave., Carol Stream, IL 60188
2. *Target Marketing,* North American Publishing Co., 401 N. Broad Street, Philadelphia, PA 19108

Part V

Getting The Order

Chapter 18

Selling the Job

Marketing is all well and good for establishing your name and encouraging enquiries, but it's not always enough. At some point, you may have to make a few actual sales.

Sales calls. Many counselors rely heavily on the transom method of getting new business. All this requires is that you sit in your office and wait to see what falls in. Others recognize that it doesn't hurt to go after a new account when things are slow or you want to grow. Some clients simply lack initiative and need prodding. You can consider your approach to them as a favor. Many a client has been left in the wrong hands because a good counselor failed to step forward and say what had to be said.

Sales calls are good for more than business.

The sales call needn't be a disagreeable experience. You don't have to call on strangers unless you're new in town or new to the business and have no connections of your own. Sales calls work best when you have had at least some previous contact and when the call can be at least partly social. You can use the sales call to find out something about the person and the business, to make a good impression and possibly to win a friend. Use the warm-up period to identify common connections and interests. Maybe you share a taste for vintage wines and downhill skiing. Wouldn't it be a shame not to find out?

A few counseling firms use salespeople who are not counseling professionals. Sophisticated clients laugh at such efforts. No full-time salesperson can hope to be as effective as a working counselor who has credentials and knows the field.

Rules for making sales calls. Certain rules apply whether you are calling on the prospect or the prospect is calling on you. The steps are the same as they would be in calling on prospects for legal, medical or accounting business:

1. *Establish yourself as a decent person and an expert.* Until you do, prospective clients won't buy what you're selling.
2. *Qualify the prospect.* Find out as much as you can about the organization and the individual before you make the call; then use the call to find out more. Can they pay the bills? Are they serious about hiring a counselor? Will you have a conflict of interest that prevents you from taking the assignment? Ask

questions to learn the answers and to show your interest in them and their problems. Let prospects know you have done your homework, but don't appear to be conducting a major campaign to get the account. Prospects probably think you ought to be too busy for that, and they may be right. Occasionally, though, persistence with an important prospect does pay off.

3. *Find out what the prospect thinks the problem is.* Encourage the prospective client to spell out the problem in detail. You can ask questions to hasten the process or fill in the blanks but be sure to let the client state the problem before you try to redefine it. Listen for the music as well as the words.

4. *Identify the actual problem—or opportunity.* Ask questions, offer tentative descriptions, probe. This will give you a better understanding of the client's problems and a head start on the solutions. It will also demonstrate your interest. (See Chapter 19 for more on how to define the problem and close the sale.)

5. *Establish the prospect's price range.* How much does the prospect expect to pay for the service? How much do you want? What would the competition charge?

6. *Show how you can solve the problem.* That's what you'll be hired for, if you're hired.

7. *Deal with any objections.* Is the prospect afraid to spend money? Worried that the size of your firm is wrong for the job? Concerned that you will turn the work over to an underling rather than do it yourself? Now is the time to bring out such questions and answer them.

8. *Find out how the client buys services.* Will a purchase order be necessary? Someone else's approval? A formal proposal or a simple authorization letter?

9. *Offer to close.* Tell the prospect you will send or deliver a formal proposal or ask for permission to do so. Make sure all essential elements of the assignment have been discussed and are understood. Satisfy yourself that price and terms are within acceptable ranges for the prospect.

Inquiries. When you get a nibble, whether it comes out of the blue or results from a sales call, respond like a fisherman, not a hunter or warrior. The prospective client is often wary, skeptical of the bait and your trustworthiness. Your chances of being hired are poor if, instead of taking the time to calm and reassure the prospect, you move too quickly to set the hook. Display your concern and sincerity by preparing a thoughtful presentation, asking sensible questions, explaining possible approaches to the problem and showing a genuine sensitivity to his needs.

Too much aggressiveness or vanity at this stage will send the prospect off in search of another counselor. Be careful not to come across as greedy or pompous. You are not a candidate to take over the business but merely to provide a service. What prospects want to hear about at this stage is not your impressive firm but how you can help *them*.

Set the hook first.

If you can show prospects that you are able to meet their needs, you are halfway home. You'll go the rest of the way when you succeed in convincing the people on the other side of the table that you understand the problem, know what to do and deserve their trust. (See Chapter 19.)

Selling against competition. Sometimes selling is like golf: You take your best swing and hit the green or miss the shot and slice off into the rough. Often, though, it's more like a marathon: You give the run your best effort but may have to speed up or slow down in relation to your competitors.

Don't be offended by the notion that you have to compete with other counselors for business, and don't back away from competition. Do put your case in the best light, emphasizing the specific skills, experience, connections and insights that make it possible for you to do a better job than other counselors. That's what's expected and what you're entitled to do. If you don't want to enter the fray, that's OK, too; many counselors prefer to avoid competition and can easily afford to do so.

However, those who are not among this elite group, will need to use all their assets in the race for the business. If you're small and new to the game, emphasize to prospective clients as tactfully as you can that you're wiry, flexible and eager to take charge of the job yourself, unlike the guys who are muscle-bound from other work and will run the job with a bunch of low-level beginners. If you're big, talk about how strong and deep you are compared to the others. If you're in between, show how you strike just the right balance between the big guys and the little ones.

WHAT MAKES PROSPECTS BUY?

While almost any emotion can lie behind a potential client's inquiry, those that most frequently result in counseling assignments are fear, greed and ambition. The prospect is afraid and needs protection, is in trouble and wants to get out of it or sees an opportunity and wants to exploit it. Classic examples are life insurance (basically a fear sale, but the customer's love for family and interest in a prosperous old age also apply), common stocks (a greed sale that also may protect against poverty and inflation fears) and the Empire State Building ("You can own a piece of it! Think how proud your family will be!").

Clients buy other things as well: prestige, friendship, the use of a sounding board (see Chapter 19 for a discussion of hidden agendas).

Most of all, though, they are looking for understanding and results. The counselor who can relieve the client's worries and concerns by solving a serious problem or can show the client how to make a pile of money is the counselor who will command the biggest fees.

Because it's the client's emotional unease—whether it expresses itself as anxiety, guilt, greed or ambition—that triggers the request for counseling, one thing is essential to the sale and the counseling relationship to follow: trust. Without it your technical competence means nothing. The client must feel that he will be safe in your hands, that you won't somehow take advantage of the situation. You must find ways to demonstrate your sincerity, reliability, honesty and openness if the prospect is to become a client. No trust, no counseling relationship—and no sale.

> No trust, no banana.

Questions prospects ask. Even before the initial interview, potential clients will want to know about you so they can decide whether or not you are the person for them. Among the questions you should be prepared to answer:
1. What are your qualifications as a professional?
2. What is your educational background?
3. What professional designations do you hold?
4. What are your areas of special expertise?
5. What experience have you had with problems like mine?
6. Do you have any conflicts of interest that may interfere with this project?
7. How long have you been in the business?
8. What other clients do you have?
9. What references can you offer? (Be prepared to provide names and telephone numbers.)
10. Who will be doing the actual work? If others will be involved, what are their qualifications?
11. Will you supervise the work done by others?
12. Will you see the property yourself?
13. How long do you think it will take to perform the assignment?
14. What will you want me to do in connection with this assignment?
15. What do you think it will cost?
16. How will I be billed?
17. Will you send me a detailed proposal, or should I send you an engagement letter?
18. When litigation is a possibility: Have you or your organization taken a position in some previous matter that would conflict with the positions you will be taking for me?
19. Are you available to start now? If not, when can you begin?

Why they need you. Clients need counselors for many different reasons. The following list is not intended to be exhaustive.

- *Information.* Clients often don't know as much as you do about what's going on in your field because they haven't spent their working lives in real estate, don't make it a point to keep up with new developments or simply aren't exposed to real estate problems as diverse as those encountered by an active counselor. Your access to facts can help them make more informed decisions.
- *Perspective.* The counselor's breadth of experience also is valuable for broadening the client's understanding of real estate matters. A client who is too close to the trees often needs this kind of help and sometimes knows it.
- *Objectivity.* Some problems, including the most important ones, affect us so immediately that we find it hard to judge them correctly. In such cases it's useful to consult a friend or a professional advisor who is not so directly engaged in the problem and has a better chance of approaching it objectively. Real estate counselors are in an excellent position to provide this service.
- *Endorsement.* Clients often need to have their plans and decisions ratified by someone else whose opinion will be respected, much as a borrower whose credit is questionable may want to have someone else co-sign a loan. Lenders routinely demand this kind of endorsement from would-be borrowers whose credibility has not been firmly established. So also may the client's prospective partners, investors or customers.
- *Insurance.* The counselor's investigation and approval of a project may add a desirable margin of safety that is worth paying for. That same margin may be useful later on if the client is attacked for failing to seek a professional opinion before plunging ahead with a plan that turned sour.
- *Economy.* Often the early use of a qualified counselor can spare the client wasted effort or prevent a costly wrong turn. Errors that can be prevented—or economies and successes that are made possible by early counseling—can justify the counselor's fee many times over.
- *Special expertise.* Often the counselor is needed for some special skill that the client or his usual advisors don't have: investment sophistication, local knowledge, operational experience, marketing savvy and the like. The ability to present a position convincingly is one skill that is highly valued; so is the ability to sort out a financial tangle or cure a sick project.
- *Support.* A client who is going through a bad time or is caught up in a sustained endeavor often needs a friend as well as an advisor—an informed person who will listen to his ideas, ask sensible questions, weigh alternatives and help identify the best course of action. Such a person also can provide much-needed psychological support. The counselor often is ideal for this.
- *Adjudication.* Counselors often are called upon to reconcile conflicting positions of two or more parties or to decide who is right. They may be formally cast in the role of arbitrators or simply may be called upon as people of good repute (and perhaps special knowledge) to assist in resolving a conflict.

- *Advocacy.* Clients often need someone to speak for them—someone whose voice will be heeded and whose opinion will be respected by community groups, zoning boards, courts of law and similar bodies.
- *Analytical abilities.* Sorting out the elements of a problem, finding patterns in a confusing sea of data or putting together a structure that makes sense may require the services of a real estate counselor, just as the help of an actuary may be required in setting up a pension plan.
- *Organization.* At times the counselor may be called upon to organize an effort, campaign or project on behalf of an individual, company, community organization or trade group. The task may involve making something positive happen, such as a real estate development or a new legislative act. Or it may involve an attempt to stop something bad from happening, such as a new tax or an unwanted interference with the client's business. Counselors occasionally are asked to organize a mass of data, usually in connection with a lawsuit.
- *Standard setting.* Clients who are planning to buy real estate or real estate services often need help in setting the standards to be met or in drafting a request for proposals that will elicit the kinds of bids they want.
- *Insight.* Clients may be confused, blind to their opportunities or for some other reason unable to see what ought to be seen about their situation. Sometimes a counselor can furnish the missing insight.
- *Connections.* Clients occasionally need access to significant people, companies or institutions. Because counselors often belong to several key networks, their services can be helpful.
- *Supervision.* You may be asked to monitor someone else's performance: an appraiser, a manager, a broker. Who, after all, is better equipped for the job?
- *Evaluation.* You also may be asked to judge and report on how well other people are doing.
- *Asset management.* When you are doing this directly, you are not acting as a counselor but as an asset manager. Nevertheless, counselors do regularly assist in asset management, helping with portfolio design, property selection, management supervision and other services.
- *Negotiation.* A counselor who acts as the client's agent in negotiations is not acting as a counselor and is bound by the law of agent and principal. More often the counselor is called upon to assist the client or some other party in the negotiating process, providing information and advice. Some people consider it counseling when the counselor accepts the role of agent or broker on a fixed-fee basis. If you take such assignments, be sure you understand the legal implications and do not violate your state's laws governing brokerage services and commissions.

Opportunities for counseling. Certain situations regularly call for counseling skills and services; learn to recognize them. The aroma they exude is the smell of opportunity.

1. *Unhappy owner.* Something is wrong; maybe you can fix it.

2. *Unhappy lender.* Ditto, especially when you know how to do successful workouts.
3. *Ignorance.* A little research or a knowledgeable opinion may put the client's mind at ease and possibly even solve the problem.
4. *Trouble.* Who is better equipped to recognize and shoot it?
5. *Disagreement.* You could be just the person to settle the dispute, informally or through arbitration.
6. *Litigation.* Lawyers need you as much as you need them. Even the threat of a lawsuit may bring them to your door, asking for advice, research and testimony.
7. *War.* If it comes to that, there's a need for an old campaigner's advice. Often there's also a need for staff support in the usual four functional areas of the campaign organization: personnel, intelligence, operations and logistics.

Things prospective clients dislike. Whether by instinct or from experience, clients usually will pass up a counselor who is:

1. *Too busy.* The client wants a counselor who has time to listen, to think through the problem and to deal with it correctly.
2. *Too beholden.* A counselor who is known for excessive ties to one bank, one investor or one politician seldom will be trusted as completely as one who works for many clients and maintains a high degree of independence.
3. *Too cheap.* Wise clients don't like come-ons, and seldom appreciate counselors who undervalue themselves.
4. *Too vague about fees and schedules.* Clients like to know what they will have to pay and when they can expect what they pay for.
5. *Too greedy.* They don't like to overpay, either.
6. *Too pompous.* Counselors who try too hard to persuade clients of their importance and abilities often produce the opposite impression.
7. *Too talkative.* While some clients enjoy and appreciate a good gabfest, most feel that a counselor who says too much about the affairs of other clients will be equally indiscreet about their own.
8. *Too risky.* A counselor who has been publicly disciplined or indicted for a serious offense is at a disadvantage. So is a counselor whose business is on the verge of going under or whose psyche is visibly breaking down.
9. *Too touchy.* Nobody likes to deal with a paranoid or to pussyfoot around an unnecessarily sensitive or aggressive advisor.
10. *Overconfident.* A decent amount of humility inspires trust. On the other hand, clients tend to dislike too much of it.
11. *Insecure.* The counselor should at least appear to believe in the quality and relevance of the services he provides.
12. *Incompetent or obviously biased.* Enough said.

Sales pitches not to use. The big danger is exaggeration. Don't use hype. It may be OK at the Superbowl, but not in a client conference.

Clients and prospects won't like the con artist's approaches, either. For the record only (not for use) here are some of the classics:

"Donald Trump bought this one yesterday."

"There hasn't been an opportunity like this since . . ."

"For you, this is a gold mine."

"This is a no-risk proposition."

"You'd better act now; this is your only chance."

"I've got the inside dope on this (deal, person, opportunity)."

"Only a fool (coward, stick-in-the-mud) would pass this up."

The worldly-wise seldom take calls from out-of-town solicitors who may be difficult to reach if something goes wrong. They also are wary of sales pitches that arrive by messenger instead of through the mail, which reduces the sender's risk of a jail sentence for mail fraud. Pretentious company names that poach on the established reputations of other companies (Dun & Bradstreet, Reuters, IBM), are another danger signal.

References

BOOKS

1. Brownstone DM: *Successful Selling for Small Business.* (John Wiley and Sons) 1978.
2. Evetts J: *Seven Pillars of Sales Success.* (New York: Sterling Publishing) 1990.
3. Farber BJ and Wycoff J: *Break-through Selling.* (Englewood Cliffs, NJ: Prentice-Hall) 1992.
4. Girard J: *How to Close Every Sale.* (New York: Warner Books) 1989.
5. Nierenberg GI: *Negotiating the Big Sale.* (Homewood, IL: Business One Irwin) 1992.
6. Rackham N: *Major Account Sales Strategy.* (New York: McGraw Hill) 1992.
7. Silver D: *Close Any Deal.* (Englewood Cliffs, NJ: Prentice-Hall) 1992.

CHAPTER 19

The Initial Consultation

FIRST BLUSH

Clients generally see what they expect to see at the first meeting. The counselor who is thought to be powerful, successful and hard to reach will be approached with a respect that almost guarantees a favorable impression. Even if the counselor turns out to be modest and friendly, the client usually will attribute these qualities to a praiseworthy humility, not to any constitutional defect.

All the same, make an effort to look your best when you first meet a potential client. Wear appropriate clothing and try to wear it well. Ensure that your office, however overloaded and crowded, appears to be well organized and functional, if not elegant and neat. Show by your stance, expression and words that you are interested in the client's good opinion of you and your office as well as what he has to say.

Ideally, the initial meeting should take place in your office, where you are comfortable and where the client or prospect can get a feel for the way you do business. In the client's office, or on neutral ground, you may not be at a disadvantage—the client may feel more at ease—but you won't have the opportunity to show off your people and facilities.

Wherever the meeting is held, be sure to do three things before you become too deeply involved with a client. First write down the exact names of the client, the people you will be dealing with and any other parties who may have a stake in the assignment, such as lenders and major tenants. While you're at it, also write down the client's address and any relevant telephone numbers. A good "new client" form will help you to remember who is who and where to send the bill.

Get the facts early.

Second, and even more important, check your memory and your records for possible conflicts of interest involving the parties whose names you have just taken (see Chapter 23). Such conflicts may be legal—you can't properly take a client's side against one of your own partners, for example—or merely business conflicts, in which you risk angering another client or in some way hurting your business interests by accepting the assignment. Consider all such conflicts carefully before you proceed and don't hesitate to ask for the client's thoughts about them—or to call your lawyer.

Third, ask yourself whether this is a client you really want. Prospective clients undoubtedly know a lot about you. How much do you know about them?

Once you have decided you can get down to business with a prospective client, you can begin to establish rapport. Take a few minutes to find out about the other person's interests and reactions; let him get to know you a little bit, too. Both sides will appreciate the chance to break the ice. To help this process along, it's generally a good idea to leave your desk and sit down with the client at a table or in a lounge-chair setting that reduces the formality of the occasion. Refreshments—coffee, tea, soda pop, chicken soup, juices—will make it even easier to loosen up.

It's important at this first meeting to establish at least some degree of mutual trust and liking. This is not the time to spill the beans about your kidney troubles and your failing memory, but it doesn't hurt to show a few weaknesses (as well as a degree of professional competence) at the first interview. People like to feel that you're human. Show enough of yourself to make the client aware that you are a person as well as a professional and try to get the client to do the same for you. In this way you may be not only establishing a client relationship but also a friendship that can pay dividends over the years.

This is definitely the time to demonstrate your listening abilities. Give the client every opportunity to say whatever needs to be said. Probe gently to get at any hidden agendas and show a proper interest in the client's concerns. Try to get past the client's symptoms to the underlying ailment. You're the doctor, and it's up to you to find out what's wrong. How else can you treat the right problem? (For more on this point, see Chapters 2, 18 and 22.)

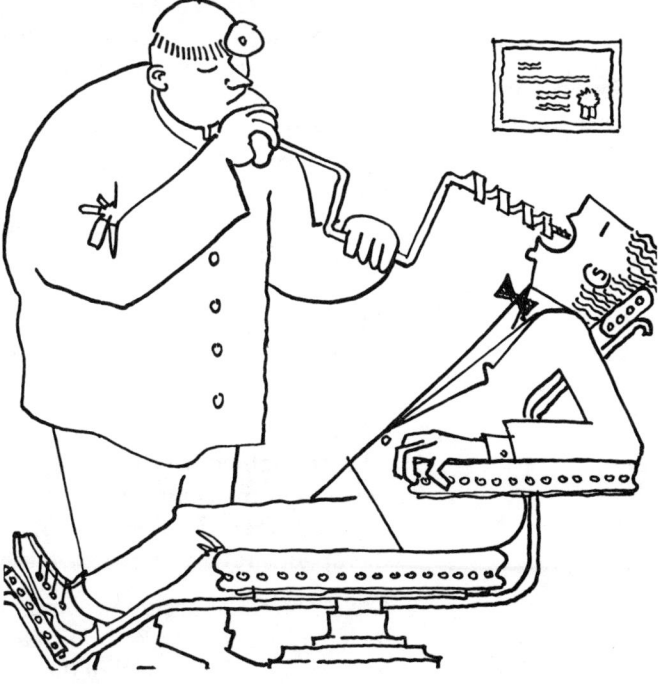

The first meeting might better be called what doctors call their first encounter with a new patient: the initial consultation. The term consultation acknowledges what really goes on in the doctor's office, which is the diagnosis or, in difficult cases, the first step toward arriving at a diagnosis. What happens at this consultation determines what will happen next: tests, on-the-spot treatment, prescriptions, referral to a specialist or a farewell handshake.

As a real estate counselor you are in the same situation; you are already counseling the client even though you have not reached an agreement with him for payment. In that respect, at least, doctors are smarter than we are; they charge for the first meeting whether or not further work follows.

Freebies. Should the first meeting be free to the client? Maybe, if the prospects of future business make it worthwhile to you, or if for some valid reason the client feels entitled to a chunk of your professional time without paying for it. Unfortunately, many people don't recognize that you are as much entitled to a fee for the first appointment as a brain surgeon. After all, you aren't offering a contingent fee arrangement to people who don't have the money for a lawyer.

Don't let yourself be induced to quote prices before the right moment arrives. You're still at the feeling-out stage, not yet ready to talk business. If pressed, you can say that your practice operates and charges like a law or accounting firm, with appropriate rates for different tasks and different people, and that you'll be able to provide a better estimate after you've learned more about the problem.

Remember that you are not facing someone who is already a client. The meeting therefore, at least in part, is a selling opportunity. Make good use of it. If the prospective client wasn't already interested in you, he wouldn't be sitting there. Chapters 16 and 20 explore the best methods of making the sale, closing the deal and converting the customer into a client. Don't be afraid to use these approaches. Your doctor does, and for your own good.

THE HIDDEN AGENDA

What the client asks for doesn't always tell you what the situation demands. An important part of the first meeting is the diagnosis: sorting out not merely what the client wants or needs in a practical sense, but also what emotions are driving him and how they should be addressed.

Explore the prospect's motives.

We are all designed by nature—and by eons of evolutionary development—to experience certain feelings and to respond to them as promptly as we can. We get hungry, we eat; we get angry, we fight—or at least feel like shouting or waving our arms and jumping up and down; we get anxious or fearful, we hunker down or run away. That's not a complete list, but you get the idea.

It pays to listen for these feelings, as they lie behind the client's stated purposes in calling on you for help. While almost any feeling can lead to a request for your services, some are apparent in almost every counseling situation.

Anxiety. The client is worried about something, usually the risk of making a mistake but sometimes the danger of losing something substantial—money, job, position in the community. Your recognition of the legitimacy of these feelings and your identification of a practical way to alleviate them can act as a sort of therapeutic relief. If you can get the client off the hot seat, you'll have a booster.

Guilt. The client has done something wrong or failed to meet an obligation and feels guilty about it. You can relieve the guilt by addressing the problem while accepting the legitimacy of the feelings in a nonjudgmental way.

Loyalty. The client wants to do a good job for company, community, country, profession, perhaps family and children. It's up to you to help.

Anger. Sometimes the client needs a way to get even or simply to attack someone who is perceived to be an enemy. At other times the client just needs an outlet for free-floating anger. This kind of situation can be dangerous unless it falls into a well-recognized, socially acceptable pattern, as, for example, when the client is involved in a dispute before the courts and you are asked to provide litigation support and testimony. Even in such situations be extra-careful if the client is carrying around an emotional overload. It may be dumped on you.

Love. Watch out for this one, too. A client who wants to do good out of love—for church, company, spouse, principles—may take offense if you do not share these feelings with sufficient enthusiasm.

Vanity. Though emotionally linked to anxiety, vanity can stand on its own as a motivator. Clients want to look good, to impress others, to avoid having their fragile self-images dented or shattered. They may feel they have to maintain unbroken strings of successes or accomplish superhuman tasks. The counselor is asked to support them in their beliefs, not challenge them. Flattery may be indicated; service may be appreciated; competition is always a no-no. The mere fact that you or your firm enjoy a certain amount of prestige may be sufficient to attract this kind of client.

Ambition. The client may be interested in fortune, fame or the next move up the corporate ladder. Can you provide the boost?

Greed. An eye for a bargain or a lucrative opportunity can bring the client to a counselor for many kinds of services. That's fine, but don't let his greed prevent you from collecting your fee.

Fear. When catastrophe threatens, people look for help. If you can give that help to them, they'll be properly grateful. But be sure to negotiate your fee before you solve the problem, and don't get caught up in someone else's disaster.

Confusion. Your objectivity and clear-headedness will let you sort out the tangle that has brought the client to your door. The rest is a matter of analysis, communication and patience.

CLIENTS YOU DON'T NEED

It isn't only the client who doesn't pay on time that you may want to reject. The laws are beginning to close in on your freedoms but—at least for now—you may still have the right to refuse any client who strikes you as unappealing or dangerous. Your office is not an emergency room, and you haven't yet sworn a Hippocratic oath.

Among the high-risk types you may want to turn down as clients are these:

1. *Neurotic, psychotic or hostile personalities.* If they are obvious as such even to your untrained eye, they stand a good chance of giving you trouble later on.

2. *Litigious people and other troublemakers.* A lawsuit can cost you more than you can afford, even if you win.

3. *People with hidden agendas they won't disclose.* Why let yourself be used?

4. *People with mobster connections.* Don't get entangled.

5. *Con artists, liars, dopers, lushes and people who are always right.* They can make your life miserable and seldom offer much in return. Who needs them?

6. *Known enemies of your present clients.* Whose side are you on?

7. *Freeloaders.* Some people will hire you for one job and feel entitled to ask questions forever after without being billed. Others won't even give you the first job. In either case draw the line quickly. Their doctors won't let them in the office without expecting payment; why should you?*

8. *Frauds.* Don't get caught up in somebody else's crimes.

How to say no? Sometimes it isn't easy. Powerful and intimidating would-be clients can be hard to refuse. A calm but firm statement that you have a conflict may be sufficient, or you can plead overwork. Better yet is to ask for a big retainer. After all, wouldn't you really rather be on the golf course or rearranging your files?

DEFINING THE PROBLEM AND CLOSING THE SALE

Once you have established some degree of rapport and learned what a prospective client thinks he wants, the next step is to figure out what the actual problem is. Clients often find it difficult to articulate their needs. They may ask for an appraisal report or a feasibility study when what they really want is help in pricing and marketing a property or deciding whether or not they should buy the site next door. Your responsibility as a counselor is to help them sort out the true requirements of the case.

Identifying these requirements may take a little time and a certain amount of sensitive probing, but the time and care you spend at this stage of the counseling process will be amply rewarded by the time and expense you save later. Try to identify all the issues correctly from the beginning. Be patient; test your ideas by watching the client's reactions to them, and listen attentively for facts, feelings and hidden agendas.

---

*Because there are so many providers of unpaid services in the real estate world, some freeloaders find it difficult to believe that you actually insist upon payment for your work. It may be worthwhile to treat them politely in some cases. Remind them gently that free advice is seldom worth more than it costs, that your time is valuable and that you are not in the business merely for your pleasure. If you are qualified to furnish counseling services, you are entitled to payment. Be reasonable, be patient, be nice if you must, but be firm.

Defining the problem is often the most valuable service you perform for clients. When you can, charge for it.

TYPES OF PROBLEMS

A prospective client's problem may be simple and direct:

> "I want to get an appraisal that will convince my banker to lend me $1,000,000."
>
> "Do me a feasibility study for this project. I want to know if it makes economic sense."
>
> "I need a marketing plan so I can get the best price for my property."
>
> "Help me to figure out the best financial structure for my purchase."
>
> "I need a development plan for this business park to help me see where I'm going."
>
> "Make me an office market study for a project that will come on stream in three years."

When the client and the counselor know exactly what they mean by the terms they use, they can quickly arrive at a common definition for the problem. The counselor, nevertheless, should make sure that both parties understand the boundaries as well as the substance of the problem. If the client requires a feasibility study, for example, both parties should agree on the market area that will be explored and the techniques that will be used as well as the nature of the project that is envisioned.

When examining a prospective client's problem, ask questions until you are satisfied that you have the answers you must have to do a good job. Try to elicit as much relevant information as possible. "Tell me about your project" is a better question than "How many square feet will your project contain?" although you may have to ask for that information as well if the client doesn't volunteer it.

Other problems are less easy to describe and define:

> "What went wrong?"
>
> "How can I get out of this mess?"
>
> "Is my manager doing a good job?"
>
> "What should I do with my land?"
>
> "Where should I put my money?"
>
> "How should I plan for the time when my tenant's lease expires?"

Patience pays.

Questions like these require discussion and thought before the counselor can establish a valid work program. Because the work program is a prerequisite to the job budget and proposal, the counselor must be careful to spell out the elements of the problem and make sure that the client agrees with the approach. The answer to "Where should I put my money?"—to take one example—

requires that the counselor know about the client's assets, liabilities, income, expenses, aspirations, abilities, health, business entanglements, family situation, life expectancy and tolerance for risk.

STEPS IN PROBLEM DEFINITION

Here are the steps you'll be taking to discover the nature and scope of a prospective client's needs:

1. Establish the client's goals.
2. Determine the available resources.
3. Consider the constraints that limit what can be done: physical, legal, ethical, organizational, chronological, political, psychological, economic, financial.
4. Explore the possibilities.
5. Define the problem.

CLOSING

After you have won the prospect's confidence and defined the problem, you'll still need authorization to do the work. This is called closing. It is a familiar topic at sales meetings and in real estate publications.

There's no point in making the offer to close before the prospective client is ready to do so. Watch for the signs that he is prepared to go ahead: nods of agreement, indications of an awareness that you really do understand the problem and how to deal with it, a long pause. You'll know when it's time.

The key to closing lies in the invitation. Find a way to open the door sweetly and let the prospect know it's time to formalize the work relationship. "Are we about ready to talk about the next step?" is one way to get things moving. Another way is to suggest the next step and ask for the prospect's agreement: "It seems to me that what I ought to do now is..." (Chapter 19 suggests other ways of moving toward closing.)

How to say things to clients. Ease into the offer by making sure the client concurs with your assessments of the problem and has some notion of how it can be solved. You can then propose a course of action: "It seems to me we have a good grasp of the problem. Here's what I think we ought to do next... Does that make sense to you?" If the answer is positive, you can respond: "All right. I'll prepare a written proposal that spells it all out, and then we'll sit down together to go over the details."

When the client's organization is large and its purchasing procedures are unknown to you, try something like: "How does your organization like to process this sort of thing?" or "Whose OK will you have to get for this?" The person to whom you are speaking may not have a ready answer, but your question at least gets the process started.

There's nothing magical about any of these words. Use your own, adapted to the situation. It's important, though, to state the proposed course of action firmly when the time comes: "This is what I plan to do," not "Would you like me to . . .?" If the client disagrees, you'll know it soon enough.

Follow-through. At this stage it's essential to move quickly and get the written proposal in the prospective client's hands as soon as possible. Get on the stick. Clients appreciate promptness in a counselor, especially at the beginning of the relationship. (For more on proposal writing, see Chapter 21.)

References

BOOKS

1. Holtz H: *The Consultant's Guide to Proposal Writing.* (New York: John Wiley and Sons) 1986.
2. Johnson S: *Yes or No: The Guide to Better Decisions.* (New York: Harper Collins) 1992.
3. Nierenberg GI: *Negotiating the Big Sale.* (Homewood, IL: Business One Irwin) 1992.
4. Rackham N: *Major Account Sales Strategy.* (New York: McGraw Hill) 1992.
5. Silver AD: *Close Any Deal.* (Englewood Cliffs, NJ: Prentice-Hall) 1992.

Chapter 20

Fees, Budgets and Bids

SETTING FEES

In ancient China, the Zen masters' first rule of Buddhism was: "No work, no eat." From this rule we can derive the first principle of real estate counseling: "No pay, no work."

HOW MUCH?

When setting your fees, you need to consider your costs as well as typical levels of compensation in the counseling market. The main thing is to set your fees so you will be rewarded properly for your valuable time. This is for the client's sake as well as your own; if the pay is too little, you'll be tempted to cut corners on the job, which won't help him any. Poor earnings also can lead to your malnutrition and brain damage. Worse, they tend to devalue your services and hurt your reputation as an advisor.

Ask yourself how much you think the job is worth. Is the property big, rare or complicated? Are the issues of vital importance? Does the assignment require special expertise or a rapid turnover? If so, the job can't be done by every Tom, Dick, Harry or Jane and should be priced accordingly. If on the other hand it is a bread-and-butter assignment almost anyone can handle, the work can be priced more conservatively.

If you don't trust your own judgment about pricing, consult others: institutional buyers of counseling services, fellow counselors, other clients, perhaps your spouse. Until they graduate from grammar school and lose perspective, your children can provide valuable counsel. Sometimes the best person to ask is the client: What does he expect to pay? How much can he afford? The answers may be more generous than you think.

As a practical matter the counseling market often sets the level of compensation. Certain types of analytical studies have well-established price tags. The best sources of information about them are not necessarily your fellow counselors, who may be competing with you for a particular job. Much better are frequent purchasers of counseling services such as bankers, insurance companies and pension fund managers. Another good source is your own law firm, which, if you have chosen it well, knows everything.

Remember these three essential rules for setting fees:

1. Never charge much too much.

2. Never charge less than you can get.

3. Charge more for hurry-up and disagreeable or dangerous work.

DRAFTING THE BUDGET

Unless a job is open-ended or inconsequential, it deserves to have a time-and-expense budget. Who will be involved? How many hours will be spent? What outside experts will have to be paid? How much of a cushion should be allowed for mistakes?

If you have a project manager who will be responsible for conducting the job, have him develop the budget and accept responsibility for it. A problem with this option is that the project manager may overestimate the job to reduce the danger of being criticized for overruns. You can control this risk by reviewing each item with the manager before you approve the budget.

Budgeting requires careful consideration of *all* the costs involved in a job, including indirect costs such as office overhead. Your accountant can help you identify cost centers and allocate these costs properly. It's up to you to remember that they are incurred whether you get them back or not.

The Federal government, particularly the Small Business Administration of the Department of Commerce, provides excellent assistance to budgeters. So do the many governmental departments that solicit proposals from the private sector. As an example, Form 60 of the Office of Management and Budget (Approval No. 29-R0184) lists the information required by OMB from would-be providers of research and development.

Some jobs are easy to budget; others aren't. The less experience you have, or the more unusual the job, the greater should be your allowance for errors and accidents. You may want to make specific provision for contingencies, although some budgeters accomplish the same purpose by inflating the time estimate to leave a little room.

The budget will be useful in project management as well as in bidding. It also will help you decide what kinds of jobs to pursue in your selling and marketing efforts. Why chase work that won't make a profit—or that won't make as much profit as other kinds?

SAMPLE PROJECT BUDGET

Job number:
Job title:
Client name:
Project name:
Location:
Project manager:
Proposed staff:
Outside contractors:

TIME CHARGES:

Consultant A _____	(#)___ hrs. at $_____ =	$
Consultant B _____	(#)___ hrs. at $_____ =	$
Consultant C _____	(#)___ hrs. at $_____ =	$
Total		$_____

SUPERVISION $_____

JOB EXPENSES:

Travel	$
Lodging	$
Meals	$
Auto rentals	$
Telefax	$
Toll telephone	$
Maps and plats	$
Photography	$
Messenger Service	$
Computer time	$
Secretarial	$
Printing and Duplicating	$
Total	$_____

OUTSIDE CONTRACTORS

Name:	$
Service:	
Name:	$
Service:	
Name:	$
Service:	
Total	$_____
TOTAL DIRECT COSTS	$_____

INDIRECT COSTS:

(rent, heat and air conditioning, janitorial, insurance, stationery, telephone, incidental, duplicating and fax, library, maintenance, parking, licenses, taxes, memberships, contributions, advertising, public relations, secretarial, general administration, depreciation)

at ____ % of direct costs $_____

TOTAL $_____

BIDDING

Clients want to know how much you expect to charge for your work even before you know exactly what they want done. Some clients are merely curious and will hire you, or not, regardless of the amount you quote. Others care more about money and may even be soliciting bids from other firms.

What will the market bear?

With merely curious clients all you have to do is appear to be reasonable. Use your own common sense and that of your colleagues. How much would a person ordinarily expect to pay for the service? Is that amount consistent with the importance of the problem and the benefits to be reaped? Can the client afford it? Is the job worth it? Will the client's accountant or stockholders find it out of line?

Competitive bidding. With clients who are seeking bids from you and other competitors, you may have to sharpen your pencil. In such cases you should always prepare a budget and review it with care. Check the going prices for similar services and in general follow the procedures described earlier under the heading *How much?*

You soon will learn that some clients buy only on the basis of price, while others care more about the quality of the work and the reputation of the provider. You can disregard price buyers unless you are a mass-producer indifferent to professional standards. The better clients will care about *you* at least as much as they care about the price you quote. Spell out your special qualifications, describe your approach, explain how you expect to meet the client's needs and show that your price is justified. Often your bid will be accepted.

Try to find out beforehand how many bidders the client is soliciting for proposals. If the list is long, you may want to take a pass; why get lost in the crowd? If the list is short, see if you can find out about the other bidders. Are they at, above or below your level of quality and performance? Tailor your bid accordingly.

Don't be shy about asking what kind of budget the client has in mind, even in a bidding situation. If your bid is too far below the amount the client expects, he may consider it to be an indication that you don't appreciate the demands of the job; if it's too high, the client may cross your name off his bidder's list. If the budget itself is too small, or you suspect your chances are slim because there are too many bidders, this is the best time to find out.

Some bids are informal, given orally (dangerous except with established clients) or in a brief letter. A letter can work well when all the prospective client wants to know is whether your figure is competitive and affordable, leaving the drafting of the engagement letter until later on. Safer and better in most circumstances, however, is a formal proposal that spells out all the details (see Chapter 21), though there is always the risk that the prospective client will use your letter to shop around for a lower bid.

It's always a good idea to set a time limit for accepting your bid, both to stimulate a prompt response and to protect yourself against cost increases. A limit of 30 days isn't unreasonable. Sometimes you may want one even shorter.

Regular clients. Good clients—the ones who keep coming back, pay on time and appreciate your work—deserve special treatment. Keep a record of the jobs you do for them and the amounts you charge. As long as your charges for new jobs fit your historical pattern, the client is likely to remain happy. If you are forced to increase your charges significantly, thereby raising eyebrows and encouraging disagreeable thoughts, you may want to take the client to lunch and explain the reasons for the increase. Let him know that you want to be fair and will reduce the bill if you can cut costs.

In the long run you may find it practical to undercharge on some jobs and make up the deficiency on others. Some clients would rather keep the bills within a relatively narrow range even though the amount of work varies from job to job. If your relationship with a client is sound, you can often accommodate this preference.

Some counselors are inclined to charge new clients a little less than the assignment is worth in the hopes of pinning down the job or at least gaining the client's attention. A better policy is to quote a little *higher* in such cases, for two reasons:

1. You don't want your good clients to find out that you are charging others less than you charge them; and
2. Clients need training. If you underquote on the first job, they will expect similar underquotes on subsequent work. A correct estimate on the first assignment lets them know right away what they should think you're worth.

NEGOTIATING THE TERMS

Everything you know about negotiation can be useful in working out your professional contracts. If you don't know enough about negotiation, learn it. Excellent books (see the References) and seminars are available to help you.

There is one important difference between negotiating in the counseling situation and negotiating with a stranger to buy a car. Because you wish to work for the client as an advisor and guide, you can never remain completely at arm's length. Negotiate with that client almost as you would with a family member or a friend. You can't risk interfering with the trust relationship on which counseling depends.

Not your enemies.

So be friendly, be fair, be as open as you can in discussing fees and fee arrangements. Offer choices. Explain why you must charge what you charge and get paid when you are supposed to. But don't forget that you are in business and are negotiating for money that's important to you, your firm and your family. It's your right and duty to strike the best bargain you can without compromising the counseling relationship.

You don't want to begin any negotiation until you have enough information about the other party. You also don't want to start with a bad attitude. Be cheerful, confident, worthy of a fair shake and entitled to your principles. You'll do better, and the client will like you better for it.

Start, if you possibly can, in a favorable setting. You're probably safest in your own office where your confidence is highest. An experienced counselor, however, can do equally well or even better in the client's office where the client will be more at ease and his guard may be down.

Wherever the meeting may be held, try to ensure that the surroundings are uncluttered and tranquil, that there will be no interruptions and that the furniture will be comfortable enough (if too comfortable, the parties will tend to slow down and may get sleepy). Best is a table to spread out the papers and lightweight chairs that people can move around to suit their comfort. A few toys on the table may help to put the participants in the right mood.

The discussion generally starts with a warming-up and feeling-out session (see Chapter 19 on the opening stages of the first meeting). Once that has been completed, the negotiation proper begins when you make an offer to do the work for a stated price. The response you get from the client then determines the direction of the conversation.

Sometimes it pays to offer a basic product that can easily be modified, as car dealers do, and then focus the discussion on options. This type of negotiation reduces tension and keeps the client in a buying frame of mind. Be careful, though, to protect the essential elements of the assignment. You don't want to sell the client a car that has been so trimmed down it won't run.

If you sense that you're going to be in a bargaining situation, keep your first quote a little high to leave some room for negotiating. It's all right to back down when the client offers a good reason, such as that the price is too high for his budget. When you must lower your price, though, be sure to do it in the right way: Look for tasks that can be eliminated, deadlines that can be eased or payments that can be speeded up to justify the price reductions. Ask the client to give something up, too. Any car salesman or building contractor can show you how this process works.

Negotiate the entire deal, if you can: tasks to be performed, terms of payment, graphics and photos, number of copies of the report to be delivered, deadlines, special conditions. Aim toward a written contract that will specify what happens if something should go wrong—death, incompetency, or bankruptcy, for example—before anything actually does go awry. Get the biggest starting payment you can, such as a third to a half of the total fee, in a lump-sum contract or an advance on a periodic-payment contract.

Close the negotiation on a friendly note after you are sure the client is satisfied with the arrangements. After all, the contract still must be written or rewritten and signed. More importantly, you will be working with the client through the course of the job and perhaps on future assignments. You don't want him to be thinking at the outset that you're careless.

Things to negotiate for. Following are some worthwhile items to try for in your negotiations:

- Good fees
- Reasonable deadlines
- 50% payment in advance (100% if client is questionable)
- Progress payments that keep you a month ahead
- Extra money for good results
- Additional charges for work not originally contemplated
- Full reimbursement for job-related expenses
- Convenient starting date
- Timely access to the properties
- Prompt delivery of relevant information by the client
- Relief from deadlines in unusual circumstances
- Fixed number of meetings on convenient dates
- Prohibition against using your work in public securities offerings
- Protection from liability for errors that are not your fault, including environmental and toxic-substance matters

Deposits and staging.

PAYMENT ARRANGEMENTS

Get as much money as possible in your pocket *before* you start work; 50% is not out of line and is acceptable to many clients. For out-of-town jobs or for clients whose good faith or ability to pay is in question, you can insist on 100% up front.

If the job is likely to extend over a long period, ask for staged payments. Try to schedule the payments so you are always a little ahead of the client and will receive enough to cover your costs if the job is discontinued for any reason. Clients may reasonably ask for a schedule that lets them withhold 10% or so from each payment until the job is finished to their satisfaction, as construction buyers usually do, but you should resist this option.

Frequent customers and large institutions may not be willing to pay in advance, preferring to wait until the work is completed and found satisfactory. Some clients, including many public bodies, will force you to wait even longer. Unless you are willing to play banker, and sometimes least-favored creditor in a bankruptcy, approach such situations with caution.

Time and expenses. Most counselors work by the hour or day, charging fixed fees when they can. Hourly rates of $50 to $500 are common, with the higher rates commanded only by senior counselors in major cities. Court time and special services can run higher. Some counselors charge only by the day or half day, making no adjustment for smaller units of time. John Robert White of New York City, one of the most respected counselors in the industry, makes it a rule to charge half days at 60% of the daily rate, a practice worth emulating.

Example:

Consultant's yearly earnings:	$60,000
Payroll taxes and other direct costs at 33 1/3%:	$20,000
Total	$80,000

Productive time (this is a reasonably productive consultant): 1,600 hours/year

Cost per billable hour: $80,000/1600 = $50/hr

Billable rate: 50 x 3.2 = $160/hr

Make hourly rates high enough. Ask yourself what would happen if you doubled the rate at which you are now selling your precious time. How many clients would you lose? Are they clients you care about?

Hourly rates can easily be shopped. Check with your accounting firm, your law firm and your friends in the consulting field to see what the going rates are. If your people and reputation are better than theirs, you can charge more. Cynics will tell you that shops with low hourly rates use faster clocks anyway.

If you insist on relating hourly rates to costs, a good rule of thumb is that the hourly rates should be at least triple the direct payroll cost of the person involved. A lower multiplier can be used if the person's time is nearly 100% billable, but that is seldom the case. Counseling personnel have to spend a certain amount of time attending meetings, reading trade journals and in other ways keeping up-to-date and minding their individual stores.

Out-of-pocket expenses for travel, lodging, meals and incidentals are usually reimbursable under time-and-expenses contracts. So, often, are computer time, toll telephone calls, maps, photographs and similar items. Some firms also expect payment for secretarial and administrative costs and for general supervision, which may be justified if hourly rates are set accordingly.

Fixed fees. Clients generally would like to know what the total cost will be before you start, not after you finish. For that reason many clients prefer fixed fees or at least a cap on your total *per diem* charges. Fixed fees may be inclusive or may provide for reimbursement of expenses.

A fixed fee can mean extra profits for your firm if you have good people and manage the job properly. But it also can mean a loss if you underbudget, so plan with care. Avoid caps if you can; offer the client, if you must, the choice between hourly rates and a fixed fee, pointing out that a cap is one-sided, as you bear all the risk of a cost overrun and have no offsetting hope of an extra profit.

If your fee is fixed, be sure to allow for the extra costs associated with urgent jobs or those that require greater-than-usual responsibility. A rush job or an especially delicate job is worth more money.

Staged and phased fees. Many counseling fees are quoted in stages. Tasks and limits are described for each stage, and prices attached. When the contract allows it, clients like the freedom this manner of payment gives them; they may stop paying when they feel they have received enough or if they become dissatisfied with the counselor's work. Counselors like the phased fee as a way to get things started without asking the client to undertake a big commitment.

The first phase may run only a few thousand dollars, usually for a preliminary investigation to determine whether a larger project is justified. If the results are positive, later phases may cost much more; if negative, the client has learned what he needs to know without wasting large amounts of money.

Value billing. Like accountants, counselors love to debate the wisdom of value billing. Some feel they should charge only for the time they spend on the job without regard to the results they achieve. This helps, they say, to guarantee professional objectivity and to prevent the advisor from becoming overly entangled in the client's affairs. Others believe that the value they add through their services should be recognized financially.

Value billing sometimes is charged at a percentage of asset value, profit, cost recovery or some other base. Be careful not to structure it in a way that is likely to bias your judgment or interfere with your responsibilities to the client. You don't want to be accused of either unethical behavior or excessive greed.

Percentage fees, and other fees keyed to some base amount, can be set at a flat rate or on a sliding scale. The percentage may kick in only after a threshold is reached. Sometimes the rate goes up as the magnitude increases, creating the opportunity for a substantial profit. This arrangement can be in the client's interest if the higher fee corresponds to a bigger gain for the client as well, so don't rule it out automatically.

There are strong arguments both pro and con on the subject of value billing. Consult your own belly-button on this issue or solicit the opinions of your principal clients. If you, or they, feel that value billing is a good idea, then you can explore the idea further, trying to work out formulas for compensation that will reward you properly without interfering with your professional objectivity. If on the other hand you sense a certain chilliness when the topic is raised, you may want to back off quickly and resume your conservative old ways.

Retainers. Many clients are willing to put a counselor on retainer in the hope of getting preferred service while barring him from working for the client's competitors. Counselors like these arrangements because they help to stabilize revenues. They also encourage the client to call often with questions and problems.

The retainer agreement usually stipulates that the counselor will keep the full amount regardless of the services rendered, but may charge more if circumstances warrant, or renegotiate the agreement. Contracts may run for a year or longer, but are usually cancellable on reasonable notice. Whatever the deal, it's a good idea to get the first month's payment in advance.

References

BOOKS

1. Goozner C: *Business Mathematics The Easy Way.* (New York, Barrons Educational Series) 1991.
2. Finkler SA: *Finance and Accounting.* (Englewood Cliffs, NJ: Prentice-Hall) 1992.
3. Jorgensen E: *Successful Real Estate Sales Agreements.* (Burlingame, CA: Axiom) 1986.
4. Livingstone JL: *The Portable MBA in Finance and Accounting.* (New York: John Wiley and Sons) 1992.
5. Siegel JG, et al: *The McGraw Hill Pocket Guide to Business Finance.* (New York: McGraw Hill) 1992.

Chapter 21

The Proposal

WRITING THE PROPOSAL

Once the problem has been defined and the client has been prepared, the counselor is in a position to draft a formal proposal that forms the basis of the counseling contract. While it doesn't have to be elaborate, the proposal should be attractive and look professional. It should be a reasonably detailed document that tells the client what to expect and gives the counselor some degree of protection against future complaints about mistaken or inadequate performance. The document accordingly should be drafted with care and, when practical, reviewed by legal counsel.

A well-drafted proposal defines the problem by, for example, describing the property that will be analyzed and the purpose of the analysis; states the fees that will be charged and when these fees will be paid; and specifies at what points, if any, the client or the counselor can stop the work and settle the account. The proposal may also list the tasks to be performed, the resources to be used and the dates by which the tasks will be completed, subject to any specified contingencies. Finally, it recites the counselor's qualifications and lists any assumptions and limiting conditions to which the work is subject. A sample proposal follows.

MODEL PROPOSAL

Blanktown Development Company
Attention: Mr. Barney Blank
Senior Vice President
Post Office Box 111
Blanktown, Any State 12345

Re: Northeast Corner Sixth and Main - Smithtown, Any State

Dear Mr. Blank:

Based on our understanding of your request, we propose to study the feasibility of adding other compatible uses to the 30,000 square foot supermarket you plan to build on a 3.5 acre site at the northeast corner of Sixth and Main in Smithtown.

The supermarket and related parking for some 260 cars will, you have advised us, require about three acres. This will mean that any additional space would demand a multilevel configuration. We will consider various possible configurations and recommend one or more for you to discuss with the architect.

Our work will focus on market and financial aspects of development and not on engineering, legal or accounting issues, except to make note of any apparent conditions we encounter. No engineering studies, soils tests, environmental studies, architectural services or accounting services are contemplated.

In the course of our work we will:

1. Inspect the property and its surrounding area to become familiar with the location as it relates to the road net, land contours, nearby development, competitive projects and regional anchors.
2. Evaluate prevailing economic, demographic and commercial development trends in the Smithtown economy as they relate to the site.
3. Analyze the market for retail and commercial uses in the relevant market area around the site, describing current demand and supply trends, current rents and absorption of rates.
4. Inventory major competitive retail and commercial projects in the market area and, to the extent practical, review current leasing experience including occupancy levels, rent levels, building types and sizes and the nature of the tenants being attracted.
5. Examine any existing constraints upon development, such as zoning, utilities, parking restrictions, easements and similar items.
6. Review our findings in relation to your plans for the new supermarket.
7. Based upon the foregoing, offer our conclusions as to the prospects for various compatible uses, setting forth what we believe to be the optimum site configuration for the amount of space likely to be marketable, projected rental rates, estimated absorption period and the principal types of users to which the project should be directed.
8. Prepare an economic analysis of the development in order to estimate your potential return on investment.

We will present our findings either in person or by telephone, accompanying our oral report with a written analysis appropriately illustrated with maps and photographs. Both the oral and the written report will be subject to our usual

Statement of Assumptions and Limiting Conditions, a copy of which is attached. Time required to complete the work is 45-60 days, subject to circumstances beyond our control and to your prompt delivery of the property information set forth in the attached list.

Our fee for this work, which will include a personal visit by Conrad Counselor, CRE, to the site and his close involvement in the study, will be $9,500 plus out-of-pocket expenses and computer time, which in the usual course, should not exceed 10% of the base amount. This fee is payable $4,750 upon authorization, $4,750 prior to delivery of our written report, and the balance within 30 days thereafter. You may accept this proposal and initiate the work by countersigning the attached copy of the proposal where indicated and returning it to us together with a check for $4,750 to cover the initial payment. The letter will then constitute our memorandum of agreement. Unless previously accepted this proposal will expire and become invalid on _____.

As you will see from the attached materials, our firm is well qualified to undertake this assignment. We have extensive experience in development planning that includes nine supermarket projects in the Smithtown area alone. Our staff includes three full-time real estate counselors, of whom two carry the CRE designation. Staff working on this assignment will be under the direct supervision of Conrad Counselor, CRE.

We hope that this proposal meets with your approval. Please let us know if you have any questions or would like to discuss the assignment further. We look forward to working with you.

  Very truly yours,
  ANY STATE COUNSELORS, INC.
  By: _____
    Abel Counselor, CRE

Attachment
APPROVED AND ACCEPTED THIS _____ DAY OF _____ , 19__
BLANKTOWN DEVELOPMENT COMPANY
BY:_____
  (Authorized Signatory)

Statement of General Assumptions and Limiting Conditions

This report is subject to the following general assumptions and limiting conditions:

1. No responsibility is assumed for the legal description or for legal or title considerations. Title to the property is assumed good and marketable unless otherwise stated.
2. The property is assumed to be free and clear of liens and encumbrances unless otherwise stated.

3. Responsible ownership and competent property management are assumed.
4. Information furnished by others is believed to be reliable, but has not been verified in all cases and no warranty is given for its accuracy.
5. All engineering information furnished us is assumed to be correct. Any plot plans and illustrative materials are intended only to assist the reader in visualizing the property.
6. It is assumed that there are no hidden or unapparent conditions of the property that render it more or less valuable. No responsibility is accepted for such conditions or for arranging for engineering studies that may be required to discover them.
7. Full compliance with all applicable federal, state, and local environmental regulations and laws is assumed unless otherwise stated.
8. It is assumed that all applicable zoning and use regulations and restrictions have been complied with unless otherwise stated.
9. It is assumed that all required licenses, certificates of occupancy, consents or other legislative or administrative authority from any local, state or national government or private entity or organization having jurisdiction have been or can be obtained or renewed for any use recommended.
10. It is assumed that any existing or proposed utilization of the land and improvements is within the boundaries or property lines of the property described and that there is no encroachment or trespass unless otherwise noted.
11. Possession of this report or of a copy thereof does not carry with it the right of publication.
12. Neither Any State Counselors, Inc., nor the individuals signing or associated with this report shall be required by reason of this report to give further consultation or testimony or be in attendance in court or other legal proceedings unless arrangements have been previously made.
13. This report has been made only for the purpose stated and may not be used for any other purpose. Neither all nor any part of the contents (especially any conclusions as to value, the identity of Any State Counselors, Inc., or any individuals signing or associated with this report or the professional associations or organizations with which they are affiliated) shall be disseminated to third parties by any means without the prior written consent and approval of Any State Counselors, Inc.
14. No responsibility is taken for changes in market conditions and no obligation is assumed to revise this report to reflect events or conditions which occur subsequent to the date hereof.
15. No consideration has been given to the existence of any potentially hazardous materials used in the construction or maintenance of the property, such as urea formaldehyde foam insulation, asbestos and/or any other toxic substance which may or may not be present. The counselors have made no inspection for toxic or carcinogenic materials, nor are we qualified to detect such substances.

The preceding model proposal is only an example. Your own requirements and those of your client, not to mention the opinions of your lawyer, will have a lot to do with the actual form you use. Note that the proposal spells out which expenses are reimbursable and provides for its own automatic expiration on a fixed date.

Acceptance of a signed proposal makes it a binding contract.

The proposal concludes with an invitation to accept it. Once both the counselor and the client have signed it, the document becomes a contract that binds both parties. For that reason care in drafting it is important. The contractual liability issues associated with consulting agreements can be serious; be sure the language of the proposal is clear and you understand the legal significance of that language. The proposal describes the business relationship between the counselor and the client; good draftsmanship therefore can contribute greatly to a successful outcome and serve to launch properly the long-term relationship.*

Staged proposals. Clients don't like to commit to big assignments until they know you reasonably well. You can help them—and yourself—by offering a staged proposal (see *Staged and Phased fees*, Chapter 20).

The staged proposal often describes an initial phase of work where you explore the problem and arrive at a detailed work program and budget, and later phases where you carry out the work program. Depending upon the size of the client and the job, the first phase may involve only a few dollars or a relatively large amount. The key is that the price tag on the first phase must be small enough for the client to risk it. In effect the client is saying: "I'll take a chance for $3,000 and then we'll see," while the counselor is saying: "Once we've got the first phase under our belts, the rest will be easy."

Another way to deal with this concern is to give the client the right to terminate the contract at fixed break points. A $50,000 feasibility study, for example, might be cancelable at the client's option if the preliminary findings are considered to be unsatisfactory for any reason. The client also may want to know what the cost of future studies will be. You can deal with this concern by providing a commitment to carry out the work for specified fees.

How long should the proposal stay open? That depends. Your costs may grow as time passes; you may get busy; market conditions may change. It therefore pays to include a time limit in your proposals: 30 to 60 days is not out of line; longer or shorter periods may be acceptable.

What the client will provide. Often you can't do your job without certain information that can best be obtained from the client. Specify these items in the proposal

---

* Some counselors prefer to sign the proposal only after the client has done so, to prevent the client from using it to shop around for a lower price. You may want to ask your lawyer about the best way to proceed. For further advice on this subject, consult Chapter 8 in Herman Holtz's useful book (see the References) as well as your own attorney.

letter and let the client know that, if they are not furnished in a timely manner, you cannot guarantee your performance schedule. Sophisticated clients will recognize your needs and try to give you the essentials promptly.

One way to request this information is to attach a standard list of information requirements that can be marked to show what you need and when you need it.

Schedule of Information Requirements

Item	*Delivery Date*
Legal description	
Survey	
Land acquisition data	
Market study	
Architectural drawings	
Environmental impact statement	
Construction cost estimates	
Proposed leases	
Operating budget	
Marketing program	

This list can be expanded or modified to suit the situation. The main thing is to commit the client to providing the information in time for you to perform on schedule without overstretching your capabilities or compromising the job.

PRESENTING THE PROPOSAL

While it's best to deliver the proposal in person, at the prospective client's office or your own, there will be times when you'll have to send it out by mail or messenger. In such cases you'll want to follow up with a telephone call or visit to make sure the proposal arrived and to answer any questions or objections the client may have. Don't let the proposal languish and die on the prospect's desk for lack of a little attention from you.

References

BOOKS

1. Blake G and Bly RW: *The Elements of Business Writing*. (New York: Macmillan) 1992.
2. Ivers M: *The Random House Guide to Good Writing*. (New York: Random House) 1992.
3. Holtz, H: *The Consultant's Guide to Proposal Writing*. (New York: John Wiley and Sons) 1986.
4. McVay BL: *Proposals that Win Government Contracts*. (Woodbridge, VA: Panoptic Enterprises) 1984.
5. Rowh M: *Winning Government Grants and Contracts for Your Small Business*. (New York: McGraw Hill) 1992.

Part VI

The Art Of Counseling

Chapter 22

Managing Your Clients

Clients who are worth anything eventually grow tired of a counselor who doesn't know what to do. After all, if they knew what to do themselves, they wouldn't need a counselor. This means that clients expect counselors to provide guidance as well as service.

The model for counselors is the doctor, whose business relies in large part on his knowledge and decisiveness. This does not mean that the counselor has to play God or be a know-it-all. Some problems, naturally, cannot be handled without a little research. Make sure, as your doctor does, to find out everything you need to know about your client and the assignment. Ask questions until you do. Your doctor can't take proper care of you if you won't tell him where it hurts. Why should you be expected to do better for a client who keeps you in the dark?

Clients are fallible human beings like you; they have fears, insecurities, prejudices and blind spots. The reason they turn to you is because they need help. Give it to them by shoring up their weaknesses, strengthening their understandings, correcting their prejudices and opening their eyes to the reality of the situation. They may not like what you tell them in the short run, but in time they'll come to appreciate your frankness.

Knowledge is power.

Never commit the error of playing to the prejudices of your clients. Sooner or later they will recognize that you have betrayed their interests and will not be shy about letting others know of your bad faith.

Firmness. Why be wishy-washy when what the client wants is a clear line of action? Be firm. You can do this without being impolite or arrogant if you simply make it clear that your only criterion is the client's best interests. "This is what needs doing, this is what the situation calls for" is very different from "Do this because I say so."

Firmness does not prevent you from considering alternative courses of action: "There ar two ways to do this; let's look at them both and see which one fits your needs better" is just as firm as "Here is what I want you to do." Either way, your conviction will reassure clients and convince them that you know what you're doing.

Integrity. Clients must remain convinced at all times that your principles are sound, your goals make sense and your intentions can be trusted. They are not unreasonable in feeling that you should never steal, cheat or lie. If you satisfy the client's expectations in this area, your relationship with him is likely to survive its inevitable ups and downs.

Some clients will be satisfied if you are straight with them and crooked with others. A few would even prefer to deal with this kind of counselor, counting on the counselor to do the dirty work they don't want (or know how) to do themselves. The better clients, though, expect you to behave like a morally decent person in every context, except possibly for slight tendencies to cheat on the golf links.

Remember that clients who appreciate dishonest manipulations frequently find themselves caught up in nasty legal situations that entangle their advisors.

Communication. Clients don't like to be bothered with meaningless messages, but they do like to be informed regularly about things that matter. Let them know what you are doing for them and make it a point to inform them of any news that affect their interests. Send them a book or a gadget at holiday time and cigars, flowers or champagne on happy occasions. Many clients appreciate lunch once in a while; some also may appreciate a reprint of an article on a topic of interest to them, particularly if you wrote it and it mentions them favorably.

A final word on this topic: Try to answer the client's letters, memos and calls with reasonable promptness. If you're tied up and can't answer on the day the message is received, have your secretary call to explain. Clients don't like your being busy with other peoples' affairs, but they expect it.

Loyalty. Nobody wants a counselor to be a toady or to make major sacrifices in the client's behalf, but most clients appreciate a reliable and consistent interest in their well being and a willingness to put your own needs aside in favor of theirs when the situation demands it. The rule of ethics in the professions demands that the client's interests come first, at least when their interests are legitimate.

On the other hand, as a counselor you almost never owe more to the client than first-rate service and professional objectivity. Don't let yourself be seduced into adopting the client's manias and vendettas. He is entitled to your loyalty as a professional, not as a friend, relative or lover—unless you happen to fill those roles as well or aspire to.

Discretion. Be scrupulous in safeguarding your clients' confidences. Keep private information in a secure place and be careful how you use it. Nobody likes a blabbermouth. Clients also have a legal as well as a moral right to your discretion.

Compensation. Make sure you are paid. Your clients should understand that you are working for money. Any failure in this area on your part may lead clients to suspect that you have ulterior motives, such as a desire for some portion of their anatomy.

As a professional you are entitled to send bills and to receive payment within a reasonable period. Don't be shy about it. It's your bread and butter, and the client, if worth keeping, knows this and respects your needs (see Chapter 12).

One further point: Charge enough. Clients tend to value you according to your own estimate of what you are worth. Don't disappoint them by undercharging, or they will get the wrong idea (see Chapters 19-21).

THINGS NOT TO BE WITH CLIENTS

It's seldom a good idea to adopt poses with your clients. In particular try not to be:

- A comedian. Everybody likes humor, but nobody wants to listen to a compulsive jokester.
- A big star. Let the client feel more important than you, at least occasionally.
- A hustler. Ambition is OK, but clients seldom enjoy being treated like rubes.
- An ideologue. Unless you're prepared to make a career out of counseling the like-minded, it's best to avoid insisting on your own beliefs.
- A snob. How should the client know what a remarkable muckety-muck you are? Why should the client appreciate it?
- A gossip. People who tell tales out of school are apt to betray confidences or talk about their clients in places where they'd rather not be mentioned.
- A bore. Spare your clients the things they don't need or want to hear. It's better to leave the impression that you know more than you are saying.
- A know-it-all. Most people don't appreciate the counselor who seems to know everything about everything and doesn't hesitate to put that knowledge on display.
- A stuffed shirt. Like the know-it-all, the stuffed shirt thinks far too little of others, including clients. Clients who are looking for a god should look in church.
- A name dropper. Do clients want their names dropped? Will they really be impressed with the people you know or just turned off?
- A toady. Be your own person, or you won't last long.
- A Pollyanna. Call things the way they are, not the way the client wants them to be.

TURNING CUSTOMERS INTO CLIENTS

Customers aren't truly clients until you become, in their opinion, the only real estate counselor worth thinking about. At that point, you are no longer a provider of services but a trusted advisor.

How can that be accomplished? For most counselors there is only one reliable way, and it takes time and care. You have to convince your future clients, through repeated experience, that your intentions are honest, your skills sufficient, your service reliable, your judgment solid, your character true-blue and your advice generally correct. That, plus good communications, will do the job over a year or two. From then on all you need to do is avoid breaching your clients' trust, insulting their character and getting them into trouble you can't get them out of again.

This process can be accelerated by delivering significant successes to clients. Counselors who solve big problems regularly and make money for their clients are valued at the top of the scale. Like corporate turnaround experts, these counselors will be sought out eagerly and well rewarded.

HOW TO SAY THINGS TO CLIENTS

They way you express yourself can be just as important as what you say. Usually, there's more than one way to express a thought. Why not choose one that keeps the client on your side—and lets your message get through? See the following examples.

Closing the deal:
- "We could start by..."
- "What would you say to..."
- "Here's what I suggest..."
- "If we're serious about this, we ought to..."

Testing the waters:
- "What do you think might happen if we leave it alone?"
- "Have you tried..."
- "What kinds of solutions have you been thinking about?"
- "What do your partners/attorneys/management people think should be done?"
- "Where do *you* think we should look for the answers?"
- "Who do you think might have a problem with this?"
- "When did you last take a look at..."
- "Let's consider for a minute what might give us the best results."

When more work should be done:
- "It might cost a little more, but I think it would be worth it to..."
- "If the budget will stand it, we ought to..."
- "Suppose we tried..."

Making your recommendations:
- "Here's the way it's starting to look to me."
- "All the facts suggest we ought to think about..."
- "There's obviously more than one way to go with this, but here's what I believe we ought to do."
- "Probably the safest thing to do is... But there's another possibility I'd like you to consider."
- "I think it's clear from what we've seen that... Don't you?"
- "Does that make sense to you?"

Client demands something unreasonable:
- "I doubt that would be such a good idea. It would..."
- "I'd be glad to look into that, but I'm afraid it might..."
- "That's an interesting idea—with a lot of interesting implications. Have you thought about...?"
- "That's an intriguing suggestion, but I don't think it'll work unless..."
- "I agree that's an important issue, but let's hold on a minute until we..."
- "I'd like to oblige, but (my firm has a policy, I'd have a problem with my code of ethics, it's just plain wrong)."
- "Let's remember what we're trying to accomplish here."
- "Why should you let that bother you?"
- "I'm surprised you would think a thing like that."
- "OK." (With some clients, this is the only possible answer.)

These phrases may seem to be too tentative; after all, the client does want direction from you, and you don't want to appear indecisive. But language of this kind does, in fact, offer direction in a respectful way that invites agreement while leaving room for other opinions. You will know when it's time to be firm.

Here are some rules for conversing with clients:
1. Use "we" whenever you can—except at the beginning ("you") and the end ("I").
2. Find out what the client thinks.
3. Find out, if you can, what the client's associates and advisors think.
4. Test the waters before you jump in.
5. Use the passive voice to avoid premature commitment.
6. Keep the client's anxieties at a minimum so your messages will get through.

7. Show that there is an objectively correct answer (or range of answers), even though you may not be absolutely sure what it is yet.
8. Guide, don't push.
9. When wronged, question the behavior, not the intention. "Why should a reasonable person like you think a thing like that?"

WHAT CLIENTS DON'T LIKE TO PAY FOR

Clients don't want to waste their time and money on unnecessary communication with you. Here are some things to avoid:

1. *Verbiage.* Keep your communications as brief as you decently can without compromising your presentation.
2. *Boiler plate.* Hold it to a minimum in your contracts and reports.
3. *Unnecessary exhibits.* Each exhibit should make a meaningful contribution. Filler is unwelcome.
4. *Leather binders and other attempts to gussy up the presentation.* There are some exceptions to this rule, but most of the time a neat and simple binding will suffice.
5. *Wasted time.* Plan your jobs accordingly.
6. *Excessively fancy offices.* Quality and roominess are all right, but ostentation encourages the belief that you don't mind wasting the client's money. It also may suggest that your vanity will make you hard to deal with.
7. *Expensive advertising campaigns.* A good wine, many feel, shouldn't need a big bush.
8. *Things they don't need to know.* Enough said.

PROBLEMS AND COMPLAINTS

Every now and then you'll have to face a dissatisfied client, one who, for one reason or another, doesn't like your report, your advice, your bill or your failure to complete work on schedule. Clients can become nasty at these times, and it's all too easy to react defensively or angrily to them, thus risking further damage to the relationship and your reputation.

Try to keep your balance when such problems and complaints arise, as they will. Remember that you are a serious and respected professional who wants to do a good job and succeeds most of the time. If there is a good reason for the client's dissatisfaction, try to correct the problem graciously and without delay. If there is not, try at least to show a little sympathy and a desire to make things better.

If the client is really angry, by all means wait for the anger to dissipate before you try to respond. After a while most people become embarrassed about their own emotionalism and will be more willing to look at another side to the question. When something is actually wrong, it's a good idea to say so, promising to correct the damage as best you can. Show a willingness to make things right at your own expense, and the client, however annoyed, will at least appreciate your attitude.

If you have the touch, you can use the client's anger and guilt to turn the situation around. A long complaining letter from a client who is justly dissatisfied with your office's performance actually can present an opportunity to cement the relationship. Instead of answering the letter point for point, try calling the client, say you agree 100%, apologize for mishandling the assignment, explain how it happened and ask for a chance to come over and discuss the situation in detail so you can be sure to get it right the next time. The client, if worth keeping, should appreciate the gesture as well as your willingness to straighten things out.

It doesn't always work, but generally speaking, the best response to a complaint is to make a series of statements along these lines:

1. "You're right. This one got past me, and it shouldn't have."
2. "I'm sorry it happened and will make sure it doesn't happen again."
3. "I want to make things right with you. Tell me what you think I should do."

No reasonable person can stay angry for long in the face of such a reply. As to the unreasonable ones, you can get along without them.

CLIENTS IN A HURRY?

Some counselors keep a sign on the desk that says: "Your failure to plan does not constitute my emergency." What the sign might better say is: "Your failure to plan constitutes my opportunity." Clients should pay more for emergency service, and usually expect to. This is not just because of the extra strain emergency work puts on your life and organization, but also because rush jobs cost more money to perform: overtime pay for your people, messengers and telefaxes rather than mail deliveries, extra charges for after-hours heating and air conditioning. Rush jobs may also force you to push other important work aside while you tend to the client's emergency. Who knows what client noses will be put out of joint—and what opportunities will be lost—if you say yes to this improvident person? Weigh the answer carefully in setting your fee.

GOLF, BOOZE, GIFTS AND BRIBES

These are not things you have to do. Unless you really enjoy playing pinochle or footsie with the client, make your excuses and go about your business. The client needs you as an advisor, not as a fourth at bridge, and will forgive you for saying no. On the other hand if you genuinely enjoy the client's company and favorite sport, by all means indulge yourself. It can't be bad for business.

There are many other things you can do to express your good will and professional loyalty. Send the client articles and clippings you think will be of special interest or small gifts on special occasions such as birthdays. Invitations to lunch or to meetings of your trade group when a speaker will be discussing a topic of special interest usually are welcome. If you have met the client's family, by all means ask how they are doing and feel free to indulge in whatever gestures of friendship seem appropriate.

At holiday time try to remember key clients, referral sources and people who have done kindnesses for you during the year with an individually selected gift or a personal letter of thanks. Do this out of gratitude and not in the expectation of a return. The gesture is appreciated and can give real satisfaction to both parties.

Culling. From time to time you may want to thin out your clientele, eliminating those who take up more time or give you more trouble than they're worth. Do it gently; after all, they can't help being the way they are, and you *did* find them acceptable in the past. Try, if you can, to refer them to someone else who may be better able to solve their problems.

References

BOOKS
1. Anderson D and Wardell MJ: *Surviving Bankruptcy.* (Englewood Cliffs, NJ: Prentice Hall) 1992.
2. Noble SP: 301 *Great Management Ideas.* (New York: Inc. Publishing) 1992.
3. Silver AD: *The Turnaround Survival Guide: Strategies for the Company in Crisis.* (New York: Dearborn) 1992.
4. Ventura J: *The Bankruptcy Kit.* (New York: Dearborn) 1992.

PERIODICAL
Management Accounting, Institute of Management Accountants, 10 Paragon Dr., Montvale, NJ 07645-1760

CHAPTER 23

The Counseling Assignment

THE COUNSELING PROCESS

Real estate counseling usually involves a sequence of tasks carried out on behalf of the client for a specific purpose or purposes, centering on a specific subject matter, making use of specific skills and materials*.

The steps ordinarily are as follows:

1. Define the problem in terms of the
    a. Client: his nature, relationship to the problem and the property, goals, priorities, needs, resources, constraints, attitudes and position.
    b. Subject matter: the kind and type of real estate, the markets in which it is involved, any special characteristics it may have.
    c. Purpose: the questions to be answered, the problems to be solved, conflicts to be settled, plans to be prepared, goals to be achieved.
    d. Form: the kind of work to be done.
    e. Materials and skills required.

2. Establish the counseling relationship:
    a. Confirm the problem definition with the client.
    b. Define the relationship.
    c. Prepare a job budget.
    d. Enter into the counseling contract.

---
* Adapted from "The Counseling Process" by Jared Shlaes, The Appraisal Journal, January 1975, American Institute of Real Estate Appraisers, Chicago; reprinted in Real Estate Counseling: A Professional Approach to Problem Solving, The American Society of Real Estate Counselors of the National Association of Realtors, 1976, Chicago.

3. Plan the assignment:
   a. Set deadlines and key dates.
   b. Check files and library for available data and methodologies.
   c. Review available resources.
   d. Allocate tasks and schedule the work, allowing for consultation and review at appropriate points.
4. Do the work:
   a. Collect the data.
   b. Form a working hypothesis.
   c. Test the hypothesis, seeking additional data as appropriate.
   d. Reformulate the hypothesis, if required, and follow with additional research and testing.
   e. Consider and compare alternative hypotheses.
   f. Reach conclusions and make recommendations.
5. Prepare the report (see Chapter 24).
6. Review the report.
7. Present the report (see Chapter 24).

This outline is flexible; adapt it as necessary to the needs of various assignments. Use it as a guide, not a recipe. Your own sense of what the client needs and the job requires should determine what you actually do.

Starting from the general concept of the work, you will need to plan and manage the specifics of the job through to completion.

PLANNING THE JOB

Good assignment planning starts with the careful consideration of two positions:* the beginning (where you are) and the end (where you want to go). All you have to do is chart the path from the first point to the second. This chart can take the form of a critical path diagram, Gantt chart or other graphic representation of the tasks that must be done and the deadlines that must be met. It can be on paper, on computer disk or in the counselor's mind. Checklists for use in assignment planning differ from case to case, but in general they include some or all of the following items:

      Statement of the problem
      Choice of report format
      Assumptions and limiting conditions
      Materials required (maps, charts, graphs, photos)
      Property description
      Community analysis
      Market research
      Site analysis

---

* Adapted from "The Counseling Process," *op. cit.*

Improvements analysis
Governmental and private constraints
Replacement and rehabilitation cost estimates
Market data search
Financial information
Analysis and conclusions

This list, of course, can be lengthened enormously. Rather than try to develop a master list that might take up an entire book, we leave the details of planning to the individual counselor.

The budget is just as important as the job plan. For guidance, see Chapter 19.

MANAGING THE JOB

Good job management is the key to profitability as well as to on-time delivery of a satisfactory report. Use any of the popular computer-based job management systems or set up a system of your own, preferably on the wall where everyone can see it.

Track the Work. Such a system may take the form of a chart like this:

DATE:	1/15	1/30	2/15	2/30	3/15
TASK:	Define the problem/JBS	Inspection/JBS, KAS	Cost estimates/ KSY	Report writing/KAS, JBS	Final approval/JBS
		Project outline/KAS	Data gathering/KAS	Comp. check/ KAS	Typing Assembly	Printing & binding
			Maps/ROQ	Photos/KAS		
			Zoning check/BBW	Site analysis/ JBS		
				Number crunching/NDS		
				Plats & charts/ BAR		
EQUIPMENT:			Car	Computer, drafting room	Word processor, copy machines	Printer, binder

or one like this:

Time in weeks	0	1	2	3	4	5	6	7	8	9	10
Job planning	—	—									
Data collection		—	—								
Field research			—	— —							
Plats and photos				— — — —						
Report writing					— — — —				
Draft presentation							—				
Revisions and final review								—			
Report production										—	

Fancier charts—PERT charts, Gantt diagrams and the like—can be used if you need them. The idea is to let you, the person who is responsible for coordinating job production, and the people who are working on the job know at all times how the various tasks are progressing and what needs to be done to complete them on time.

The system can be designed to track dollars as well as tasks and people. Tight financial control usually shows up as better results at the bottom line. However, in a small office you may not have time to follow the dollars as well as the work. If the job was properly budgeted initially and takes no more time than was planned, the dollars usually will take care of themselves.

Initial planning meeting. It helps to sit down with the project manager and staff consultants when the job begins. This is the time to discuss the results you desire and how they will be achieved. Participation by members of the job team at this stage will improve their sense of responsibility and often lead to useful suggestions. It also will reduce everyone's anxiety level because it allows the job team to reach an early agreement on tasks, procedures and the time to be spent on each task by each person. Sometimes the initial meeting will show that the job can't be performed within the available time and budget. If so, it's better to make that discovery at the beginning, not when the job is almost finished and money is already down the drain.

The good boss tries not to interfere with the progress of the assignment once the actual work program has been delegated to a project manager. If the person in charge of the job is qualified, he should be given enough authority to get it done. This builds the manager's confidence, competence and sense of responsibility. It also spares you detail work and wasted time.

All the same, it pays to check in now and then to make sure things are going smoothly and to answer any questions that may come up. Start this early enough in the job process to allow major course changes if they are indicated. Try never to let things go so far that you can't make corrections when the problem comes to your attention. And remember to pat the project manager on the back frequently when things are going well.

References

BOOKS

1. American Society of Real Estate Counselors: *Real Estate Counseling*. Chicago, IL: (American Society of Real Estate Counselors) 1984.

2. House R: *The Human Side of Project Management*. (Reading, MA: Addison-Wesley Publishing) 1988.

3. Townsend PL and Gebhardt JE: *Quality in Action. 93 Lessons in Leadership, Participation, and Management*. (New York: John Wiley and Sons) 1992.

Chapter 24

The Counseling Report

An oral report may be enough for some jobs and some clients. Often a brief memorandum will do. In many cases, though, a formal written report is required. Contents of such a report may include:*

A. Title page, setting forth:
   1. Type of report
   2. Property location, kind and nature
   3. Client name
   4. Date
   5. Authorship
B. Cover letter, setting forth:
   1. Scope and nature of the assignment
   2. Conditions, presumptions, constraints and caveats
   3. Statement of salient facts and conclusions
   4. Unanticipated findings
C. Table of contents
D. Statement of the problem
E. Sources and methods employed; acknowledgments
F. Limiting conditions and assumptions (see Chapter 21 for an example)
G. Property description:
   1. Precise location
   2. Description of the land
   3. Building descriptions when appropriate, listing all significant characteristics of the improvements

---

*Adapted from "The Counseling Process," *op.cit.*

4. Zoning description, with any needed explanations
5. Property tax data
6. Building and other codes relevant to the problem
7. Description and analysis of the immediate neighborhood
8. Area and community descriptions
9. Description of title and of any leases, contracts, or encumbrances affecting the property
10. Political or other constraints

H. Presentation and analysis of other relevant data including information pertaining to existing and anticipated demand and supply and (when appropriate) to cost, income and expense, project impact, engineering and market trends
I. Application of these data to the problem or property, leading to a conclusion or set of conclusions and setting forth the logical steps taken
J. Statement of findings and recommendations
K. Supporting documentation and graphics:
   1. Area map
   2. Community map
   3. Map of immediate vicinity, if applicable
   4. Survey, plat, or sketch of property showing significant improvements
   5. Legal description
   6. Schedule of income and expenses
   7. Schedules of data regarding competitive properties, anticipated supply, anticipated demand, prospective tenants/buyers and similar items
   8. Copies of leases, deed restrictions and other significant documents
   9. Photographs of existing or proposed improvements at the location and competitive locations
   10. Rating grids, critical path charts, decision trees, and other exhibits
L. Qualifications of the authors

Not every counseling report lends itself to this format, nor is there any reason to prepare this type of report for every assignment. There are many ways to organize your materials; any of them will be acceptable as long as it presents the facts and your message effectively. (This is not true for members of the Appraisal Institute, who must satisfy that organization's reporting requirements.)

You may find these organizing principles useful when arranging your data in a report:
- Order of importance: First things first, as in a news story
- Chronology: Start at the beginning, then go forward
- Outside in: From general to particular, as in Balzac's novels
- Logic: Follow the reasoning process

However you organize your materials, all written reports should include at least these essentials:
1. A clear statement of the problem to be solved and how you are going to approach it
2. A list of the resources consulted and the people who participated
3. A recitation of the facts
4. A discussion of their implications as they relate to the problem
5. A summary of your conclusions and recommendations
6. Supporting exhibits (pictures, maps, plats, plans, specifications, tables, charts, deeds, leases, title reports and similar items)

Whatever format you use and whatever facts you include, try to present your materials in a sequence that will lead the reader to your conclusion in a convincing manner. The purpose of the report, after all, is to share your thought processes with other people. How else can they evaluate your findings?

Include only the information you need to show the reader how you got from your problem statement to your conclusions. Anything else is waste; it clutters up the report, distracts the reader, confuses the issues and costs money. This rule applies to the language you use as well as to the report itself. Use plain, concise English to make your work convincing and readable.

SOME REPORT-WRITING RULES

1. *Don't say more than you know.* It's better to omit a fact than to misrepresent one inadvertently; it's also better to confess your ignorance than to display it unawares.
2. *Don't predict.* It's all right to make forecasts and projections or to assess the chances that a particular event may occur, but flat predictions will get you in trouble sooner or later.
3. *Say enough.* Let the reader know what your thought processes are as well as what facts you used to reach your conclusion. How else can he evaluate your findings?
4. *Don't say too much.* Unconnected facts, extraneous materials and extra sheets of paper seldom impress the client. If something doesn't contribute to the purpose of the report, leave it out.
5. *Be clear.* No sense muddying up your meaning if you know what you are talking about. Avoid jargon that only your fellow professionals understand.
6. *Write defensively.* Some day an obnoxious lawyer may decide to challenge your statements while you are writhing in the witness box. Don't say things you can't defend.
7. *Watch out for slurs.* Try not to insult the reader or his friends, even by mistake or by implication.
8. *Never assume.* The client may not know what you know or agree with your preconceptions. Spell out the facts and don't be afraid to explain.

9. *Avoid certificates.* Unless you are making an appraisal, there is seldom need for one. An unnecessary certificate adds a degree of pomposity and may expose you to unwanted liabilities.

USE OF CONFIDENTIAL SOURCES

Much of the information that goes into your reports will come from people who may consider the facts they relate to you as confidential. If they do, your use of these facts will seem, and actually may be, a breach of their trust. In such cases your source of information may be entitled to file an action for damages.

You don't want to find yourself in this position. Guard against it by being careful not to disclose anything told to you in confidence, whether by a client or anyone else, or any information a reasonable person would assume to be confidential. That includes information about property income and expenses, financial condition, market strategies and trade secrets. Sometimes you can sanitize your data to avoid improper disclosure, but usually it's best not to include potentially confidential information in your reports. If in doubt, ask the source of your facts for permission to report them and consider getting your lawyer's opinion as well.

QUALITY CONTROL

Different offices have different requirements for quality control. Sometimes a designated person or team is responsible for quality assurance; sometimes several people or departments must sign off on a report before it can be issued.

Much of the work that goes into quality control can be done in your word processing department. If your word processors have been appropriately selected and trained, they can spell, fix your grammar, catch your errors and check your calculations. If they can't, someone else will have to be given these responsibilities.

Watch your language—and your figures.

The quality control person of last resort is, of course, you. Don't release a report until you (or your representative) has flyspecked it, at least for important omissions and errors of substance. Read the report as a critic would, not a proud author. You will spare yourself embarrassment—or worse.

PRESENTING THE REPORT

If possible, present your work in person. Hand the finished report to the client (and additional copies to any others present). Then take your listeners through the report, adding personal touches when appropriate and answering any questions that may arise.

A personal presentation is desirable for at least three reasons:

1. It involves the client in a direct way. Clients appreciate your willingness to share and explain, and will be more inclined to adopt your logic and your conclusions if you discuss them personally than if you merely send the report.

2. It gives you the opportunity to watch and listen to the client's reactions. This feedback will tell you when to stand firm, when to make changes and when to plan for a bigger fee next time. In group settings a presentation will help you recognize your friends—and your enemies.
3. It opens the door to further business. You are demonstrating your interest in the client by making the presentation; you also are inviting information about related concerns that may lead to an expansion of the assignment or to other work.

A good way to introduce your report or presentation, especially if there are people in the room who aren't fully familiar with the problem, is to start with a recital of essential background information. Briefly explain where the problem is, what it is and how you went about tackling it. Then take the audience through your analysis one step at a time, answering questions as they arise, before you make your recommendations. Sometimes, especially when there are decisions to be made before the next step is taken, it's wise to sketch out a few possible directions and ask for discussion before you zero in on a specific action program which may or may not entail more work for the counselor.

If the group is larger than two or three, it usually helps to make your presentation against a background of maps, plats, charts and pictures that locate the problem and illustrate key points. Otherwise, it's enough to use the exhibits on the table or in your report. Your listeners don't necessarily know where the property is or how it relates to its surroundings and competition. Show them as graphically as you can, so they can follow your logic, add comments and correct any mistakes.

As you would in making a sale or a speech, don't get so involved in your story that you forget to watch and listen. How your audience is reacting will tell you how the wind is blowing and whether or not you're on a satisfactory course. If not, you can almost always find a way to reef your sails or jibe before too much damage is done.

ORAL REPORTS

Unless a written report is absolutely necessary, as it is sometimes under Appraisal Institute or FIRREA rules, make your report orally. Prepare for it as you would for a speech or a legal deposition. Review the facts, organize the material in your mind or on a notepad, decide how you will open and close, try to anticipate questions and have the answers ready. Keep a comprehensive record of what you said (it's not a bad idea to dictate a memo from your notes after the presentation and keep it in your files) and retain all documents connected with the assignment as you would any counseling or appraisal file. If desired, you can give a short *aide-memoire* to the client as you start the presentation or send one along later.

References

BOOKS

1. Bailey EP: *The Plain English Approach to Business* Writing. (New York: Oxford University Press) 1990.

2. Barrons: *Writing Effective Letters and Memos.* (New York: Barron's Publishing) 1992.

3. Bernstein T: *The Careful Writer.* (New York: Atheneum) 1965.

4. Blake G and Bly RW: *The Elements of Business Writing.* (New York: Macmillan) 1992.

5. Boettinger HM: *Moving Mountains.* (New York: Collier) 1969.

6. Ewing D: *Writing for Results.* (New York: John Wiley and Sons) 1979.

7. Ferrara CF: *Effective Business Writing in Ten Minutes a Day.* (Radnor, PA: Chilton Book Co) 1989.

8. Iacone S: *Modern Business Report Writing.* (New York: Macmillan) 1985.

9. Poe RW (ed): *The McGraw Hill Handbook of Business Letters.* (New York: McGraw Hill) 1992.

CHAPTER 25

Conflicts

Because we don't live in Paradise any more, conflicts do arise from time to time, and counselors often get entangled in them, voluntarily or involuntarily, as professionals or as principals. It's a good idea to know what to do when conflicts occur.

CONFLICTS OF INTEREST

The term "conflict of interest" covers a multitude of sins and near-sins. It also covers a number of acts that, in common sense terms, you may consider to be perfectly proper.

Direct legal conflicts of interest are relatively uncommon except in large firms that have many clients, such as national accounting and consulting organizations. They do, however come up occasionally in small firms, and can be painful when they arise unexpectedly, causing damage to your reputation as well as your wallet. Avoid them. When a client is on the other side of a controversy you are asked to join, watch your step.

1. The new client can reasonably fear that your involvement in the case will be tainted by your existing or past relationship with the old client. Who knows what secret arrangements you and your first client may have made?
2. The old client in turn may believe that you are using your special knowledge of his affairs to benefit the new one, and worse, that you have betrayed him by taking positions adverse to the old client's interests. Even a matter that doesn't directly involve an existing client can hurt his interests indirectly and thus be dangerous to you as well.
3. At best, both sides will suspect you of having divided loyalties. When in doubt, by all means consult your lawyer.

Other Kinds of Conflicts. They come up every day. Examples:

- A client actually consists of multiple persons or businesses, such as a corporation and its major subsidiaries, each of which has different objectives and may try to influence your opinions accordingly.

- Some time ago you recommended that your client sell an old shopping center. Now the new owner appears and wants your help in turning the property around. If you succeed, what will the old client say—and do?

- A new client wants a study that you know will be useless unless its results confirm the soundness of a prospective venture. You have serious doubts about the feasibility of the venture. Can you take the job? Under what conditions?

- An article you published two years ago declared your views on a certain topic in no uncertain terms. Now you have changed your mind, and a client is asking you to testify in support of your new opinion. Will the earlier publication destroy the usefulness of your testimony?

- Client A wants you to negotiate a rent reduction for her manufacturing company. Client B owns several leased properties in the same industrial park, is squabbling with Client A over the way she uses the loading area and won't be pleased if you succeed. What to do?

Be alert to situations of this type as well as to legal conflicts of interest. Both kinds of conflicts can damage your practice. If you possibly can, stay out of these situations entirely; the best medicine is preventive.

Other people's battles. You also will want to avoid business, personal and legal wars that won't pay for your time and may cause you grief as well as cost you money. These wars easily can arise through no fault of your own. Routine counseling work, because it involves you with other people and their problems, exposes you to reproach and sometimes to a subpoena. Active counselors usually can't escape either forever.

To minimize this risk and reduce the chances of being on the receiving end of professional liability claims, follow the advice on the subject of liability set forth in Chapter 13. Take care to perform your assignments properly, obey the rules of your profession, be courteous and fair, avoid positions you can't easily sustain—and try never to say anything that may lend itself to misinterpretation or deliberate distortion.

TESTIMONY

No matter how careful you are, a time will probably come when you will be obliged to testify in court. You will then have to undergo deposition and cross-examination by a lawyer who doesn't care a whit about your best interests. You must regard that lawyer, however friendly he appears, as hostile and potentially damaging. Because poor performance as a witness can harm your reputation as well as your ego, you must think carefully about the case and your part in it before you take the stand or the deponent's seat.

A court proceeding involves other people and interests besides your own. Who are these people? What are their objectives? How will your testimony be important to the case? From what direction will your testimony be attacked? Talk things over with your side's lawyers (and your own, if necessary) and make sure you understand how they think the case will go. While you're at it, learn the points they want to make through you and the pitfalls to be feared.

Always try to anticipate the questions the opposing lawyer will ask on cross-examination. It's his job to discredit your testimony, all of it if possible but at least the essential points. The cross-examiner will try to show you to be ignorant of or mistaken about relevant facts, inaccurate in your logic or numbers, a liar or (especially when a jury is listening) a blowhard.

You can protect yourself to some extent by remembering that you are being attacked not as a person but as a professional. Don't let opposing counsel incite you to anger, as you will appear to be a fighter rather than an authority. You are likely to lose the *mano-a-mano* that follows, anyway. So try to stay calm, balanced and ready for whatever may come. Your job as a witness is not to win fights but to help the court (and the jury, if there is one) understand the facts of the case.

Be a lover.

You can survive testifying by adhering to a few principles:

1. *Always tell the truth*. You are under oath and have a legal duty to do so. Truth-telling also will relieve you of the obligation to remember your previous lies so you don't contradict them.

2. *Prepare thoroughly before you get on the witness stand*. Know your facts cold. This frees your mind to follow the questioner's strategy and allows you to anticipate some of the questions. It also helps to impress the court with your remarkable understanding of the problem.

3. *Answer the questions*. Listen carefully and answer only the question you are asked. Otherwise, you may unknowingly spill the beans or set a trap for yourself. Worse, you may appear to be ducking the question because of a hidden nefarious intent.

4. *Don't say or claim too much*. Extra verbiage only opens the door to attack during cross-examination. It also may make you sound like a blabbermouth and a fool. Witnesses who want to be liked, even in the courtroom, tend to feel they must disclose damaging information without being asked, which is not the case. Telling the truth requires only that you provide an honest answer to the question. What you are participating in is a trial, not a popularity contest.

    Be particularly careful not to claim more expertise or knowledge than you actually have, as opposing counsel cheerfully will use any such claims to discredit you when the time comes. A common technique in cross- examination is to ask the witness early on, often in deposition, a question like: "Aren't you the leading expert on condominiums in Blanktown?" An unqualified "yes" surely will cause you trouble later.

5. *Remember your audience doesn't know much about the subject*. Explain things as simply as you can without talking down to the jury

or compromising your presentation. Define any real estate jargon you may have to use and explain your concepts in enough detail for lay people to grasp your meaning. Chances are they don't understand the case very well and will appreciate any light you can cast on it in a nonpatronizing way. Judges usually are tolerant of such explanations, which can be helpful to them and to the higher courts as well as to the jury.

6. *Speak clearly.* Too many witnesses mumble or wander around the subject. Try to be plain-spoken and direct.

7. *Be as nervous as you like.* Judges and juries can understand your discomfort and make allowances for it. They like a nervous witness better than one who appears over-confident. But try not to get rattled or to let the cross-examiner's bluffs and distortions get your goat.

8. *Don't be a know-it-all.* Nobody likes arrogance. Besides, you may claim knowledge you don't actually have—and pay for it later.

9. *Don't play too obviously to the judge and jury.* Your purpose in the courtroom is to help the judge and jury understand the facts of the case, not to impress them with your performance. They expect you to watch the questioner, not to keep your eyes on them, except when you turn toward them to make a point or explain one.

10. On the other hand *do try to establish eye contact with the judge and jury occasionally.* It shows you recognize that they are people and that you acknowledge their presence. The judge and jury are your audience, not the questioner, and audiences are entitled to respect. Most of them don't like to be completely ignored. This applies particularly to the judge in a nonjury trial, who will be determining all the issues of fact and law, but jurors, too, like to be addressed directly when you have something to tell them.

11. *Dress the part.* Look like a professional. This doesn't mean you have to wear a white shirt with a dark suit and a gloomy tie, but avoid offbeat costumes and accessories. The impression you want to make is that you are a reasonable person who respects the court, the jury, the problem and yourself.

DEPOSITIONS

The opposing side in many court cases has the right to subpoena you and your files for examination before a trial begins or while it is going on. The idea is to minimize last-minute surprises in the courtroom and to give both sides equal access to relevant information before you testify. Unfortunately, this places the witness in the uncomfortable position of having to form and disclose his opinions before the trial, giving opposing counsel ample time to formulate tough questions for cross-examination later.

No secrets allowed.

There is no real defense against this danger. All you can do is what you would do as a witness on the stand: Answer briefly, pay attention to the questions, be honest and cautious. Everything you say can and probably will be used against you when the time comes. Still, with good preparation you can make a record so convincing and demonstrate your own professional abilities so effectively that the other side may back down and settle the case.

Opposing counsel probably will attempt to ensnare you in a variety of lawyer's traps and to keep you off balance by any means available. A tactic now becoming popular, and perfectly legal in many jurisdictions, involves jamming the lens of a video camera in your face to record not only every word you say but also every drop of sweat on your upper lip. There's little you can do to protect against this and similar tactics except to strive to keep your cool. On the other hand it doesn't hurt to let the record show that the camera, or whatever other device is being applied to upset and confuse you, is doing precisely that, and that you could do a better job of informing the court if this psychological bludgeon were removed from the room, or at least pointed in some other direction.

Remember, a subpoena is *sub poena*—under penalty of law. You have no choice but to obey. Stripping your files before you produce them, or failing to reply honestly to a question during the deposition, at which testimony will be given under oath, subjects you to a possible contempt citation.

The good part, if there is one, is that your client should be willing to compensate you for the time required to prepare your testimony and present it. Get a firm commitment in writing on this point, or at least an oral agreement in front of adequate witnesses. This shouldn't be hard to do, as your cooperation can be expected to help the client's position, and any negative feelings on your part could lead to testimony that would damage that position.

A caution based on painful experience: If the trial is out of town or if you have any doubts about getting paid, collect your money up front. The client will howl, but usually will pay, and you won't have to worry about your receivable after the verdict is in.

OTHER CONFLICT SITUATIONS

Counselors frequently are called upon to participate in zoning presentations, permit hearings of various types, arbitration procedures, negotiating sessions and other situations in which people have taken sides and are fighting out the issues face to face.

Zoning and permit hearings. You may be called upon to provide testimony as an expert on issues related to a developer presentation such as the impact of a zoning change on neighboring property values or the appropriateness of a proposed land use. Prepare your case as you would for trial, working with your client's attorneys to make sure your testimony will be legally sound and compatible with the rest of the presentation. You may or may not be testifying under oath, but you will be expected to answer questions honestly and maintain a professional demeanor. Dress as you would for trial unless counsel thinks more casual clothing would be appropriate. Try to speak as you would to a group of your neighbors rather than as a professor or a visitor from another planet.

Any exhibits you offer should be large enough to be clearly visible as they will be seen at the actual hearing. Make sure they are put together so they can stand where they are supposed to and will remain intact when moved. This will spare you the embarrassment of having to crawl around on your hands and knees picking up loose sheets of paper. Exhibits of course should be preapproved by counsel, and can even be designed in accordance with counsel's recommendations.

The people listening to you—at least the ones who count the most—are ordinary citizens like yourself who are devoting their time as volunteers to hear the case, often after a hard day's work. They don't need fancy persuasion, just simple arguments supported by facts and presented in a direct and friendly manner. Remember, too, that they probably have to listen to many cases and tend to get irritable or bored when things run on too long.

On the other hand they are entitled to hear all the relevant facts and opinions, just as you are entitled to deliver them. Don't feel you have to cut your testimony short, even when the hearing chairman starts to rustle papers and cast glances at the wall clock. You are making not only a presentation but a record, one that may be important if the ruling is appealed later.

Plain talk and a good record.

The rules change from one jurisdiction to another; so check with counsel before you appear. Some questions to ask:

> Will cross-examination be allowed?
>
> Will a stenographic record be kept for possible future use on appeal?
>
> What can you tell me about the judge, jury, hearing officers, lawyers for the other side, courtroom or hearing-room arrangement?
>
> What kinds of exhibits would be useful?
>
> Who else will be testifying?
>
> How exactly does my testimony fit in?
>
> What points does counsel particularly want me to make?
>
> What pitfalls must I avoid?

Arbitration proceedings. Occasionally you will be called upon to address a counseling problem in the context of an arbitration. Typically in such cases each side selects its own expert. If the two experts fail to agree, the parties can choose a third expert or arbitrator to decide the matter. Unless the behavior of the arbitrator suggests that, like Solomon, he will cut the baby in half if given the chance, it generally pays to present your opinion honestly, completely and plainly. If the other side departs too much from the truth, the arbitrator should recognize it and come down squarely on your side.

You may be asked for help in constructing an arbitration formula that will be fair to both sides. One that works well if the findings can be expressed in quantitative terms, such as fair rent or market value, requires that each side present its figures. The arbitrator then chooses one of the two figures, not something in between. This system encourages both counselors to strive for the correct answer, as any wide departure from the truth probably will lead the arbitrator to the other side.

Many other ways to structure an arbitration are of course possible. Bear in mind that it is not uncommon for one of the parties to be dissatisfied with the results of the arbitration and decide to pursue troublesome litigation. It therefore pays to watch your step in these matters and speak carefully.

Negotiations. The counselor may be asked to serve as back room advisor to one or more negotiating parties, or may be called upon to negotiate in their behalf. The presumption is that he is an experienced negotiator and can provide useful assistance. If such is not the case, say so and suggest somebody better qualified.

Many textbooks and courses on the subject of negotiation are available to interested readers (see the References). However you choose to play your part in the discussions, remember that even a hired negotiator is responsible to the public and the truth. You don't want to damage your good reputation for the sake of somebody else's tactical advantage.

Always remember that conflicts eventually end, and as a professional you may well find yourself one day called upon to work for the other side. In the heat of combat it's wise to remind yourself that the battle soon will be over. Don't resort to personal insults, even when you show your temper in other ways; leave the door open to an accommodation when things quiet down, as they eventually will.

References

BOOKS
1. Barrons: *Winning with Difficult People.* (New York: Barron's Business Success Series) 1992.
2. Bernstein A and Rozen SC: *Neanderthals at Work: How People and Politics Can Drive You Crazy and What You Can Do About Them.* (New York: John Wiley and Sons) 1992.
3. Cannie JK and Caplin D: *Keeping Customers for Life.* (New York: Amacom) 1992.
4. Handcock WA: *The Small Business Legal Adviser.* (New York: McGraw Hill) 1992.

Part VII

Getting Out

Chapter 26

Sale, Merger or Dissolution of the Counseling Firm

The time eventually will come when you tire of the counseling load or have to put it down involuntarily. Even counselors get old, and some are mortal. The discussion that follows may be of little immediate interest to you. If so, you can skip it safely—for now.

SALE OR MERGER

If you are interested in a merger or sale of your company, whether because of your advancing years, management problems, declining health or simply a desire to get onto the consolidation bandwagon while there is still time, there are several ways to encourage invitations. One is to let the world know that the wave of the future lies with your potential merger partners. You can deliver this message through speeches, articles or interviews in publications read by the other side's senior executives. It also can be sent through company brokers, financial advisors, professional recruiters and your own law firm. If you have a specific partner in mind, your natural ingenuity will suggest a host of ways to get things started.

If on the other hand you are approached out of the blue by a potential majority partner or purchaser of your organization, don't be in a hurry to react. Sound out the prospect's seriousness, capabilities and compatibility with your own style of operations—and his eagerness to make a deal. Explore other possibilities as you go; perhaps there are other prospects waiting in the wings, one of whom may be better for you. Talk to your attorneys and business advisors to see what they think you and your organization may be worth and how you should proceed. Be careful not to accept all the prospect's statements at face value; deal makers tend to over promise and can lead you down the garden path in reasonably good faith, as their representations can always be second-guessed by their board of directors.

What price? Setting a price for your company can be relatively simple. Many likely buyers base mergers on some fraction of the annual gross fee volume of the merged firm. The fraction is greater for a well-regarded company able to show consistent growth over a period of years and able to deliver its active principals, clients and staff. The amount agreed upon, if there is a sale, will be paid out over a number of years, often without interest, and may be partially contingent, but the selling principal usually can count on a salary for a few years. In a merger you can negotiate for partner status for one or a few of your firm's principals and for manager status, important in accounting firms, for senior professional employees with administrative responsibility.

The course of the negotiations will depend on: (1) what you think you're selling (usually your reputation, skills, experience, client connections and access to networks); and (2) what the other party thinks he is buying (usually entry into a new field or market area, expertise, client list, trained staff, net income and growth). An important factor is the rainmaker, whom the other party will try to lock in for a reasonable period of time (often four or five years). They also will be interested in your client list, especially those transferable clients who will be new to their firm and represent potential customers for their other services.

What you're selling—and what the other person is buying may not be the same thing.

Other negotiating points may include enhanced retirement programs and various special benefits such as first-class travel and accommodations when on the road, automobile and club allowances, moving costs, bonuses based on new business brought in and special insurance coverages. You also will want a reasonable escape clause that won't prevent you from earning a living if you exercise it. Bear in mind, though, that many large professional firms have little flexibility in negotiating merger deals and that they will consider your business to be inherently unstable, subject not only to real estate cycles but also to your own ups and downs and your vulnerability to sickness, fatigue, age and natural decay. If you haven't taken care to develop a faithful clientele and a strong upper-level echelon, your company may not be worth as much as you think it is.

Don't forget that your partners and employees may be the logical people to take over the operations of the firm, especially when you feel a strong obligation to them or feel you have no better prospects. You can consider retaining part ownership and letting them run it for you. Even better, if you think they are ready, you can sell the business to them outright. Loyal associates who are capable of running the business may be able to do more with it than strangers could, and may deserve the chance to try.

A sale to your partners and employees usually will be made on terms the business can afford to pay out of its profits, with a relatively small down payment. Often the seller will be asked to stay on for a while to offer sage advice and bring in work. Some of these arrangements turn out well for all parties; others come to grief in various ways. A lot depends on the quality of the individuals and the soundness of their relationships. If your people have been unhappy campers, they're not likely to be happy as your employers.

LIQUIDATION

If the business can't be sold profitably and is no longer making you rich or happy, you still may be able to give it away. When that doesn't work, you can always liquidate. Before you do, take the time to prepare a sensible plan. Can you close out or settle pending assignments and collect outstanding bills before you shut down and they become uncollectible? Can you sell your furnishings and equipment while they are still in place, or will they have to be moved to a warehouse and bring much lower prices? How will you deal with your accounts payable—and your bankers?

Talk to your lawyer and your tax advisors about these and other questions that are likely to come up. The way you choose to shut down your business can affect your tax position and perhaps your surviving liabilities. You may want to settle any outstanding debts and rethink your estate plan before you get too serious with your travel agent.

WHAT'S BEST?

Should you merge, sell, liquidate or stay where you are? Obviously there is no one answer to this interesting question. Your own needs and situation will govern. Some of the issues to consider:

Age and health. How long do you plan to keep working? What other things would you rather be doing? Would you relish the challenge of building a new department in a major firm or would you rather take things easy?

Succession plans. Have you provided for your own successor? Do you have partners or a second-in-command ready to take over the reins? Will your organization be able to sustain itself if you should be hit by a truck?

Clientele. Can you service your clients from your present base or do you need a larger framework? Are key clients happy with the present structure, or would they rather see you in a larger one with more capabilities? Will they follow you to the new company? How much difference will it make if they don't?

Culture and personality. Is the potential merger partner or employer one that you respect and can work with? How well will you and your people fit into its culture? Will the rules and procedures of the new company stifle the energies that have led to your success?

Responsibility. How much do you enjoy running your own show? How easily will you be able to give it up? How much power will you have—and do you want—in the new structure?

Resources. Do you have the tools you need to serve your clientele? If not, will you have them in the new framework? Which base will better allow you to attract those resources and put them to work?

Financial planning. Do you need cash? Is your income sufficient? How much would you like to defer until later? You may be able to structure your deal accordingly.

Tax position. Your tax advisors may be able to show you an advantageous way to go. Make sure they understand your wishes and have time to think about the options.

Peace of mind. Do you enjoy the ups and downs of your own business or would you rather seek the security of a large organization where somebody else minds the store? How solid in reality is the new organization? Will its guarantees be good enough to outlast your working life?

Freedom. In any new structure you will be constrained in ways you probably aren't now. You may have to watch what you say much more closely and will almost certainly be limited in your investments and business ventures outside the company framework. You may also have to subscribe to a host of detailed regulations governing many aspects of your business life. Can you accept this, and at what price?

RETIREMENT

Few real estate counselors retire completely except when forced to do so by deteriorating health. Counselors who are physically and mentally able often practice well into their 80s because they are having too much fun to quit. Those who do choose to retire generally can find interesting work in some field associated with real estate: teaching, writing, administering a foundation, working with a community group, becoming a real estate advisor to a corporation or lending institution. You may be an excellent candidate to oversee a new civic venture or a troubled housing authority. Perhaps you have a book in you that may help other people make better decisions and reach a better understanding of their activities. Some retired counselors are able to enjoy themselves and make money doing real estate deals or managing property.

In the end, you don't really have to make a choice about retirement. Fate will generally make it for you. Just do what you can during your more active years to assure your financial security and basic good health. With both of those to sustain you in your old age, and an honorable career behind you, the future is yours.

References

BOOKS

1. Cox V: *How To Sell Your Business for the Best Price.* (Chicago: Probus Publishing) 1990.

2. Rosenberg L, Rosenberg SL: *Fabulous Places to Retire in America.* (New Jersey: Career Press) 1991.

3. Ryan C: *Cashing in Your Chips. How To Profitably Sell Your Business.* (Homewood, IL: Dow Jones-Irwin) 1989.

4. Sperry PS: *The Guide to Selling Your Business* (Dover, NH: Upstart) 1992.

5. Tuller LW: *Getting Out. A Step-by-Step Guide to Selling a Business or Professional Practice.* (Blue Ridge Summit, PA: TAB Books) 1990.

6. Ventura J: *The Bankruptcy Kit.* (New York: Dearborn) 1992.

7. Vicker R: *The Dow Jones-Irwin Guide to Retirement Planning.* (Homewood, IL: Dow Jones-Irwin) 1985.